Picture Book: Diverse Activities of Life in India

Kulvir Bangarwa

Contents
1. Crows with their Natural Way of Life in Northern India
2. Cows in Residential Areas of Northern India
3. Beautiful Heron in Northern India
4. Ducks without Water in Northern India
5. Animals and Waste Spread over Undeveloped Market Place in Northern India
6. Vehicles and People on a Road Crossing in Northern India
7. Squirrel Drinking Water in Northern India
8. Public Park after Organizing a Function by Someone in Northern India
9. Honey Bee as a Pollinator in Northern India
10. People Moving on the Road in a Town of Northern India
11. Overloaded Tricycle in Northern India
12. People Sitting on the Roof of a Passenger Bus in Northern India
13. Balloon Seller in a Residential Colony of a Town in Northern India
14. Black Ducks Drying their Body sitting on Side Wall of Water Works in Northern India
15. Pet Dog Playing with Plastic Bottle in Northern India
16. Pet Dog after having Bathe in Northern India
17. Dog Sitting on the Top of a Car in Northern India
18. Transporting Waste of Town on a Rickshaw in Northern India
19. Plastic Toys Being Sold on the Road Side in Northern India
20. Landscaping of an Institute in Northern India
21. Yoga on the Occasion of Celebration of World Yoga Day in Northern India
22. Religious Person on the Side of Road in Northern India
23. Couple Travelling on a Bi-cycle in Northern India
24. Group of Pigs on their Mission for Search of Food in the Waste on the Side of Road in Northern India
25. Peacock as Indoor Patient in a Veterinary Hospital of Rajasthan in India

26. Tribal People Moving along with their Animals on the Road in Northern India
27. Crowd of People on the Public Places in Northern India
28. Animals on the Public Place in Northern India
29. Woman Transporting Green Fodder in Northern India
30. Beautiful Vulture as an Indoor Patient in Veterinary Hospital of Rajasthan in Northern India
31. Struggle of Ants in Transportation of their Food Material in Northern India
32. Cattles with Loss of Legs as Indoor Patient in Veterinary Hospital in a Town of Northern India
33. Swimming and Bathing in Canal Water in Northern India
34. Struggle for Transporting Heavy Loads on Human Operated Tricycle/Bi-cycle in a Town of Northern India
35. Women along with their Babies Begging from Door to Door with Song for Entertainment in a Town of Northern India
36. People Travelling by Different Vehicles on the Roads at Red Light Stoppage in Northern India
37. Amazing Struggle of Bug for Transportation of Food Grain in a Park of Northern India
38. Saints Moving Door to Door for Begging with Entertainment in a Town of Northern India
39. Driving Motor Bike Ignoring Driving Rules in Northern India
40. Celebration of Worship on the Bank of a Canal in Northern India
41. Farming Community Women for Transporting Farm Produce on their Head in Northern India where Work is Worship for farmers of India
42. Farmers Transporting Farm Produce by Driving Animal Cart in Northern India
43. Overloaded Two Wheelers on the Roads in Northern India
44. Overloaded Four-Wheeler Vehicles on the Roads in Northern India

1. Crows with their Natural Way of Life in Northern India

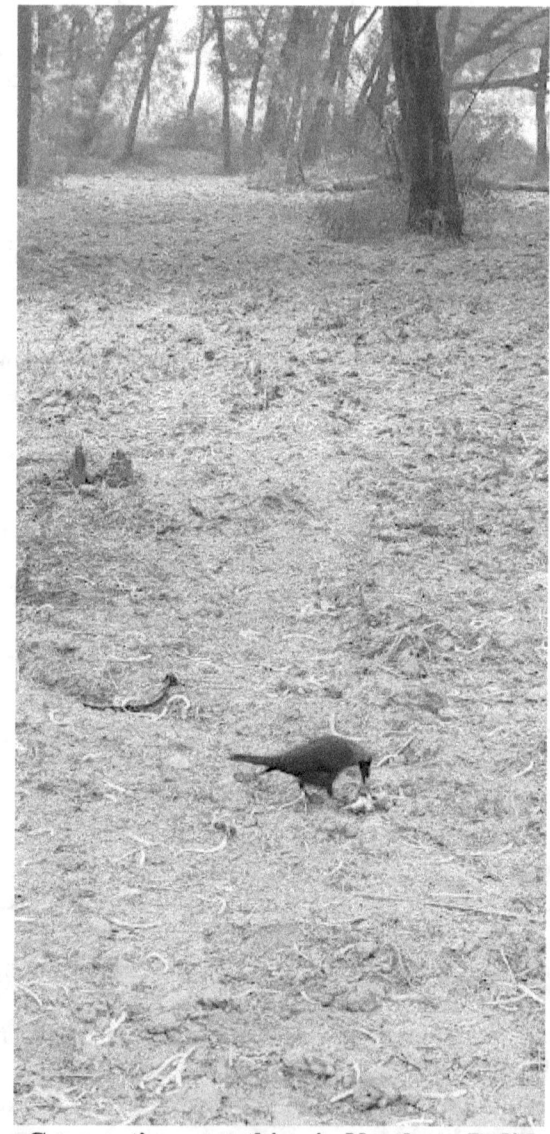

Crow eating something in Northern India

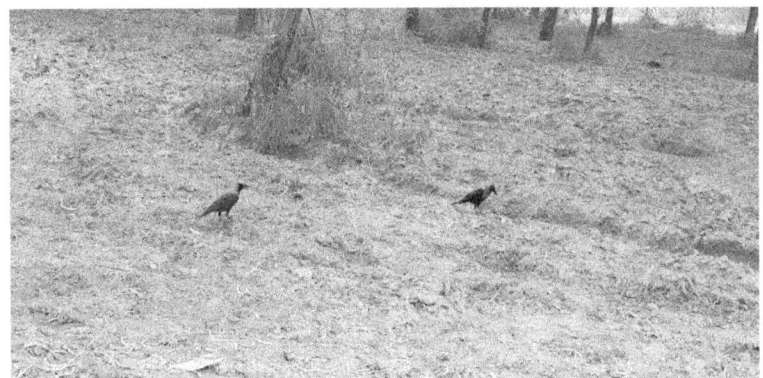

Two Crows with Natural Way of Life in Northern India

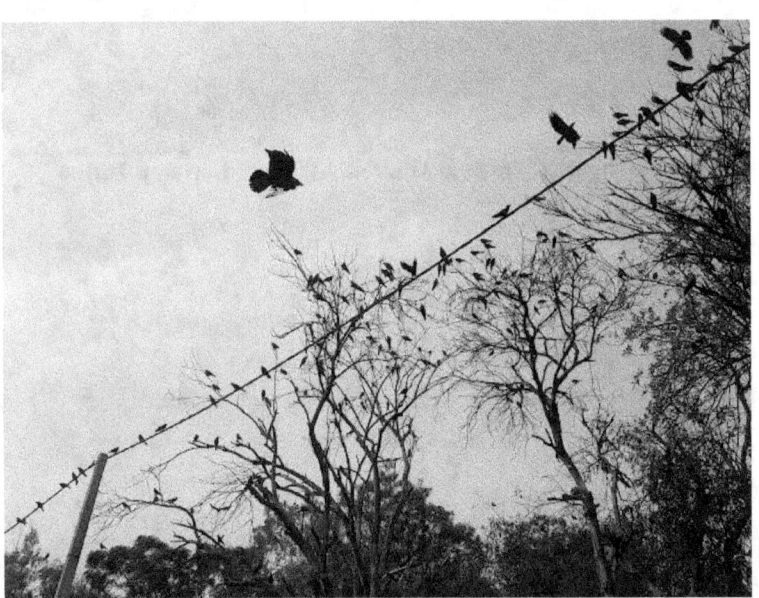

Crows with Natural Way of Life in Northern India

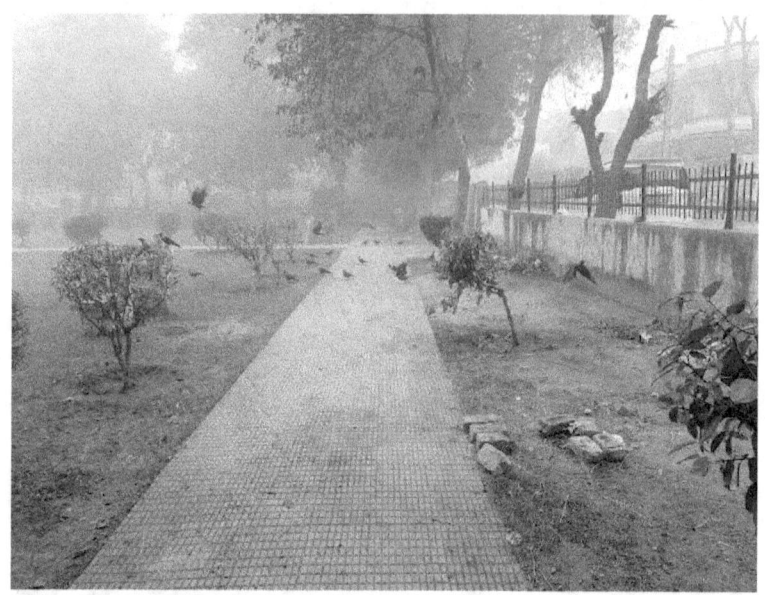

Crows with Natural Way of Life in Northern India

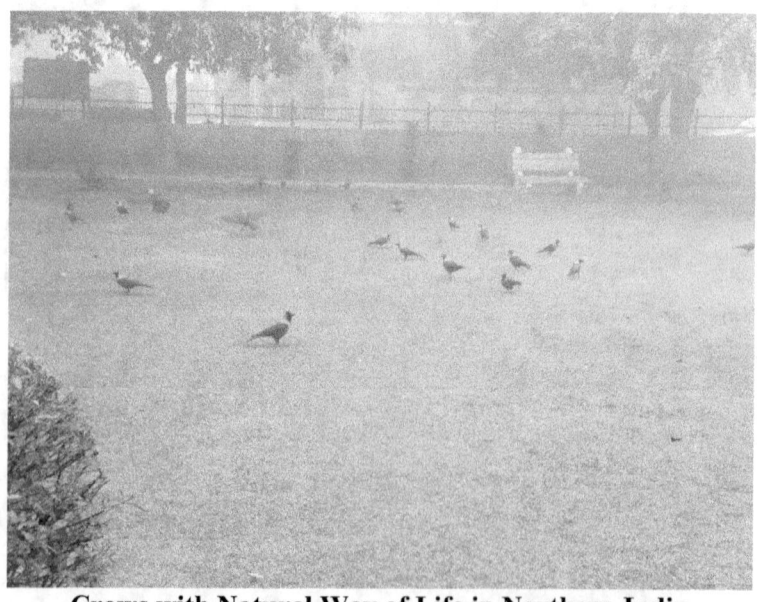

Crows with Natural Way of Life in Northern India

2. Cows in Residential Areas of Northern India

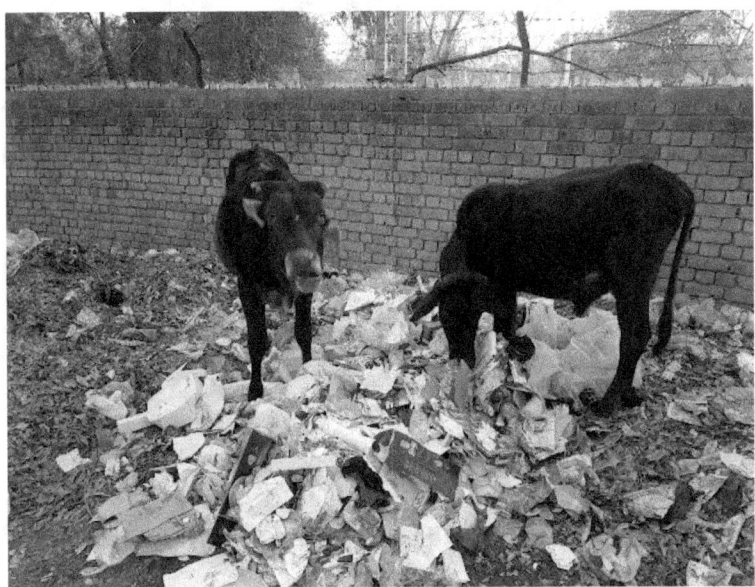

Black Color Cow and Bull in Residential Area of Northern India

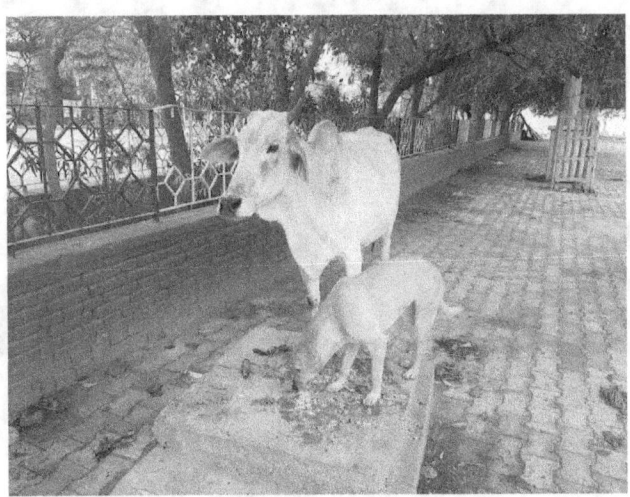

Cow and Dog in Residential Area of Northern India

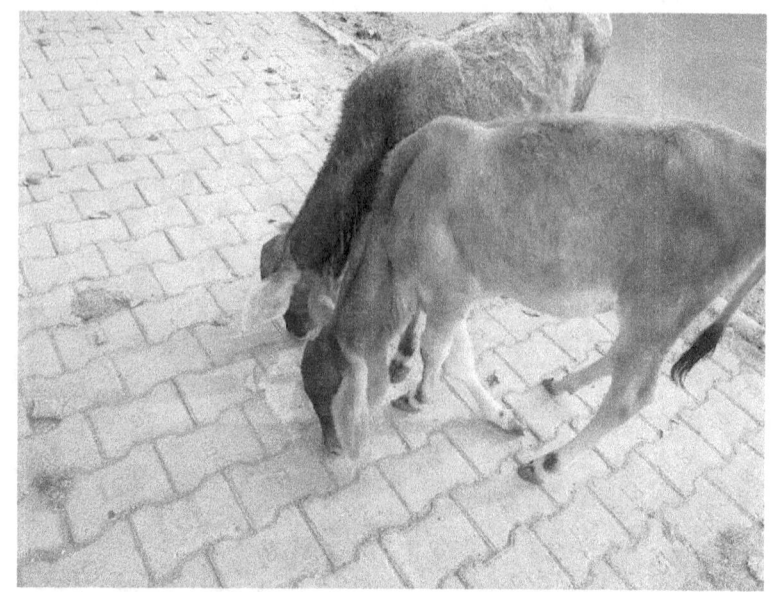

Young Cows in Residential Area of Northern India

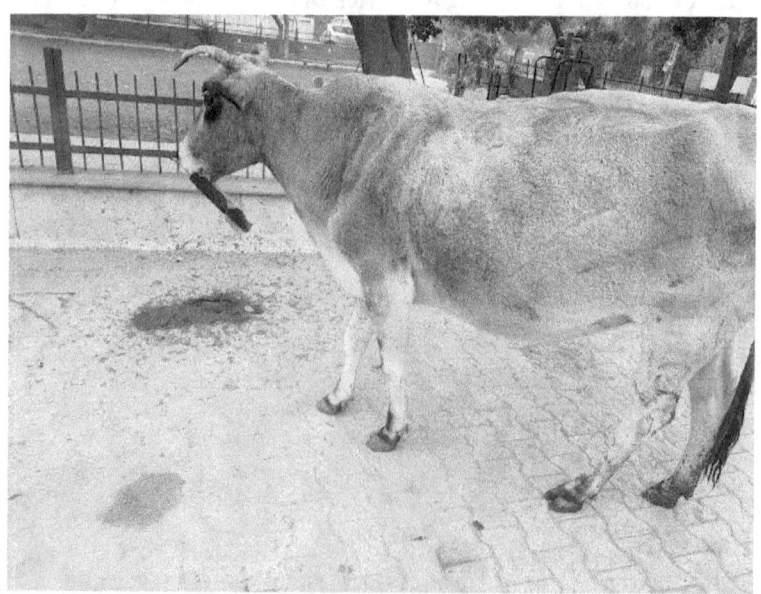

Cow in Residential Area of Northern India

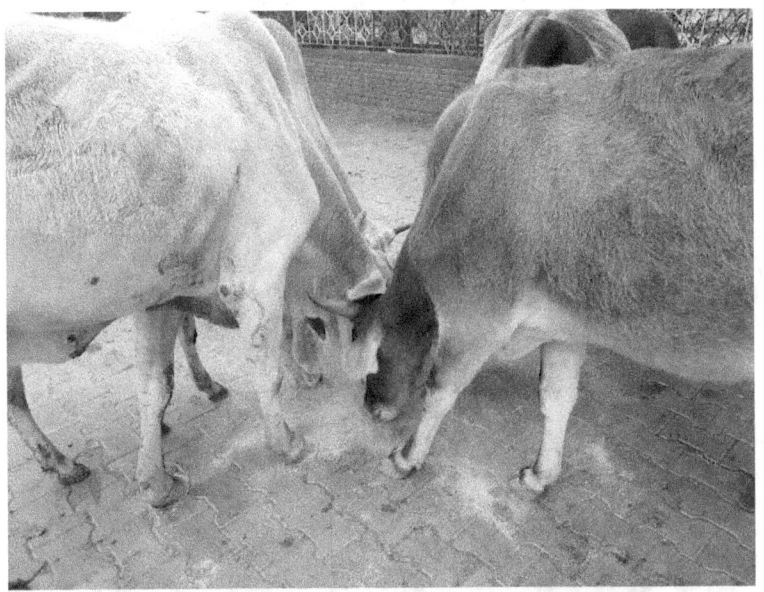

Cows in Residential Area of Northern India

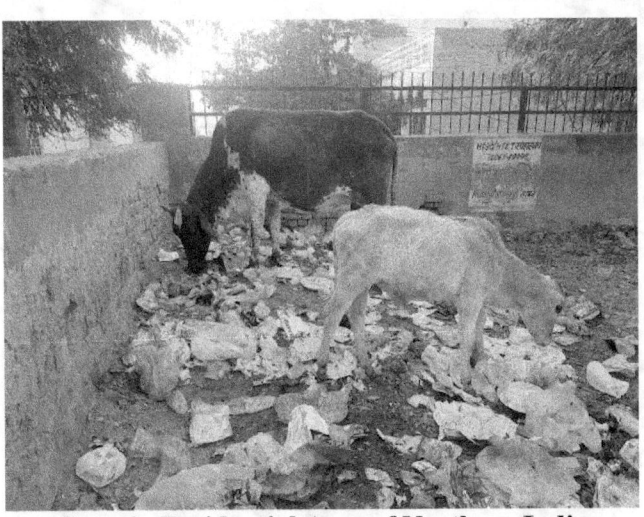

Cows in Residential Area of Northern India

3. Beautiful Heron in Northern India

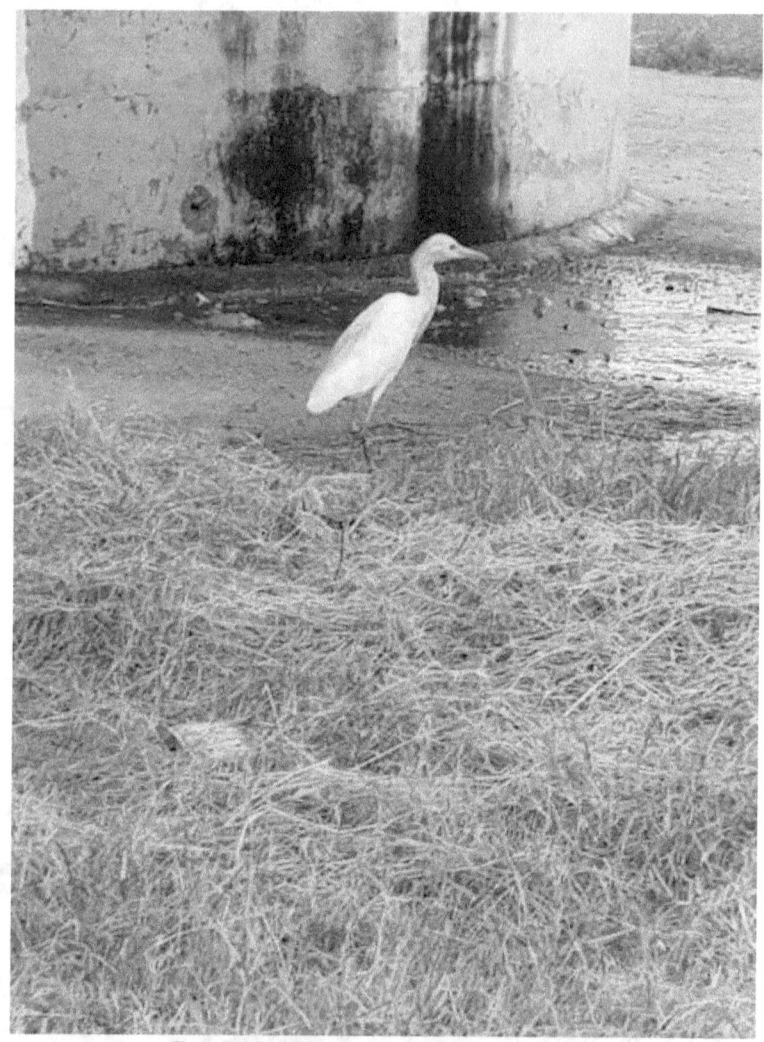

Beautiful Heron in Northern India

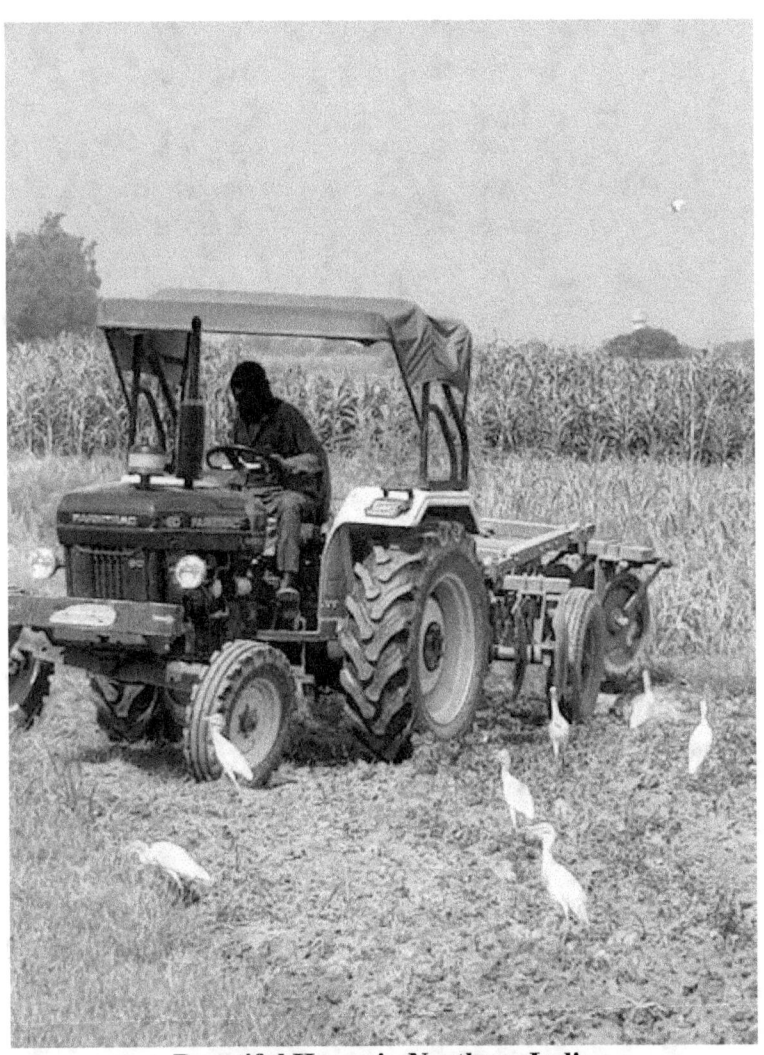

Beautiful Heron in Northern India

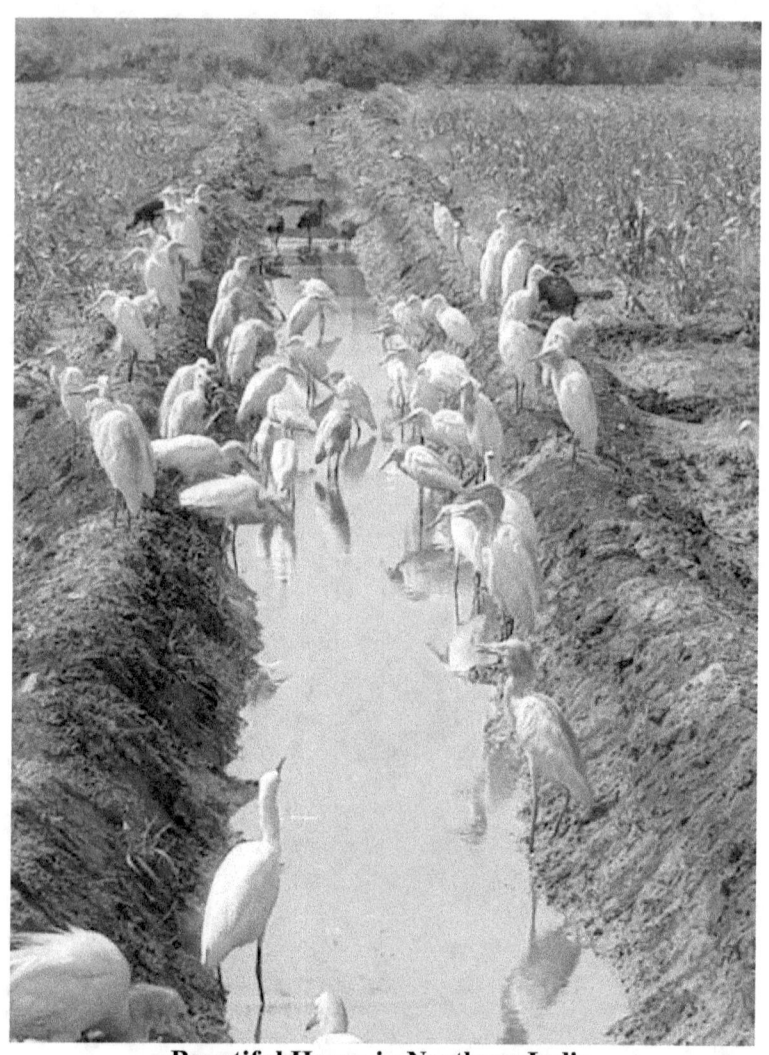
Beautiful Heron in Northern India

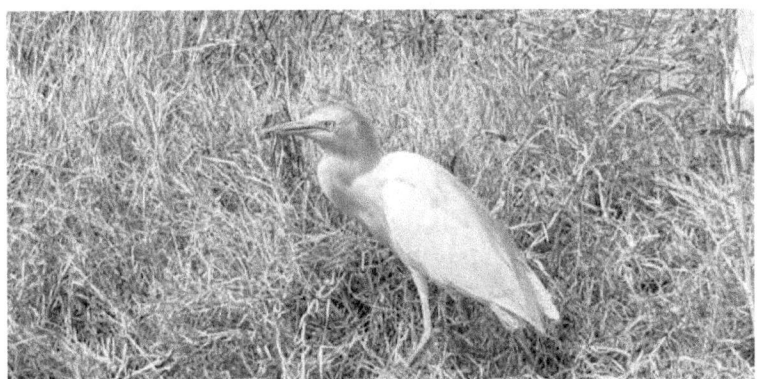

Beautiful Heron in Northern India

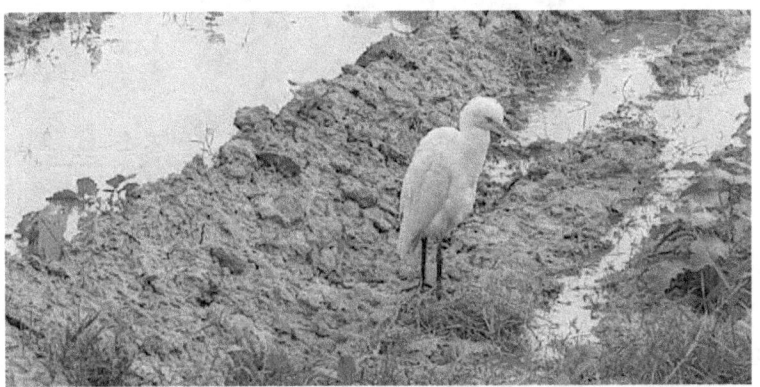

Beautiful Heron in Northern India

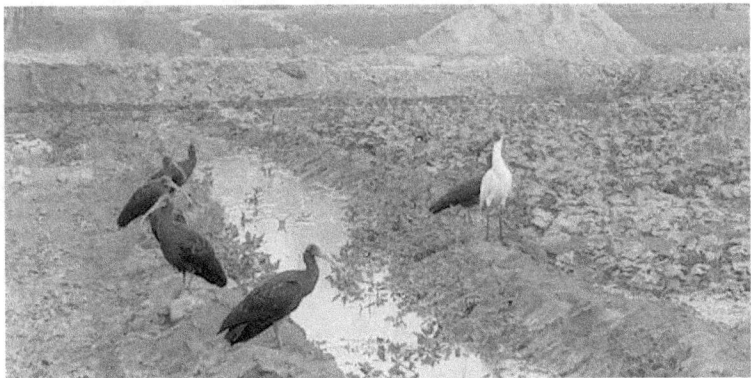

Beautiful Heron in Northern India

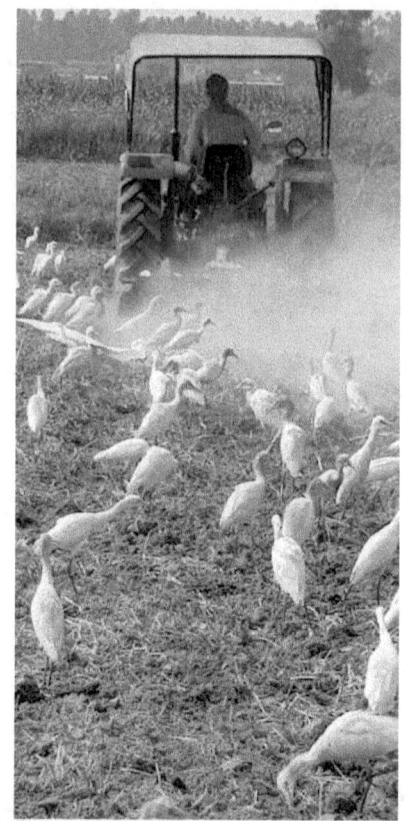

Beautiful Heron in Northern India

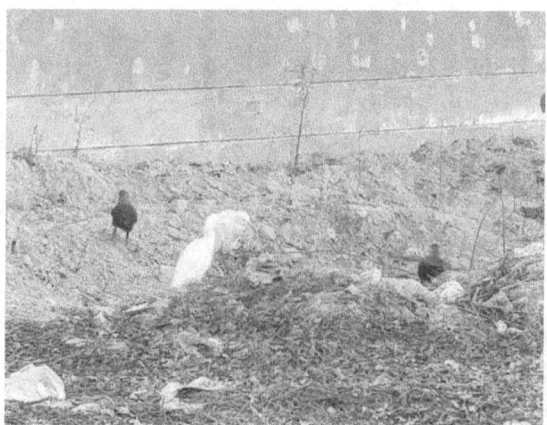

Beautiful Heron with Crows in Northern India

4. Ducks without Water in Northern India

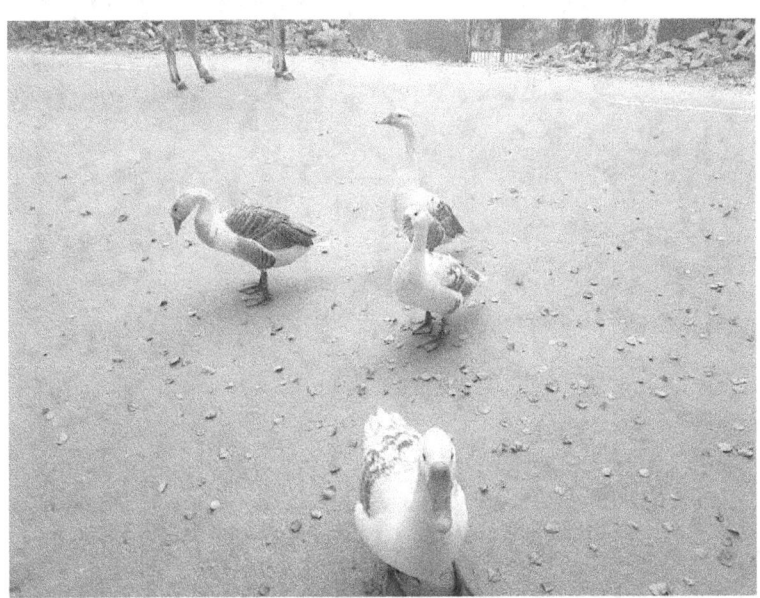

Ducks without Water in Northern India

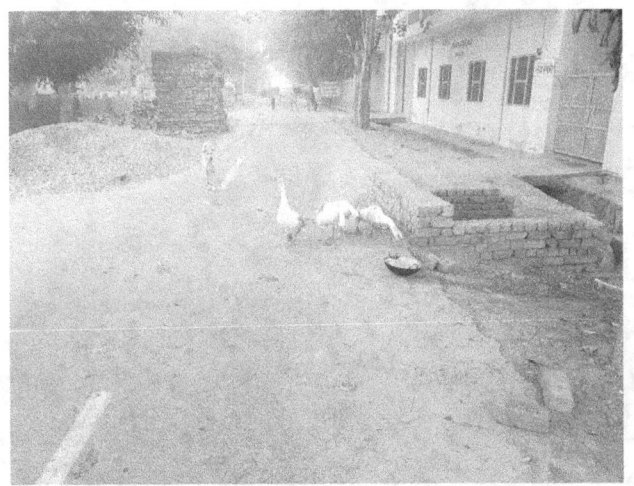

Ducks without Water in Northern India

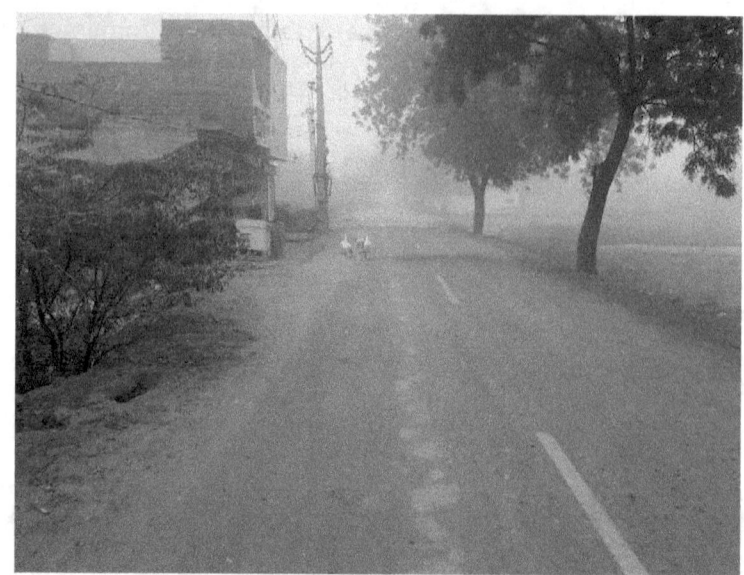
Ducks without Water in Northern India

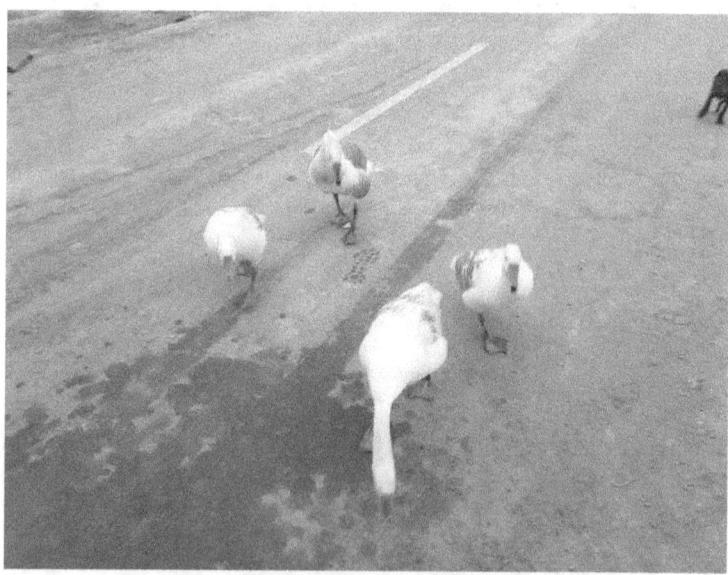
Ducks without Water in Northern India

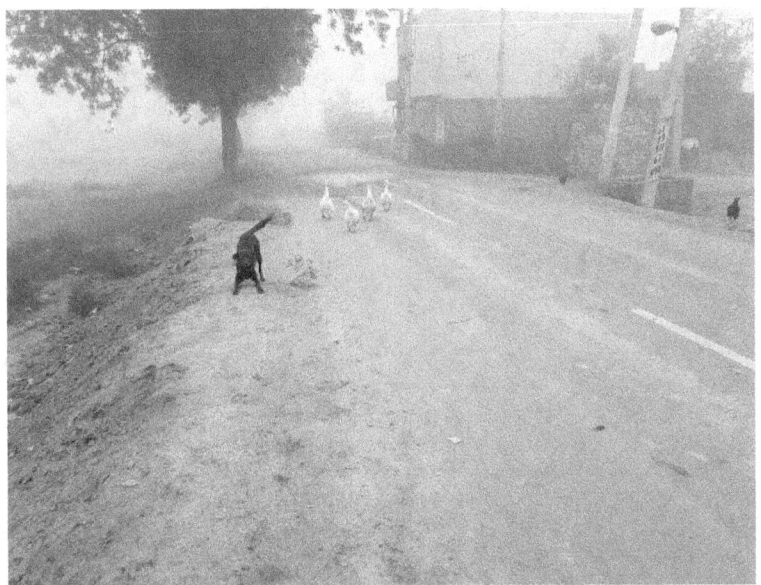

Ducks without Water in Northern India

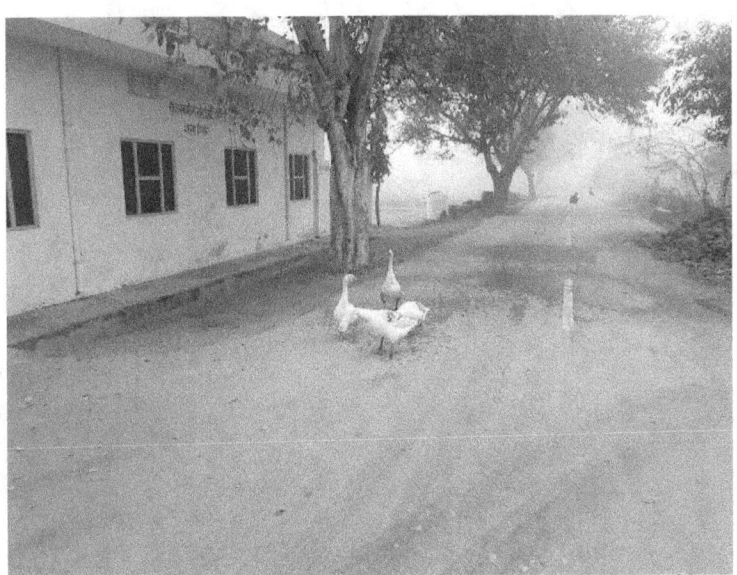

Ducks without Water in Northern India

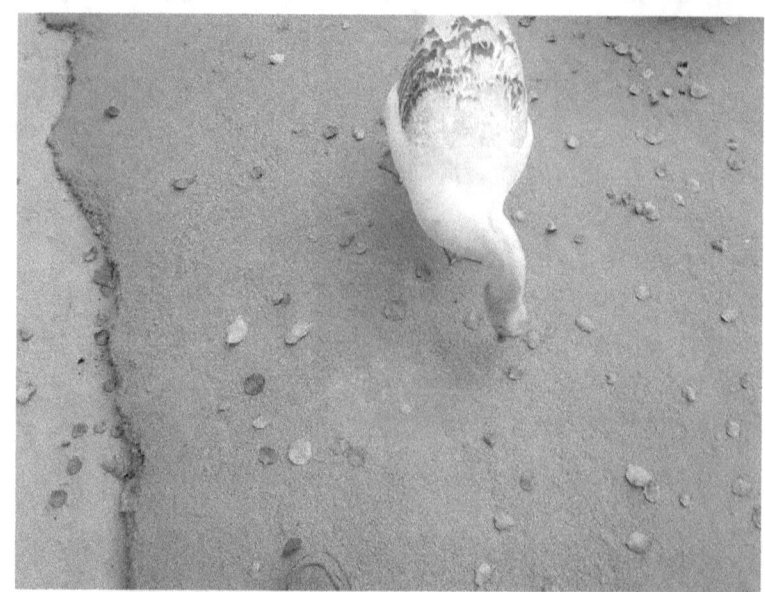

Ducks without Water in Northern India

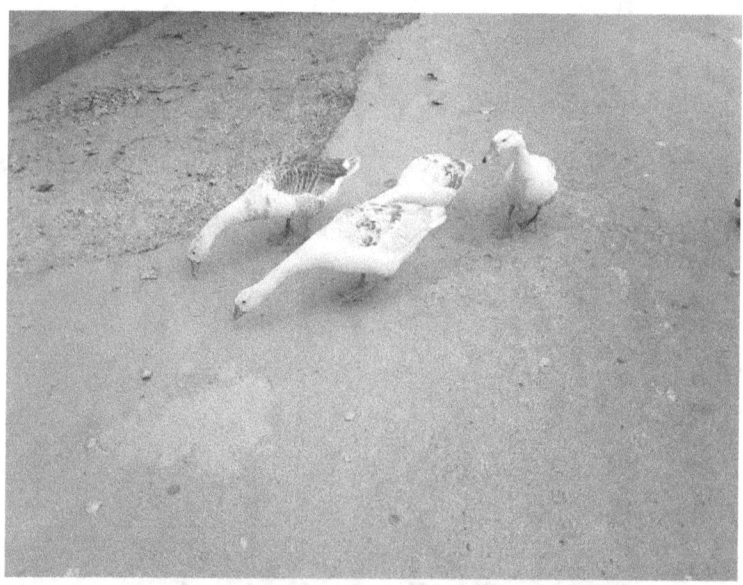

Ducks without Water in Northern India

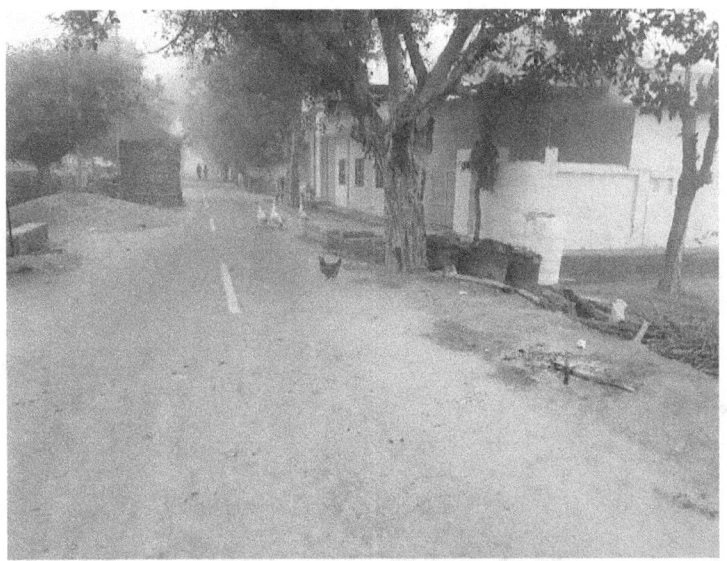

Ducks without Water in Northern India

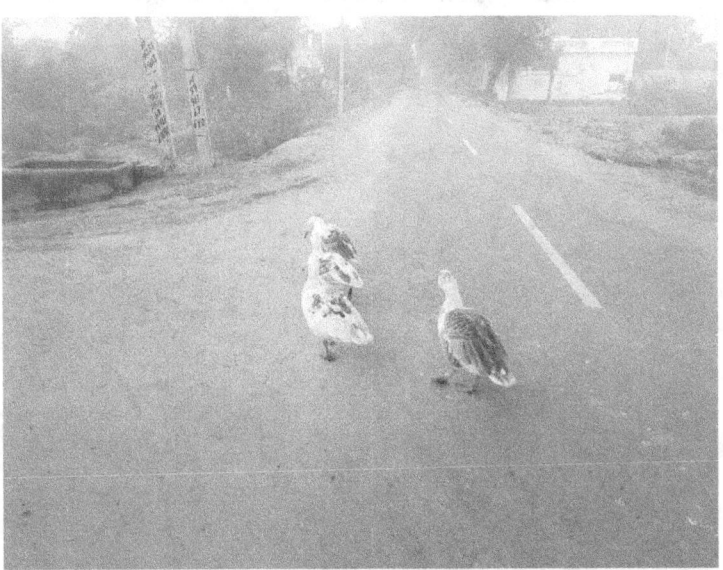

Ducks without Water in Northern India

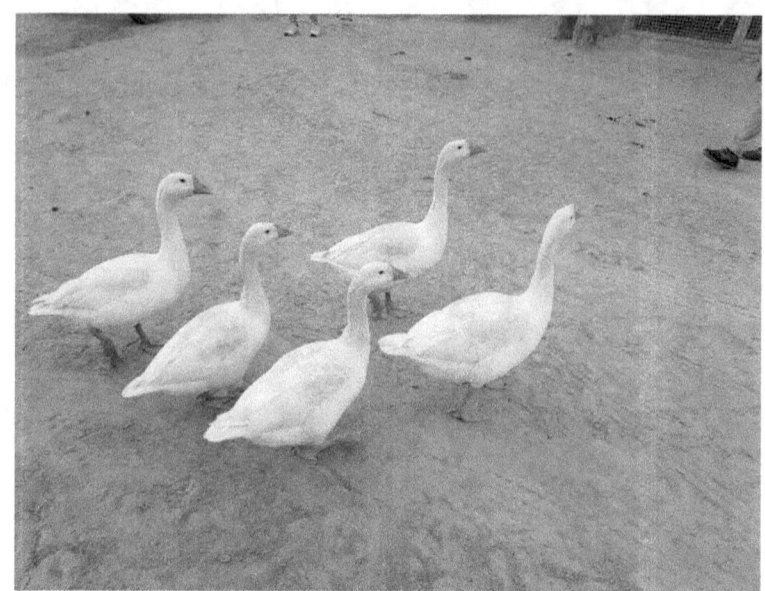
Ducks without Water in Northern India

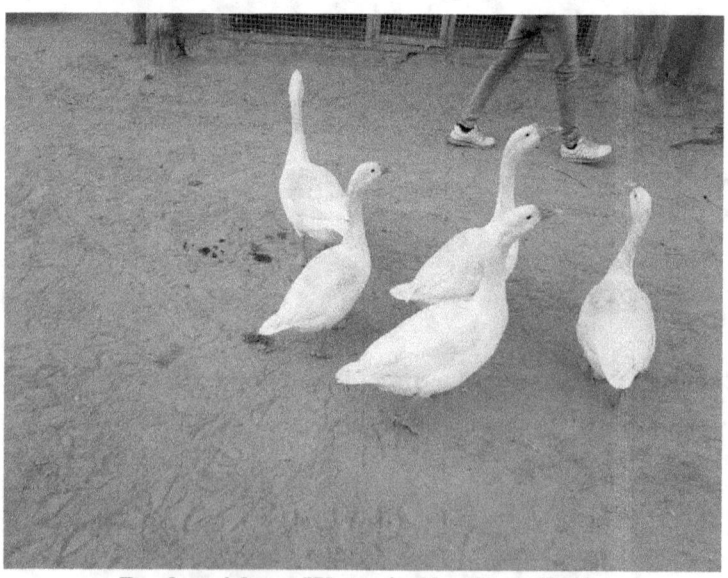
Ducks without Water in Northern India

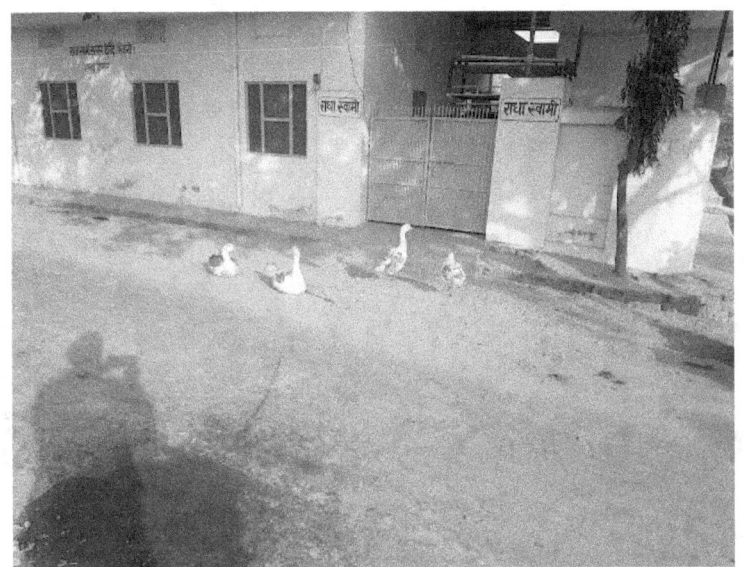

Ducks without Water in Northern India

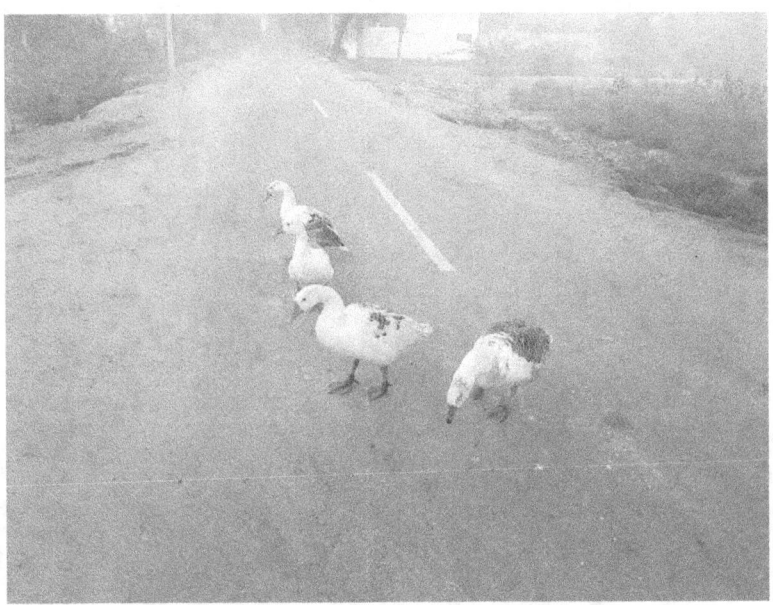

Ducks without Water in Northern India

5. Animals and Waste Spread over Undeveloped Market Place in Northern India

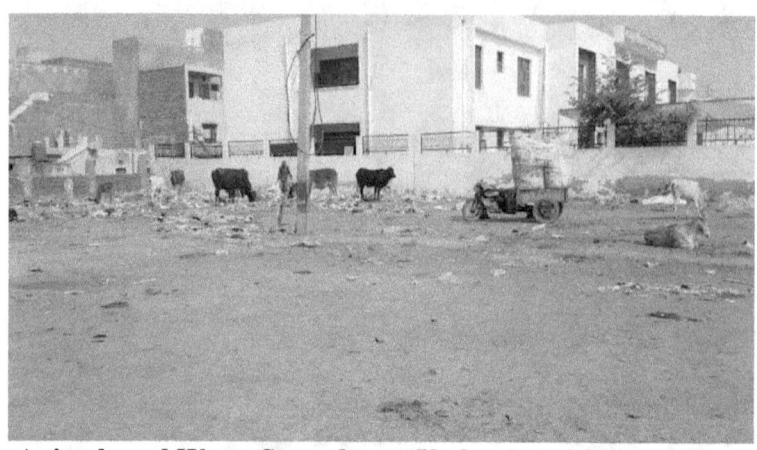

Animals and Waste Spread over Undeveloped Market Place in Northern India

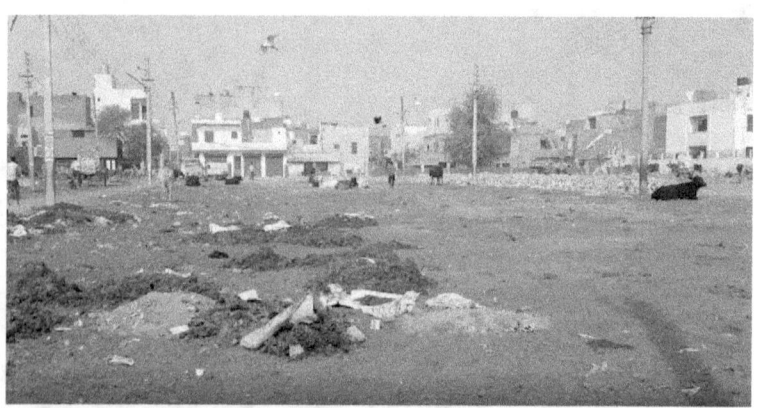

Animals and Waste Spread over Undeveloped Market Place in Northern India

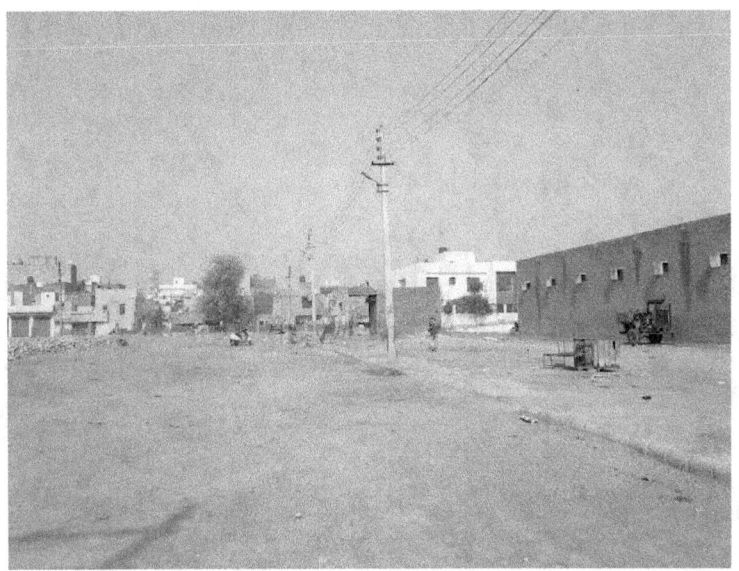

Animals and Waste Spread over Undeveloped Market Place in Northern India

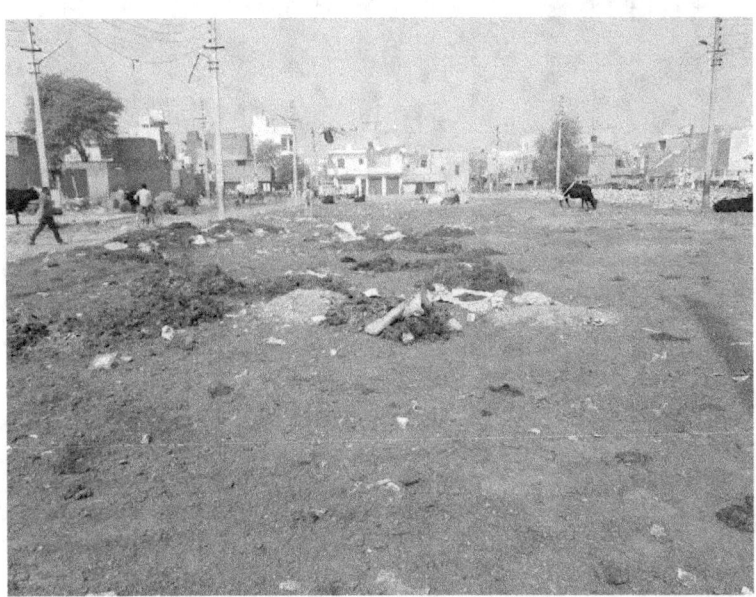

Animals and Waste Spread over Undeveloped Market Place in Northern India

6. Vehicles and People on a Road Crossing in Northern India

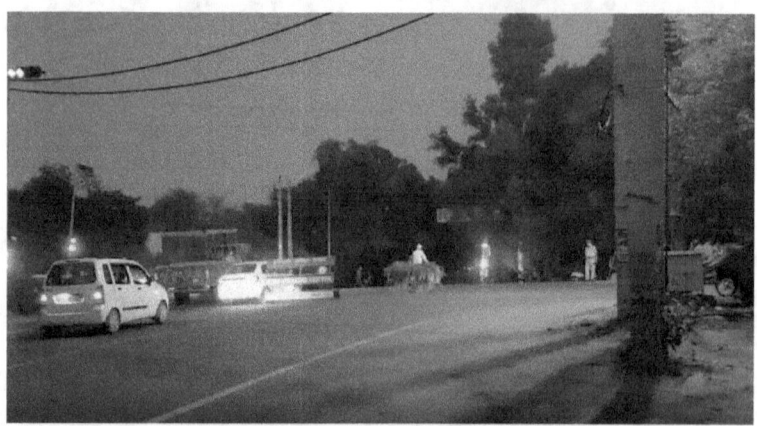

Vehicles and People on a Road Crossing in Northern India

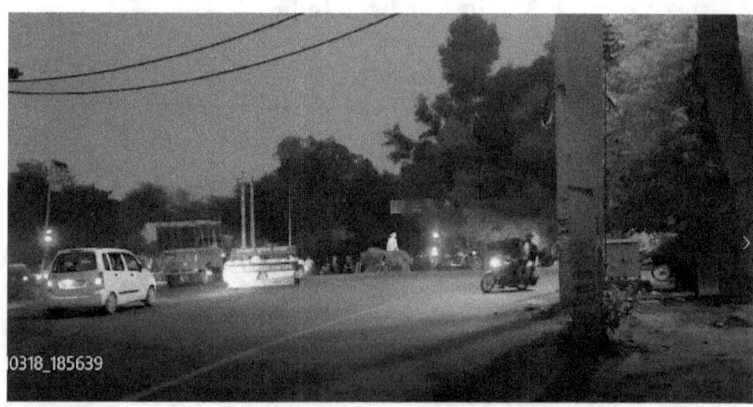

Vehicles and People on a Road Crossing in Northern India

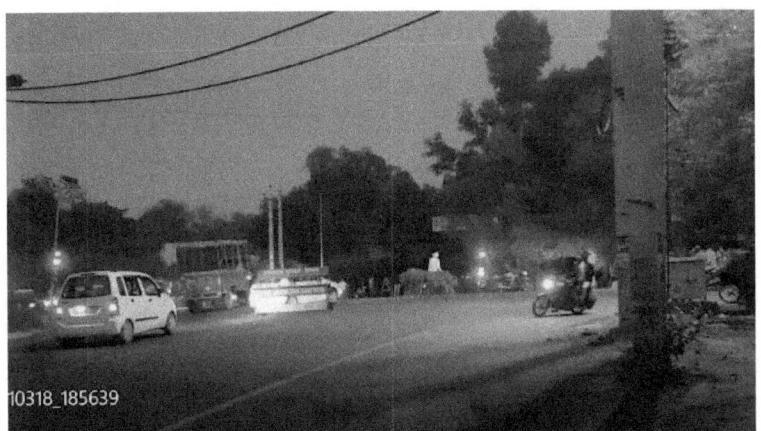

Vehicles and People on a Road Crossing in Northern India

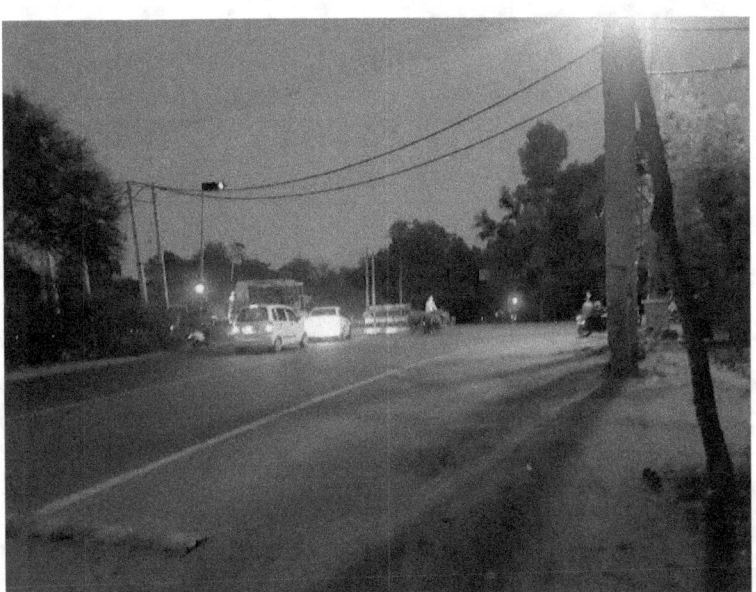

Vehicles and People on a Road Crossing in Northern India

7. Squirrel Drinking Water in Northern India

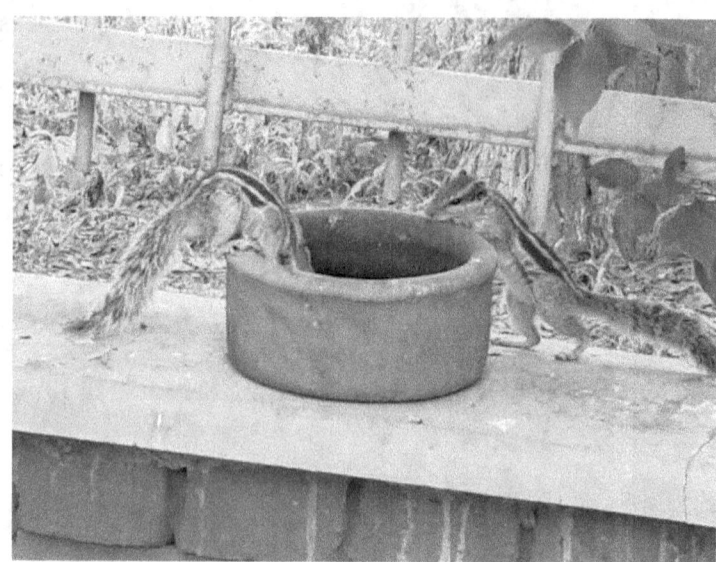

Two Squirrel Drinking Water in Northern India

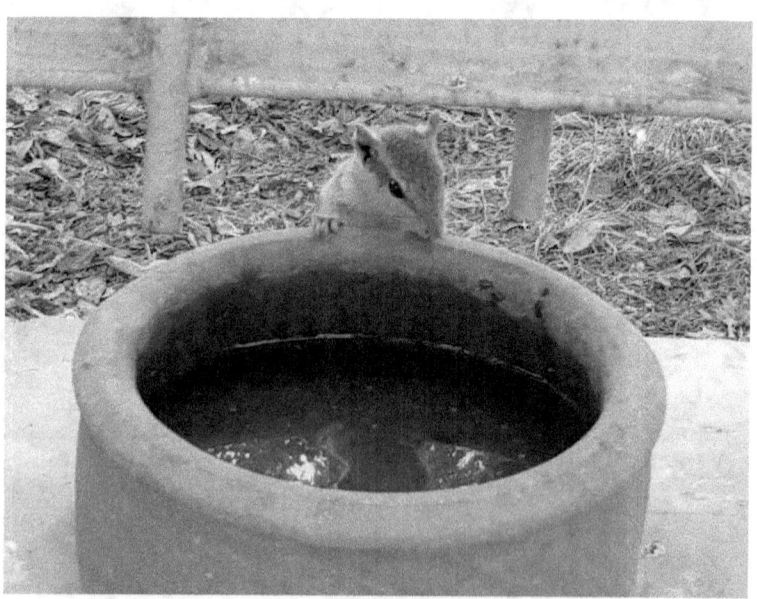

Squirrel Drinking Water in Northern India

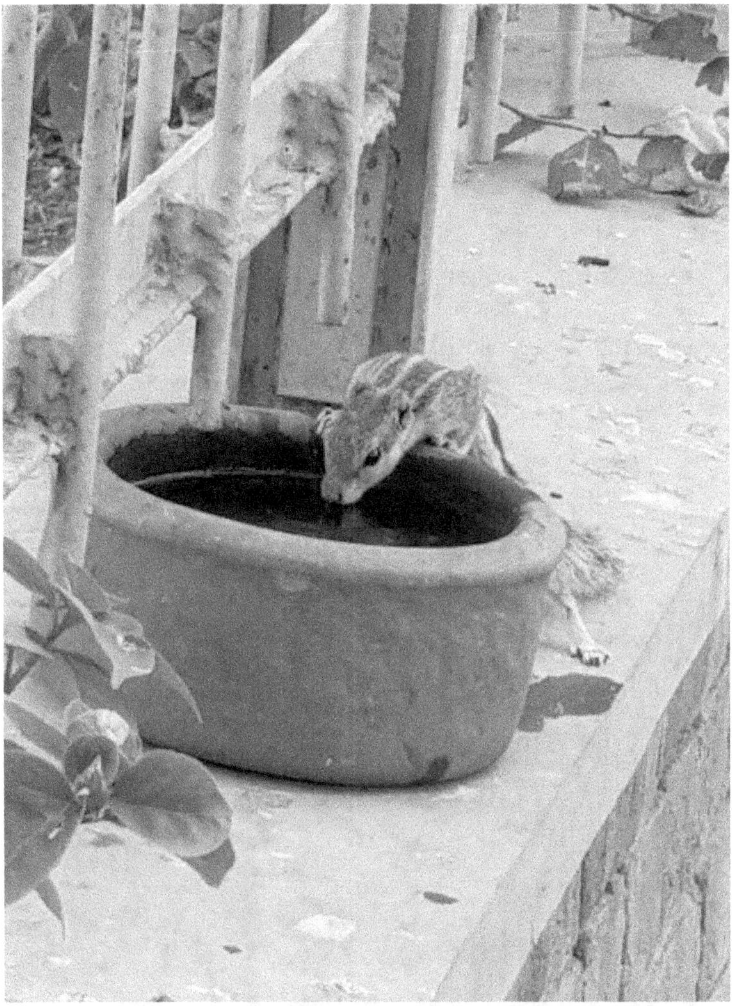

Squirrel Drinking Water in Northern India

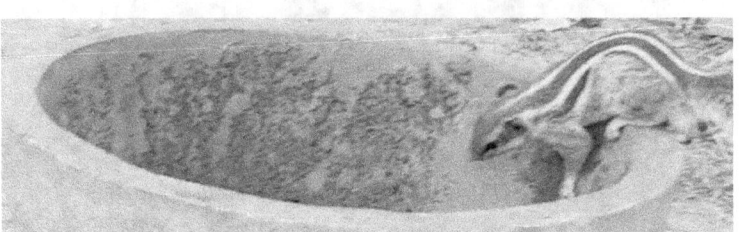

Squirrel Drinking Water in Northern India

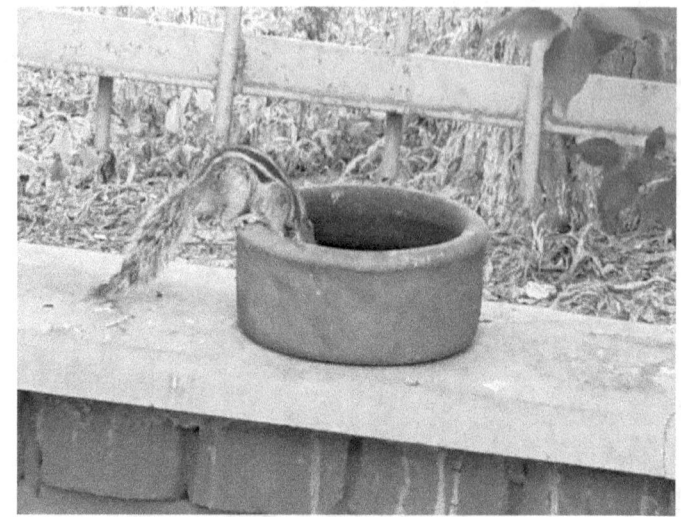

Squirrel Drinking Water in Northern India

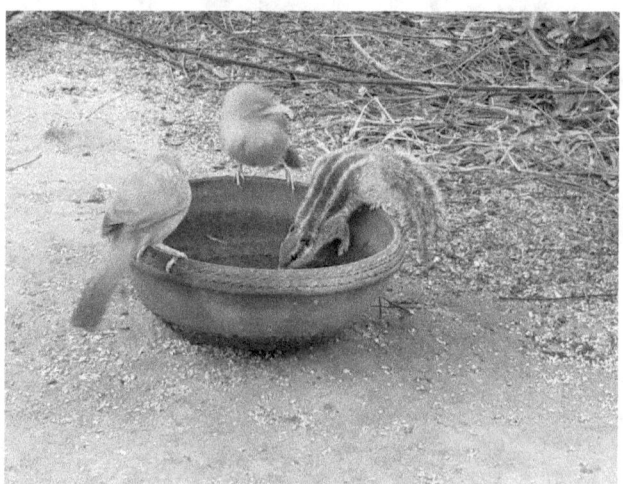

Squirrel Drinking Water in Northern India

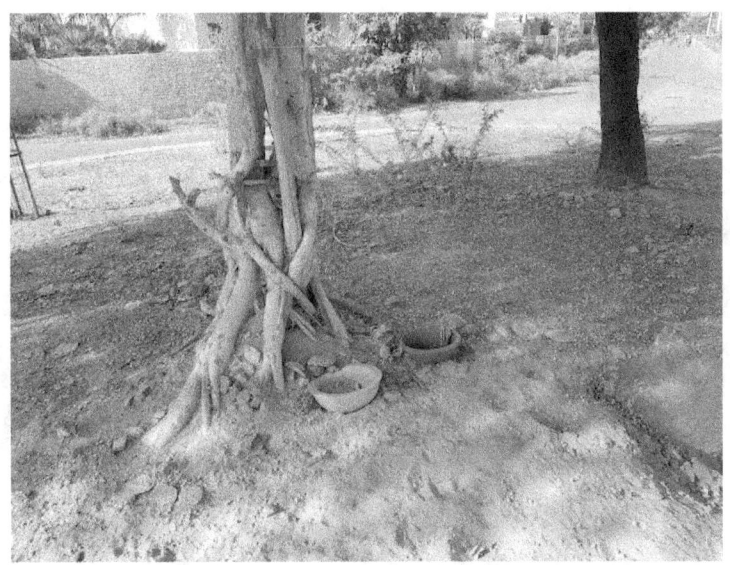

Squirrel Drinking Water in Northern India

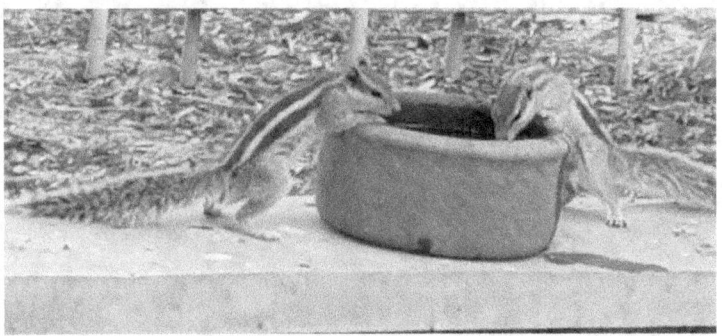

Two Squirrel Drinking Water in Northern India

8. Public Park after Organizing a Function by Someone in Northern India

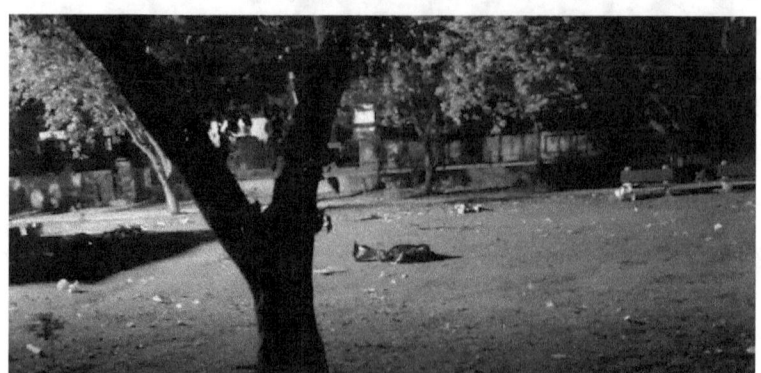

Public Park after Organizing a Function by Someone in Northern India

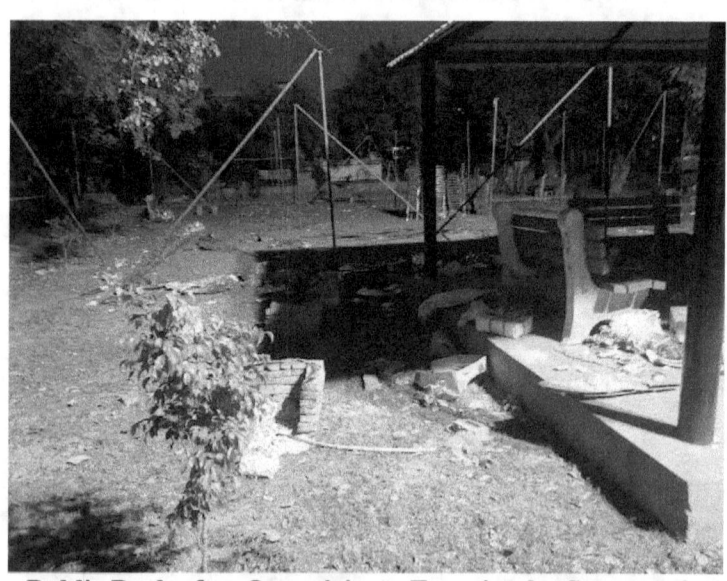

Public Park after Organizing a Function by Someone in Northern India

9. Honey Bee as a Pollinator in Northern India

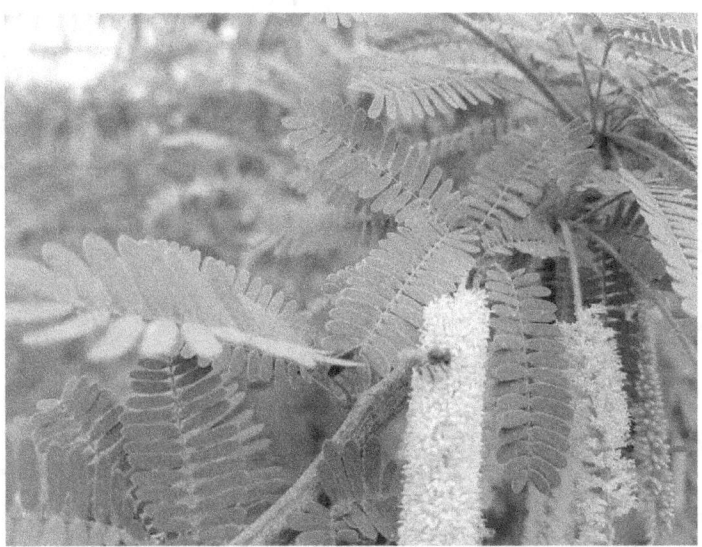

Honey Bee as a Pollinator in Northern India

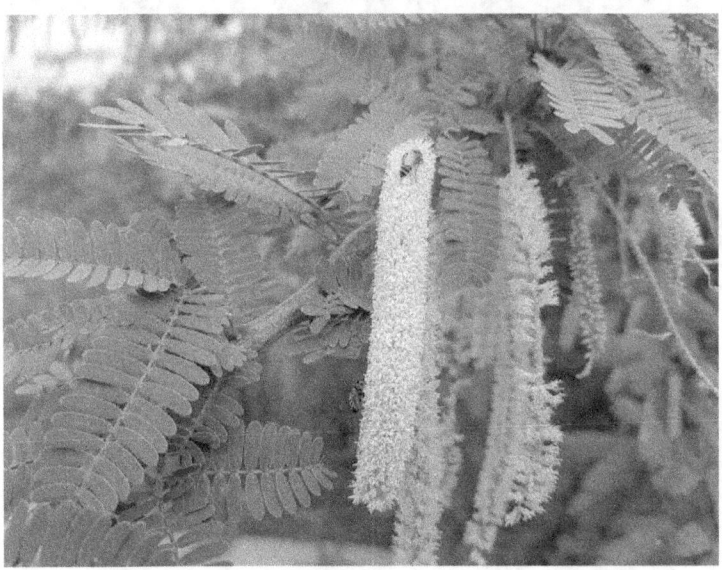

Honey Bee as a Pollinator in Northern India

10. People Moving on the Road in a Town of Northern India

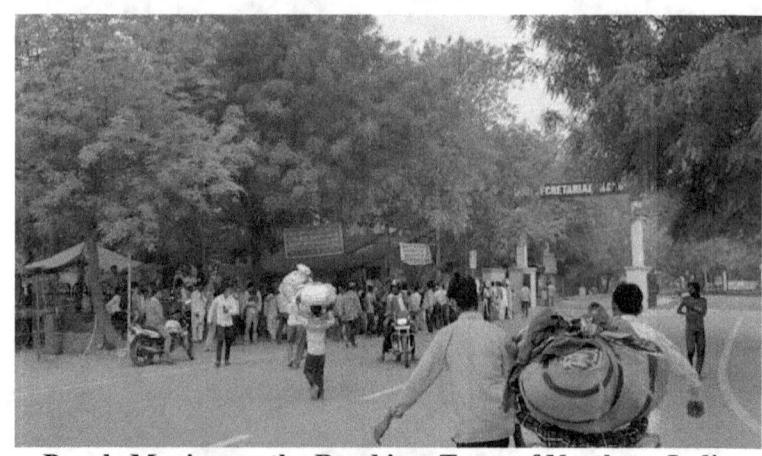

People Moving on the Road in a Town of Northern India

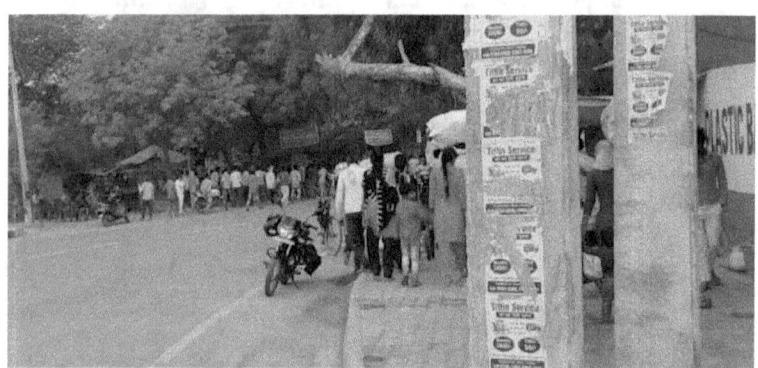

People Moving on the Road in a Town of Northern India

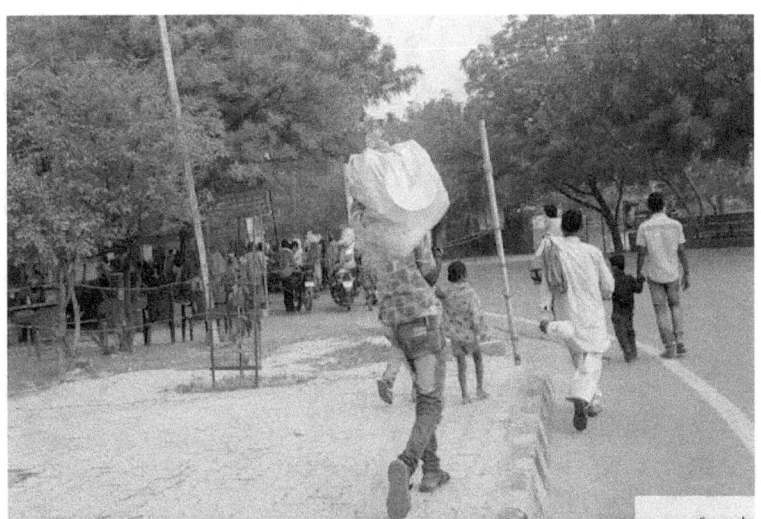
People Moving on the Road in a Town of Northern India

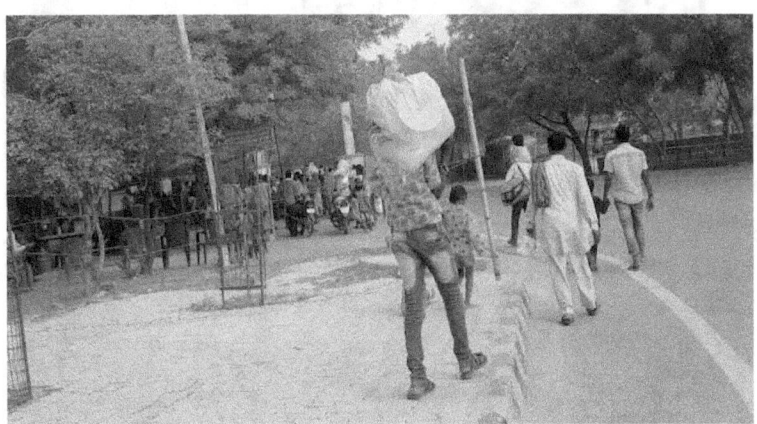
People Moving on the Road in a Town of Northern India

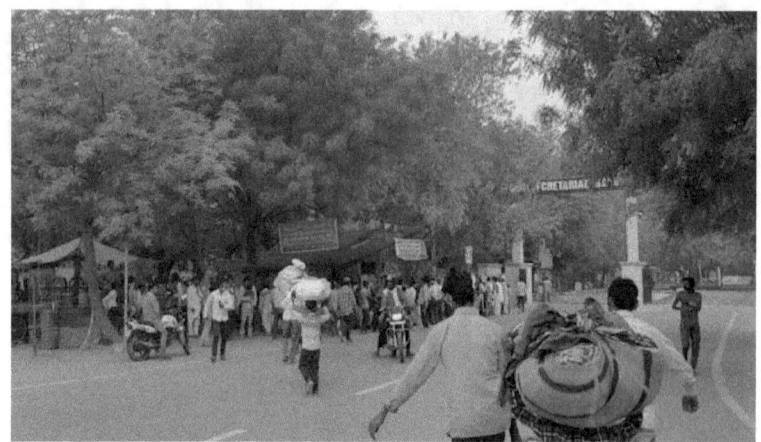

People Moving on the Road in a Town of Northern India

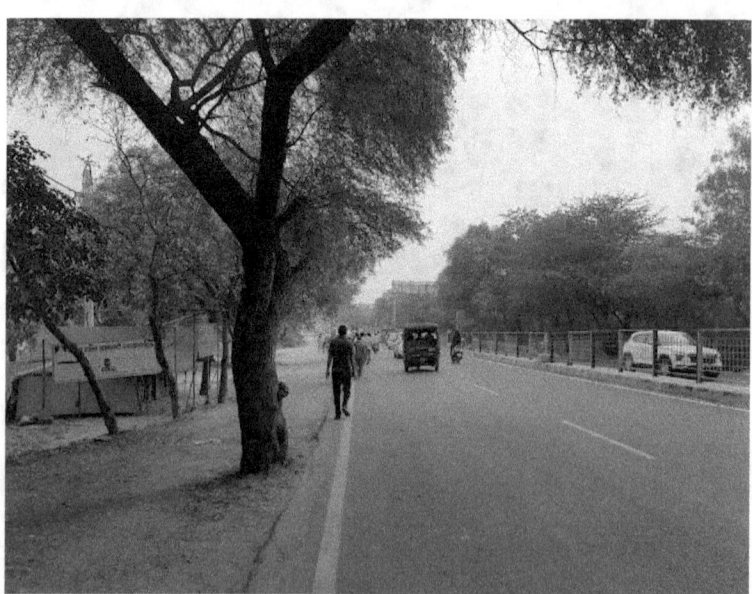

People Moving on the Road in a Town of Northern India

11. Overloaded Tricycle in Northern India

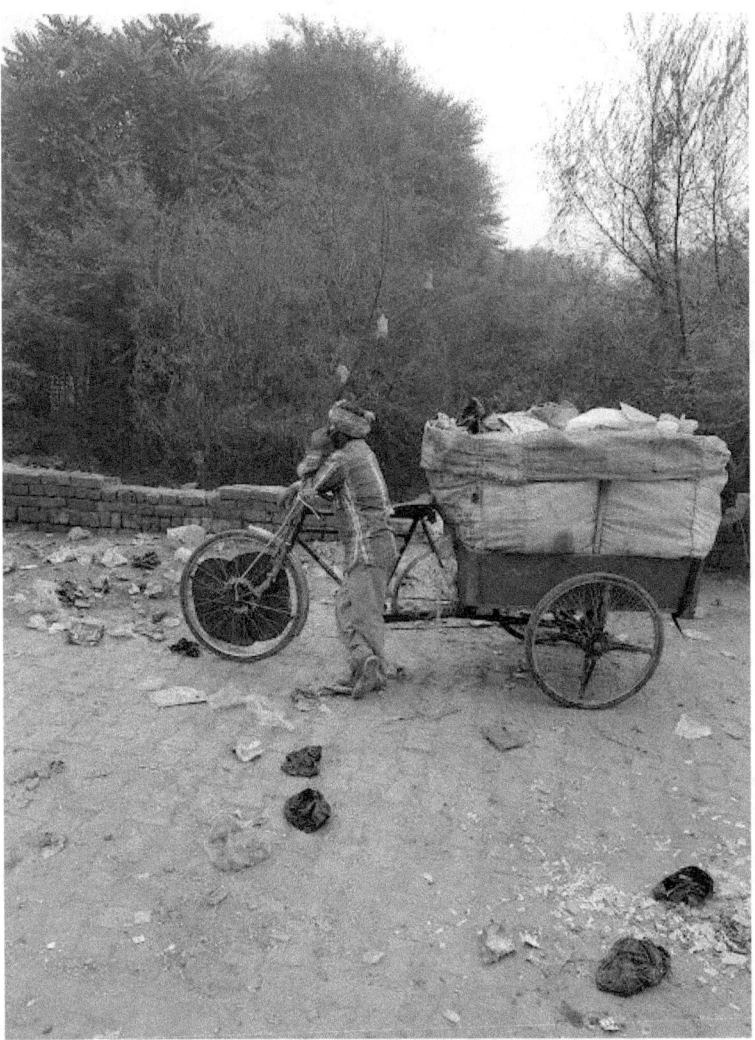

Overloaded Tricycle in Northern India

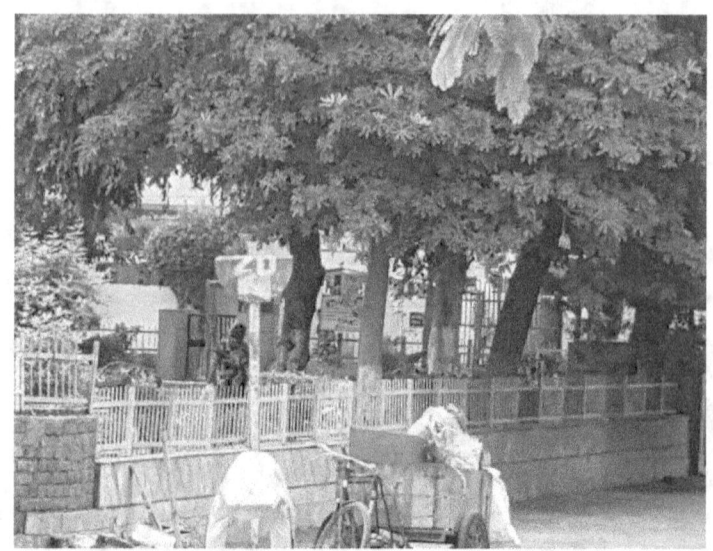
Overloaded Tricycle in Northern India

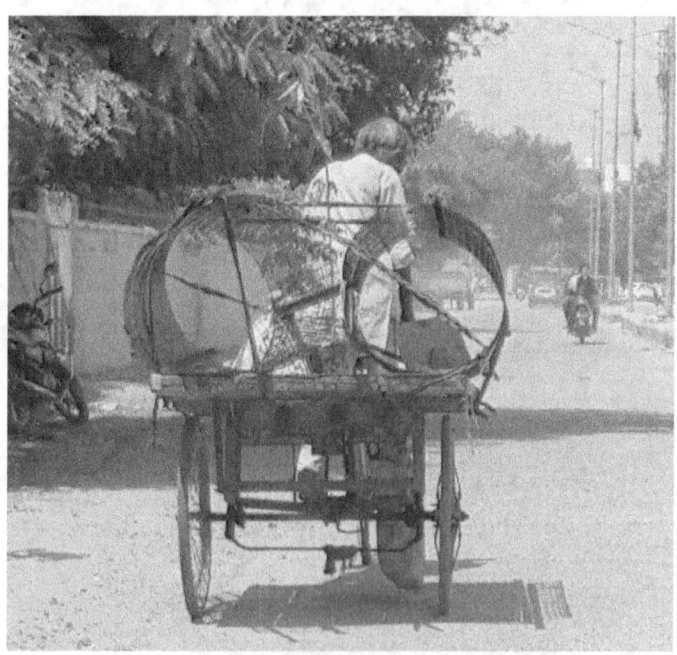
Overloaded Tricycle in Northern India

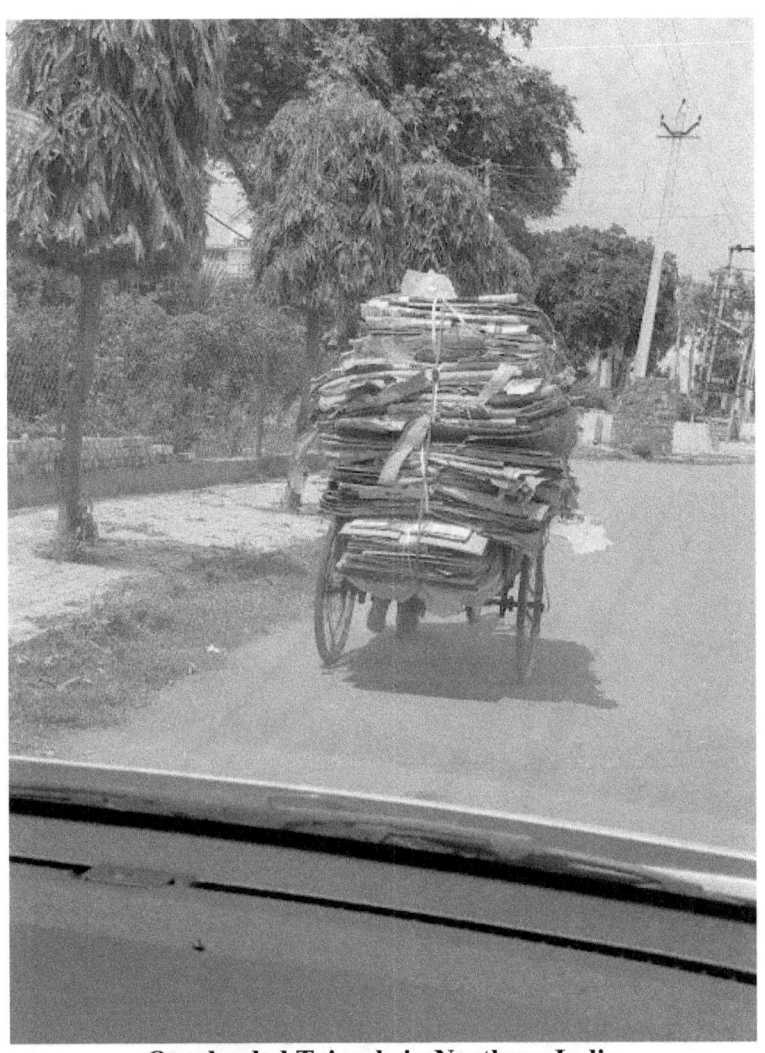

Overloaded Tricycle in Northern India

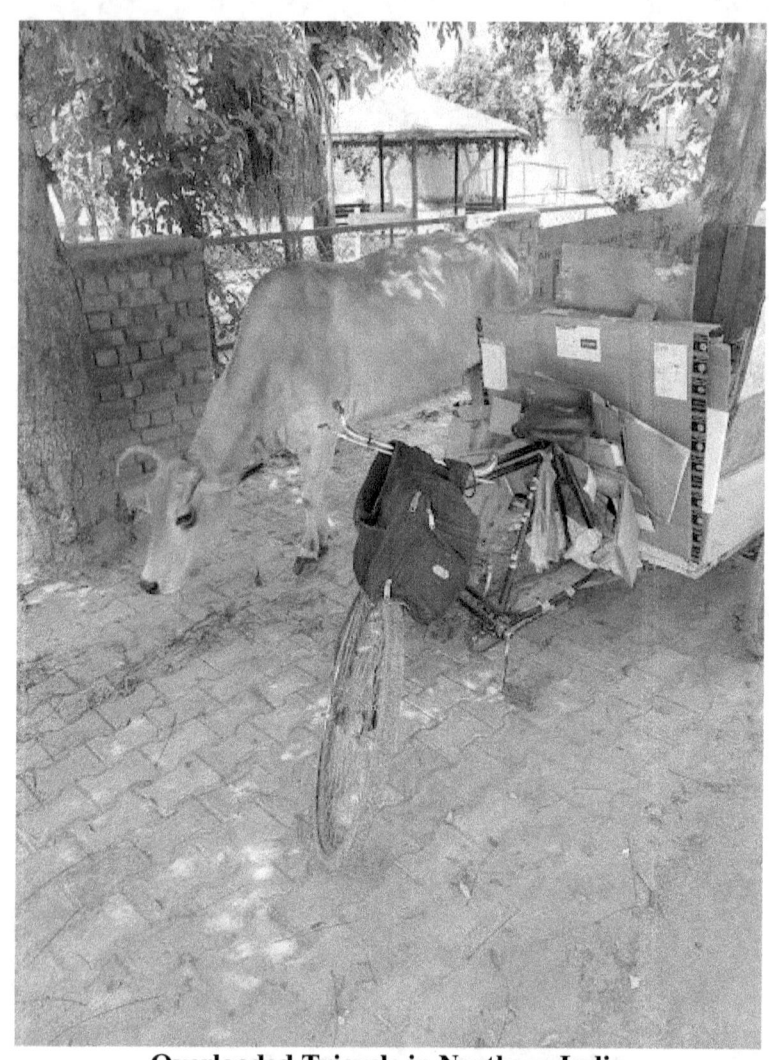

Overloaded Tricycle in Northern India

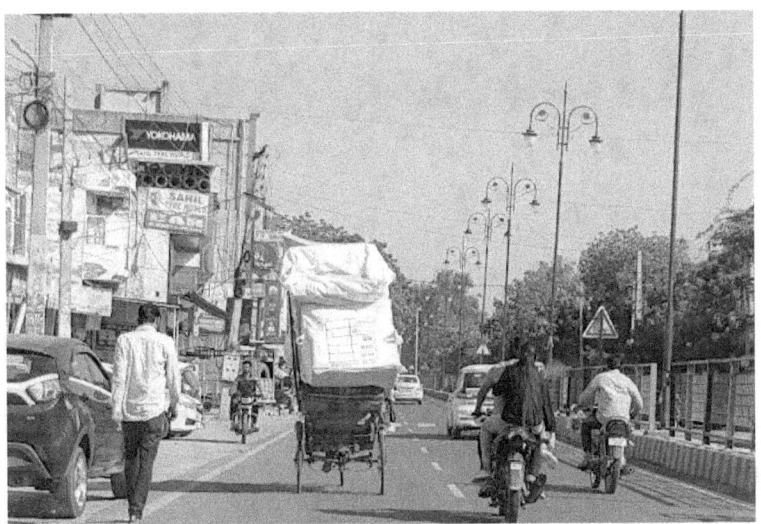

Overloaded Tricycle in Northern India

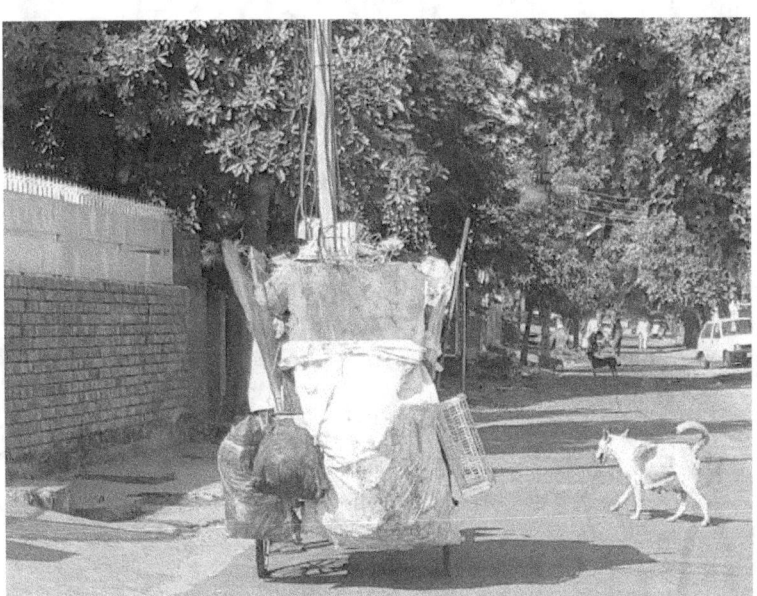

Overloaded Tricycle in Northern India

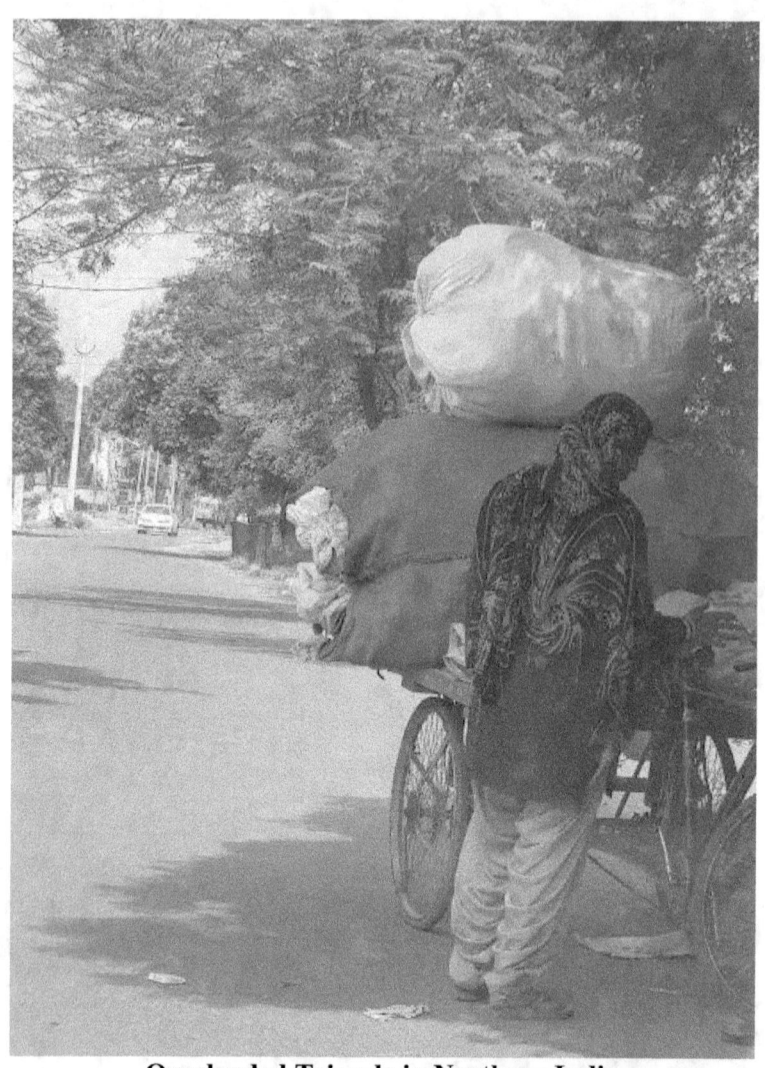
Overloaded Tricycle in Northern India

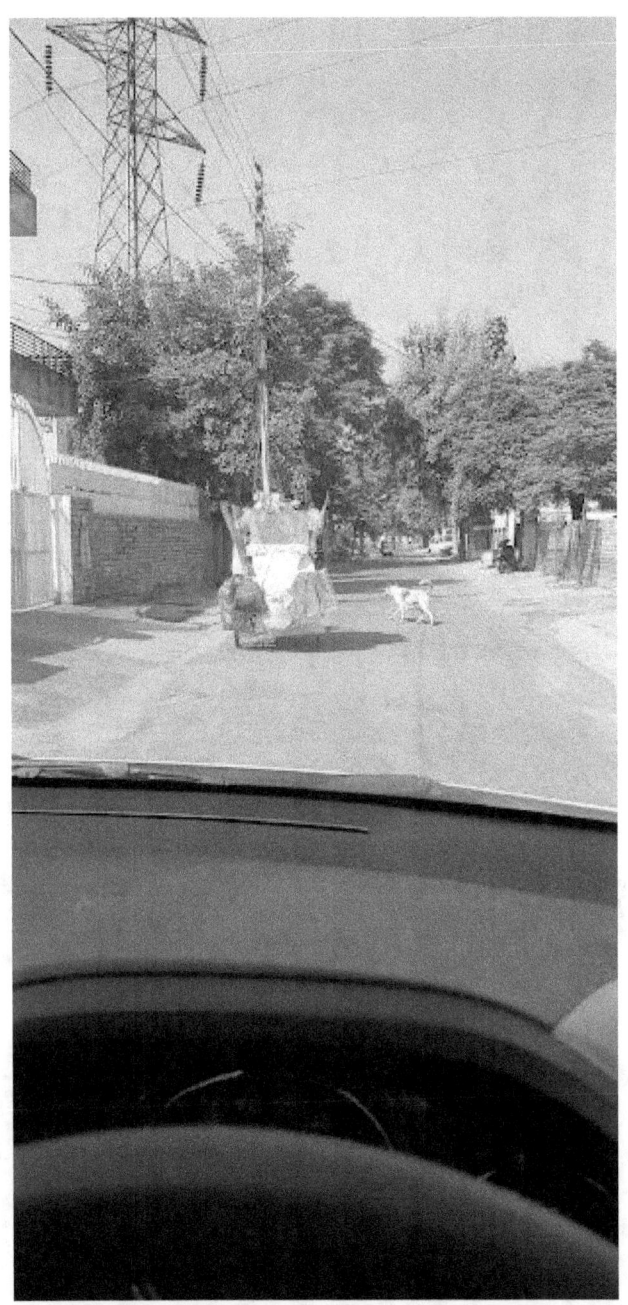

Overloaded Tricycle in Northern India

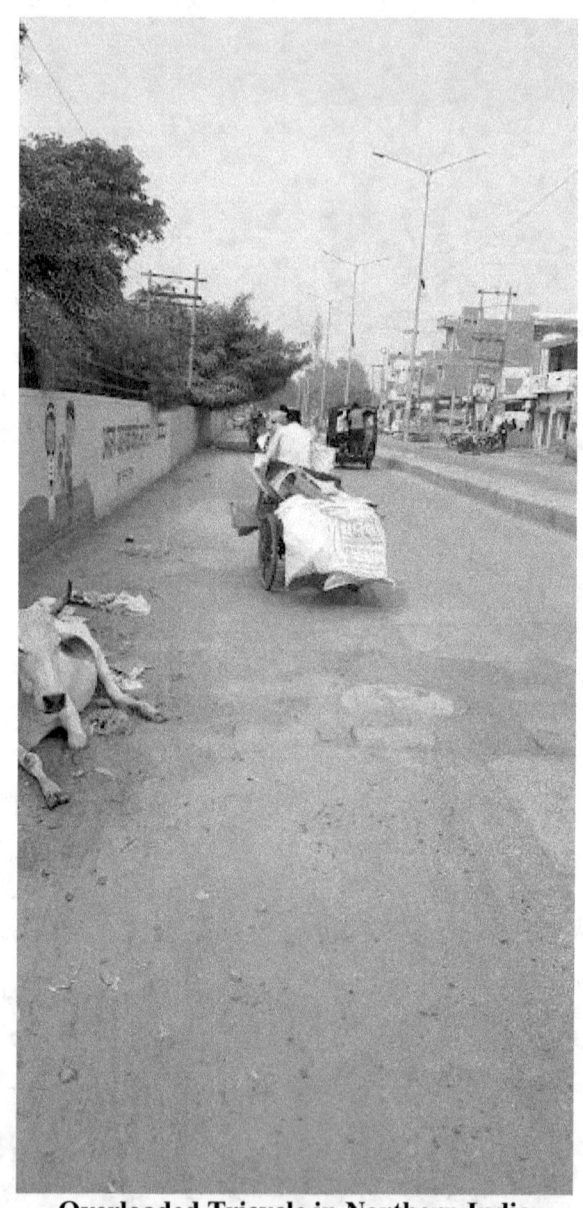

Overloaded Tricycle in Northern India

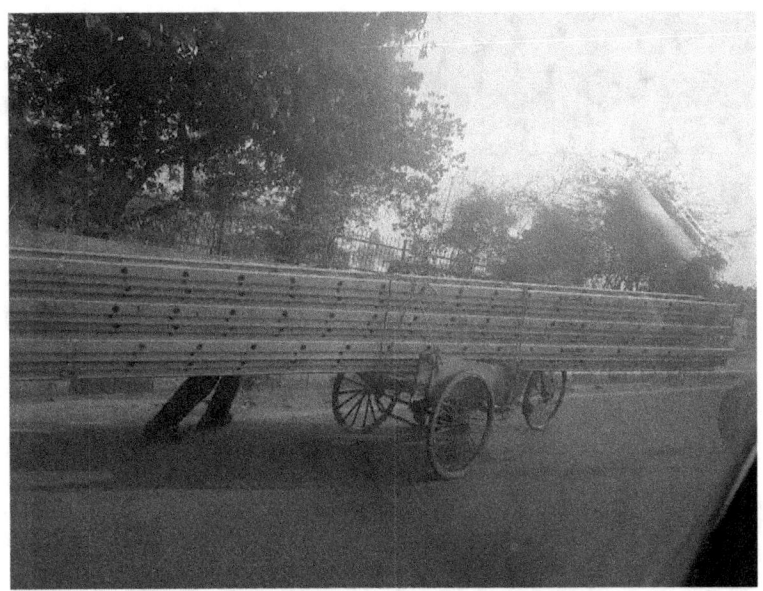

Overloaded Tricycle in Northern India

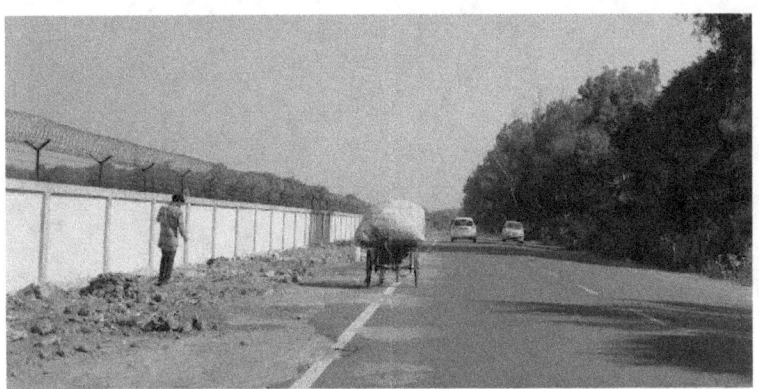

Overloaded Tricycle in Northern India

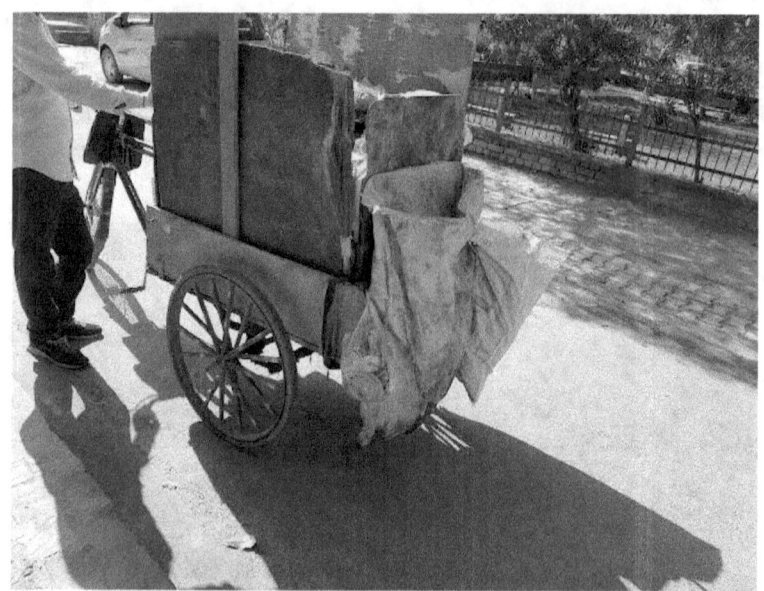

Overloaded Tricycle in Northern India

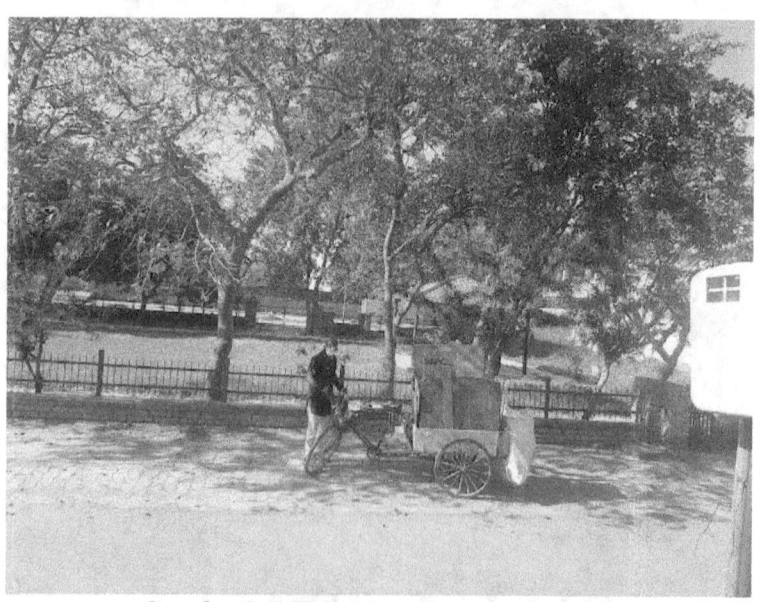

Overloaded Tricycle in Northern India

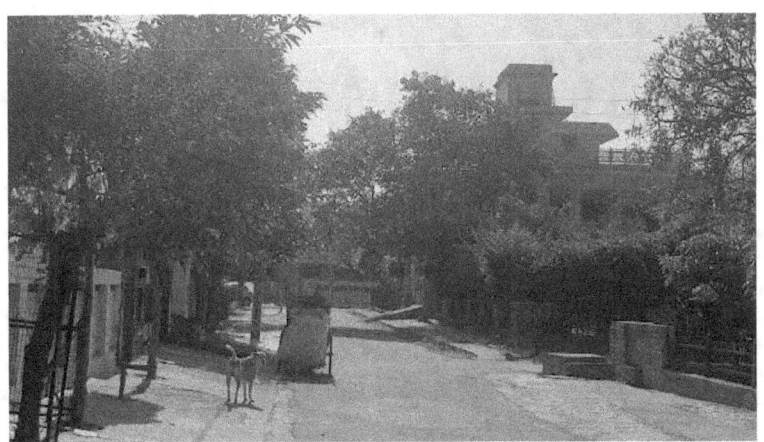

Overloaded Tricycle in Northern India

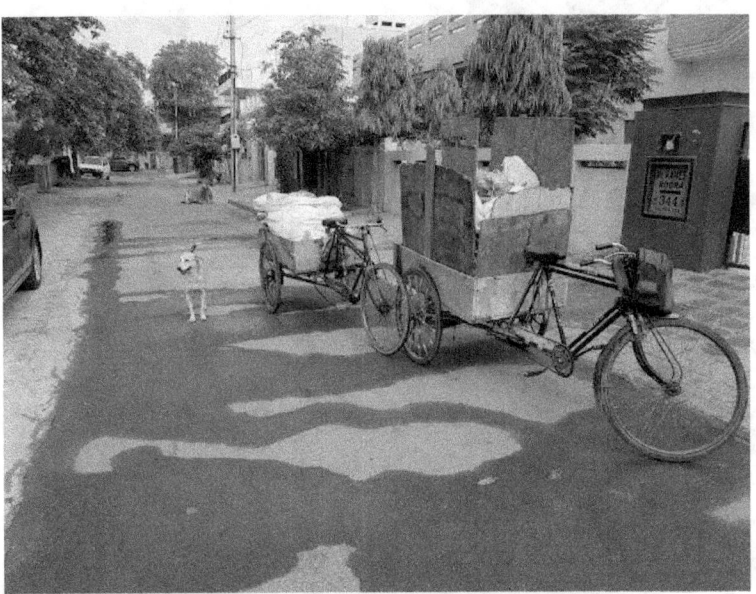

Overloaded Tricycle in Northern India

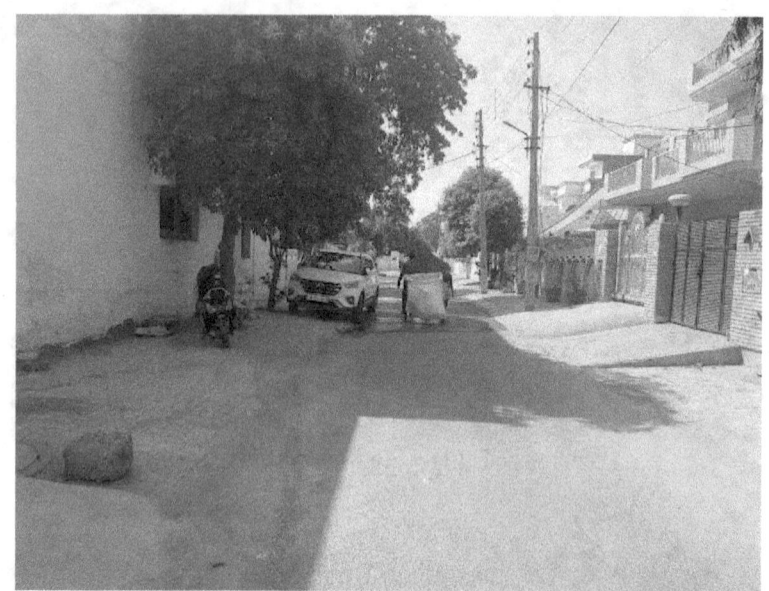

Overloaded Tricycle in Northern India

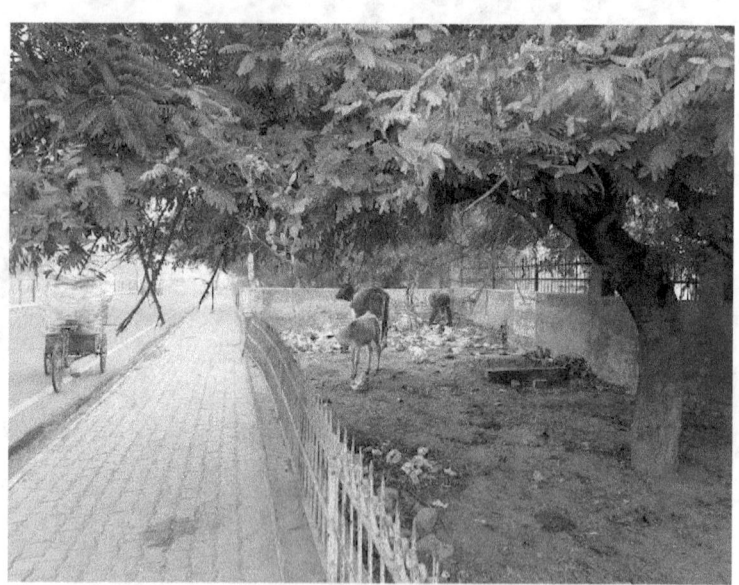

Overloaded Tricycle in Northern India

12. People Sitting on the Roof of a Passenger Bus in Northern India

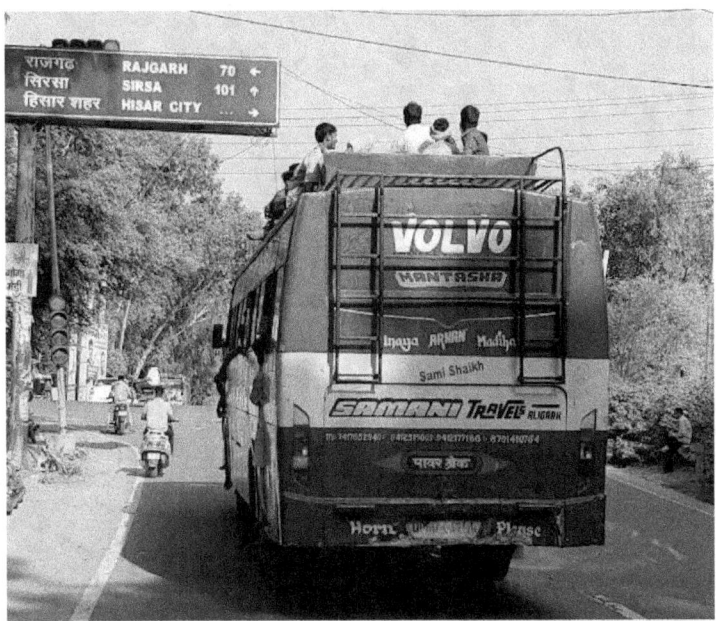

People Sitting on the Roof of a Passenger Bus in Northern India

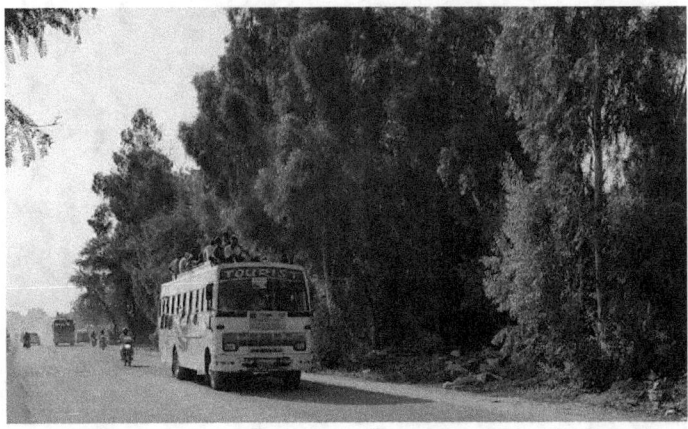

People Sitting on the Roof of a Passenger Bus in Northern India

13. Balloon Seller in a Residential Colony of a Town in Northern India

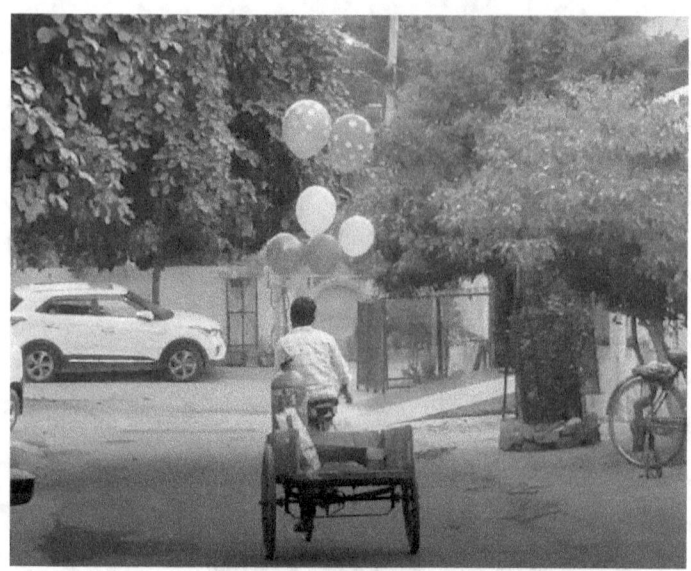

Balloon Seller in a Residential Colony of a Town in Northern India

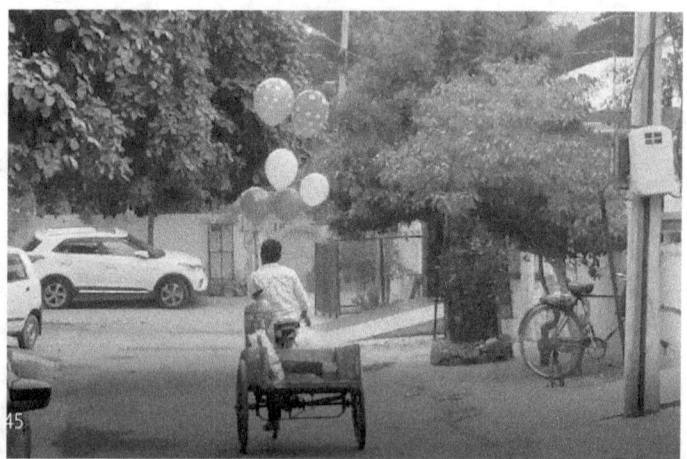

Balloon Seller in a Residential Colony of a Town in Northern India

14. Black Ducks Drying their Body sitting on Side Wall of Water Works in Northern India

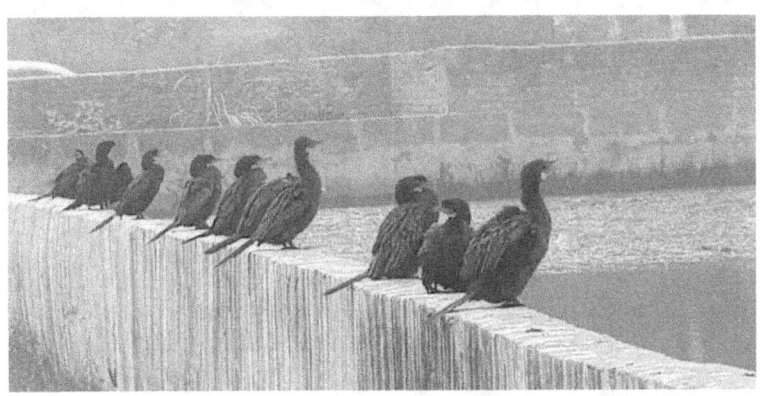

Black Ducks Drying their Body sitting on Side Wall of Water Works in Northern India

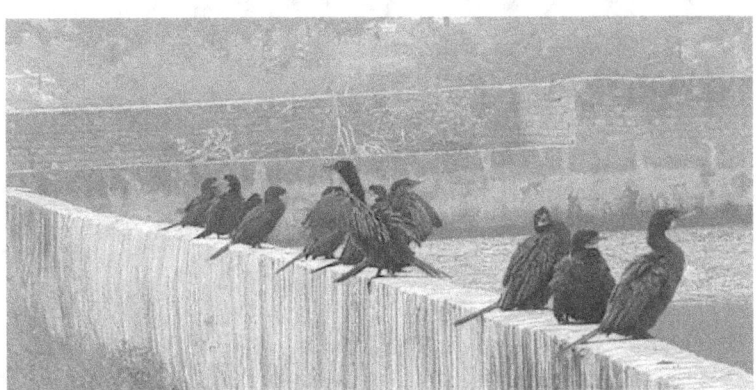

Black Ducks Drying their Body sitting on Side Wall of Water Works in Northern India

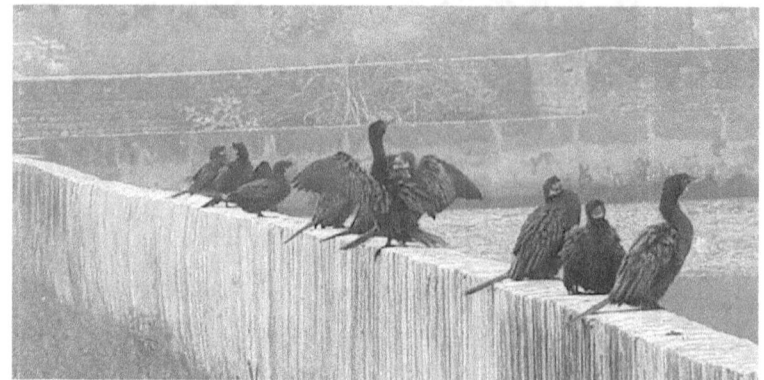

Black Ducks Drying their Body sitting on Side Wall of Water Works in Northern India

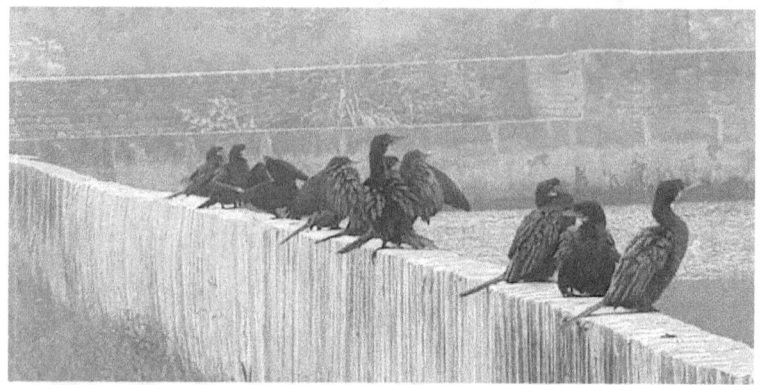

Black Ducks Drying their Body sitting on Side Wall of Water Works in Northern India

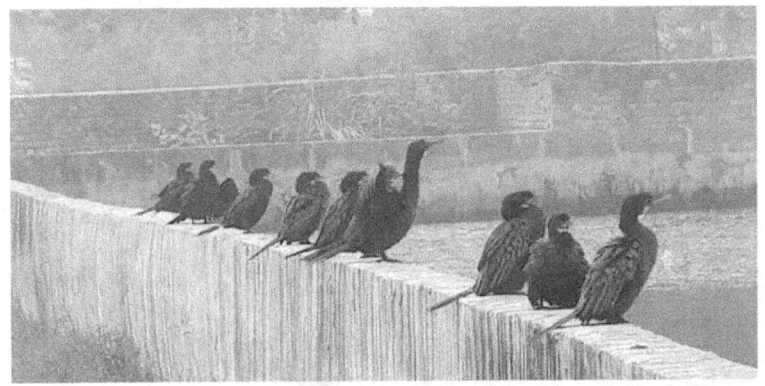

Black Ducks Drying their Body sitting on Side Wall of Water Works in Northern India

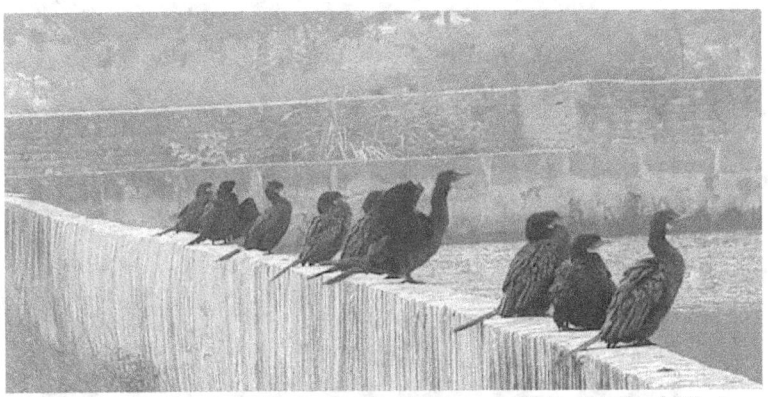

Black Ducks Drying their Body sitting on Side Wall of Water Works in Northern India

15. Pet Dog Playing with Plastic Bottle in Northern India

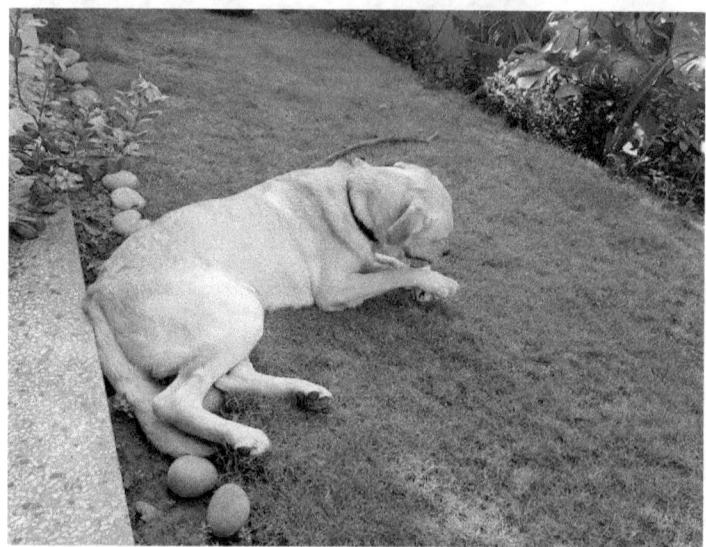

Pet Dog Playing with Plastic Bottle in Northern India

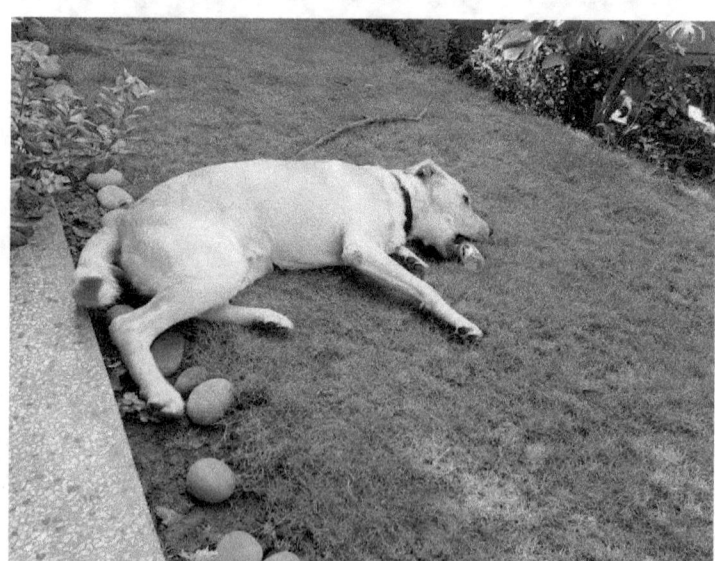

Pet Dog Playing with Plastic Bottle in Northern India

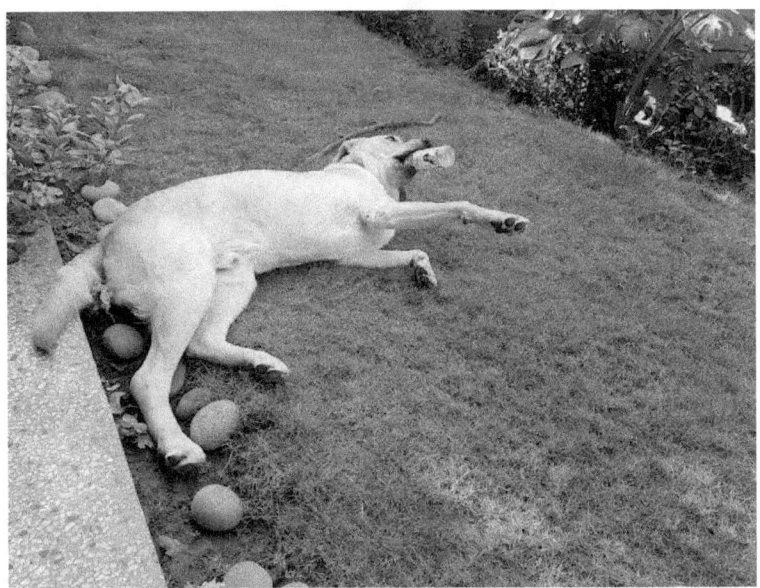

Pet Dog Playing with Plastic Bottle in Northern India

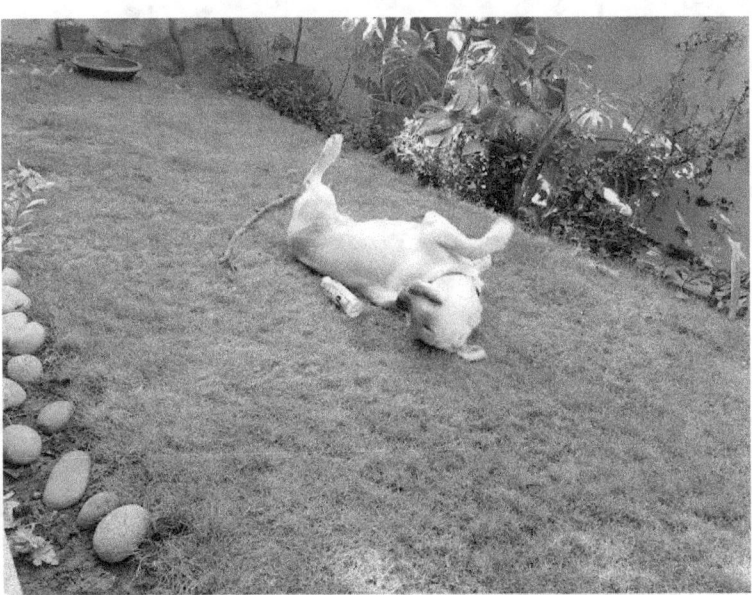

Pet Dog Playing with Plastic Bottle in Northern India

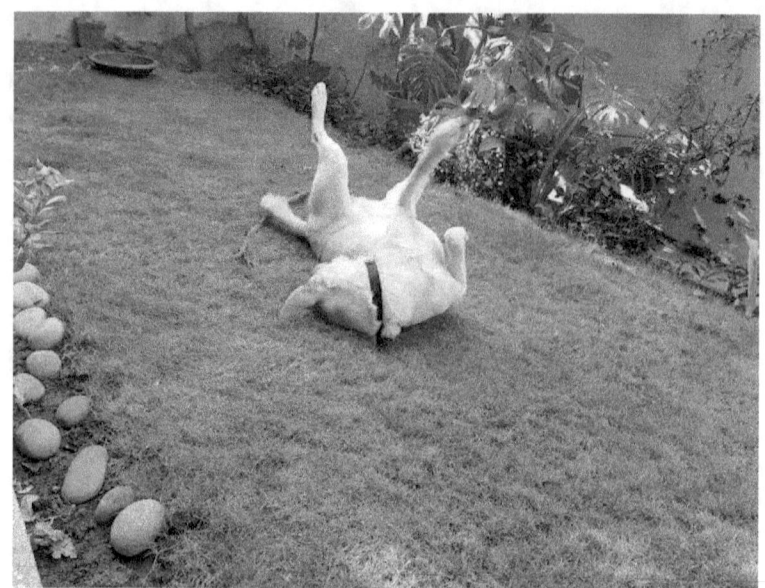

Pet Dog Playing with Plastic Bottle in Northern India

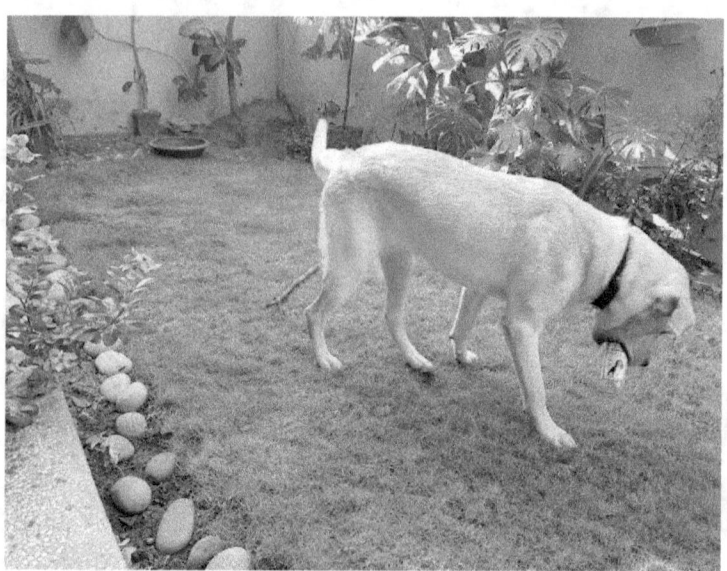

Pet Dog Playing with Plastic Bottle in Northern India

16. Pet Dog after having Bathe in Northern India

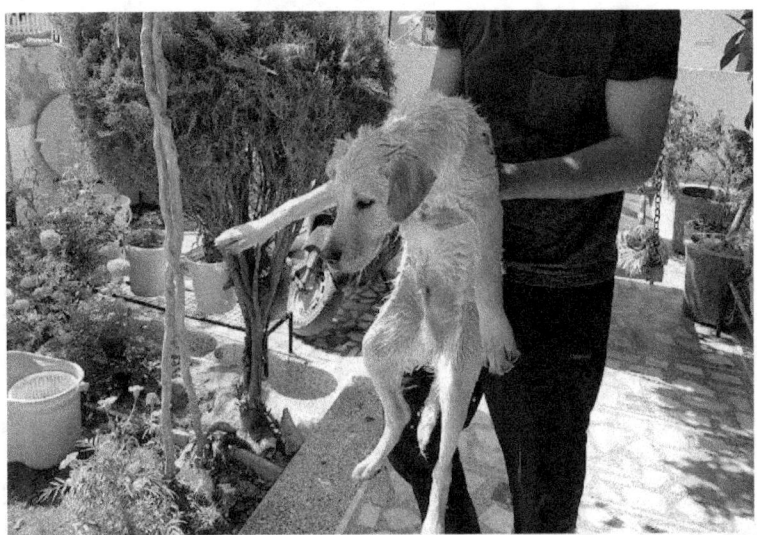

Pet Dog after having Bathe in Northern India

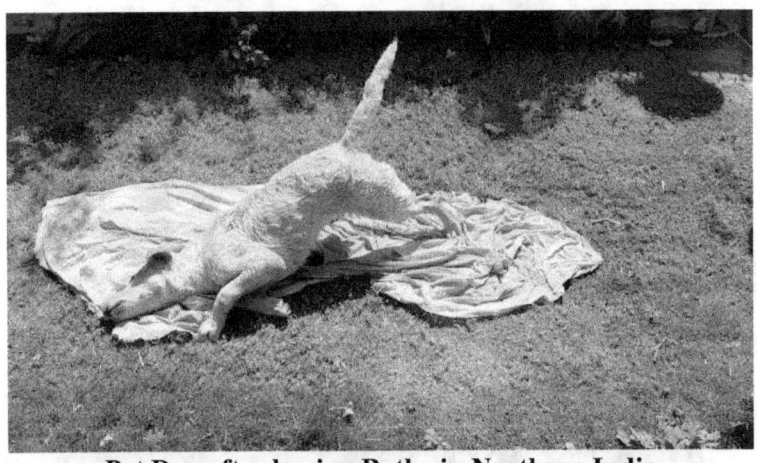

Pet Dog after having Bathe in Northern India

17. Dog Sitting on the Top of a Car in Northern India

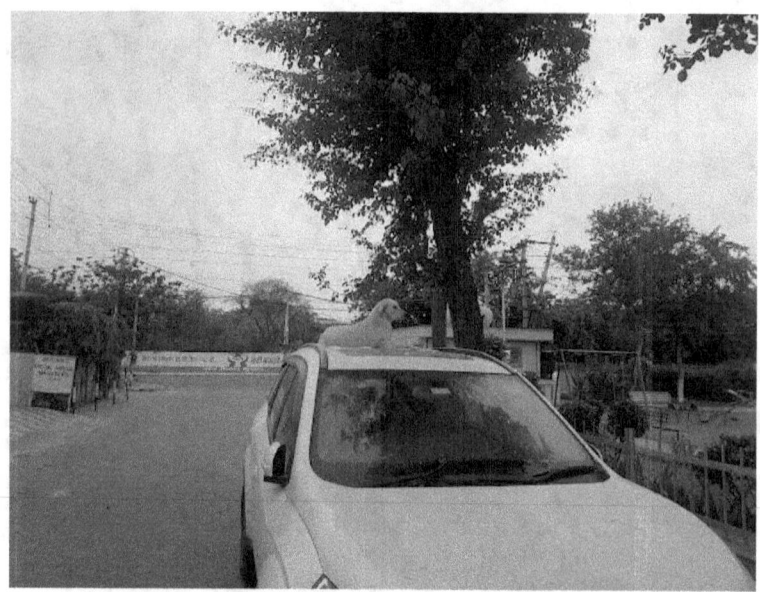

Dog Sitting on the Top of a Car in Northern India

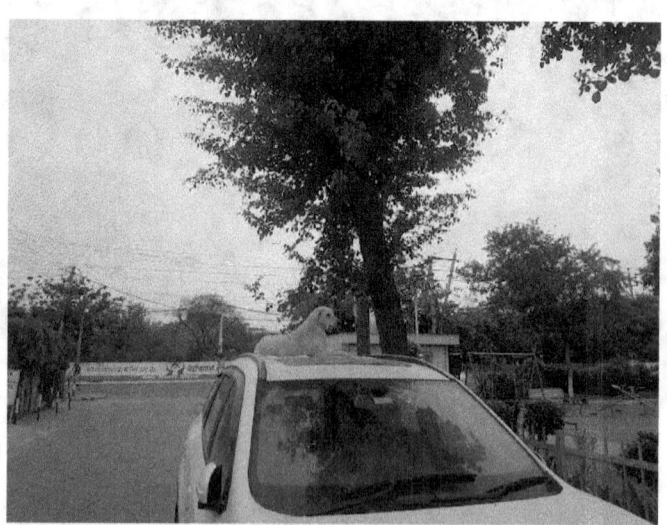

Dog Sitting on the Top of a Car in Northern India

18. Transporting Waste of Town on a Rickshaw in Northern India

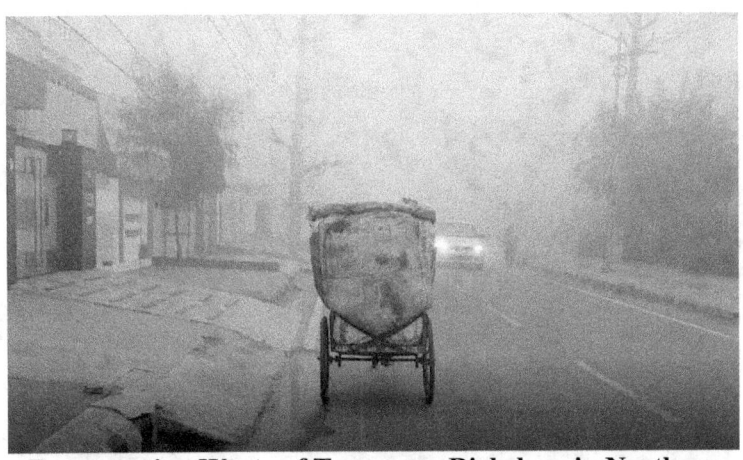

Transporting Waste of Town on a Rickshaw in Northern India

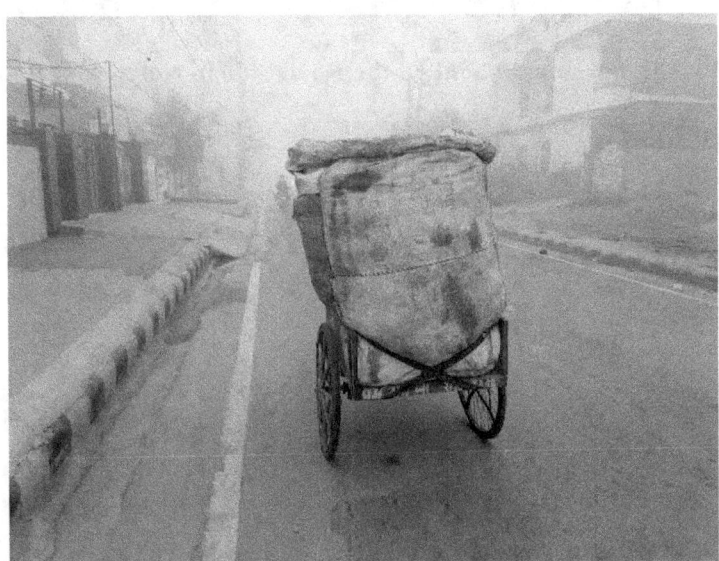

Transporting Waste of Town on a Rickshaw in Northern India

19. Plastic Toys Being Sold on the Road Side in Northern India

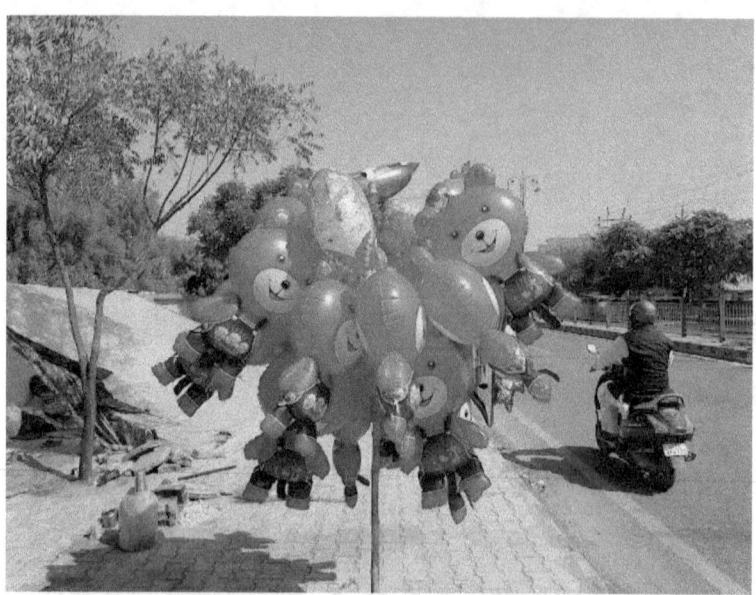

Plastic Toys Being Sold on the Road Side in Northern India

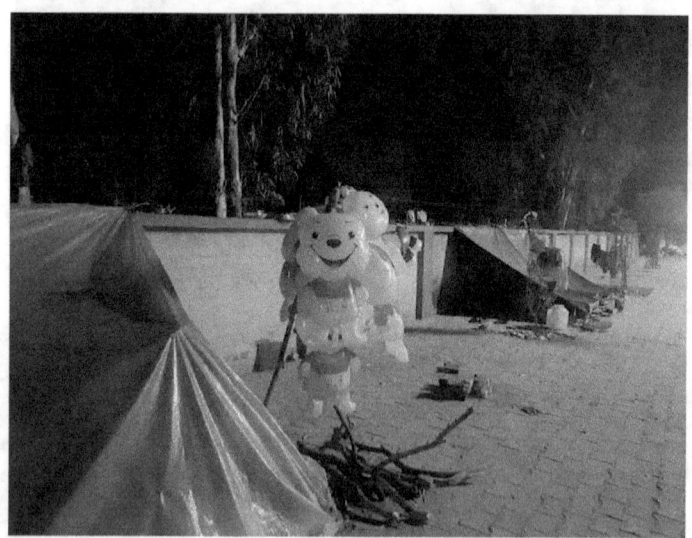

Plastic Toys Being Sold on the Road Side in Northern India

20. Landscaping of an Institute in Northern India

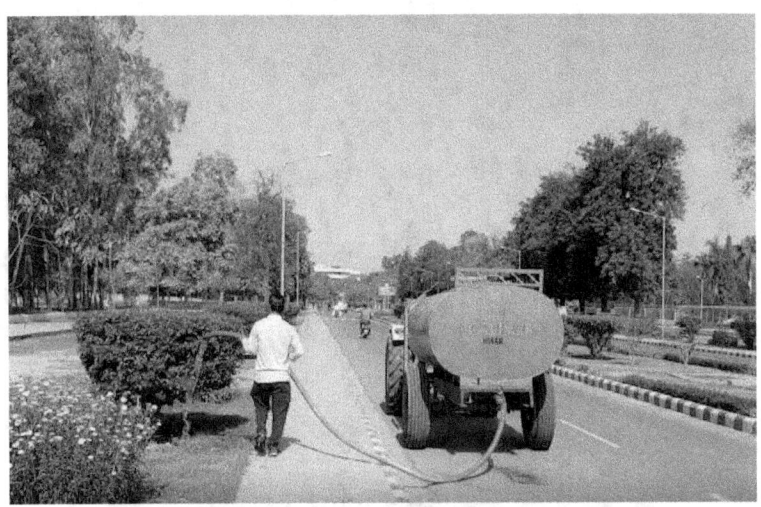

Landscaping of an Institute in Northern India

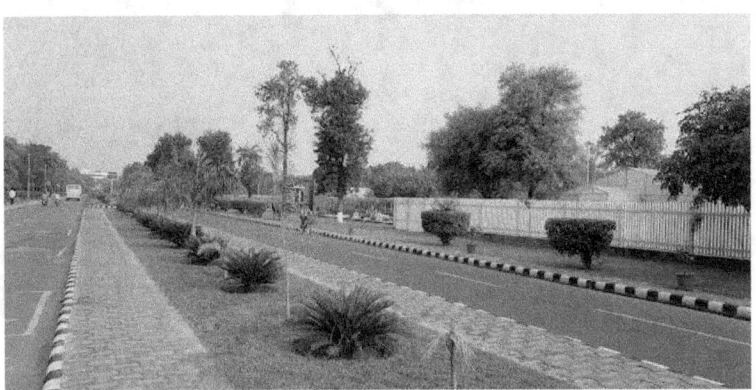

Landscaping of an Institute in Northern India

21. Yoga on the Occasion of Celebration of World Yoga Day in Northern India

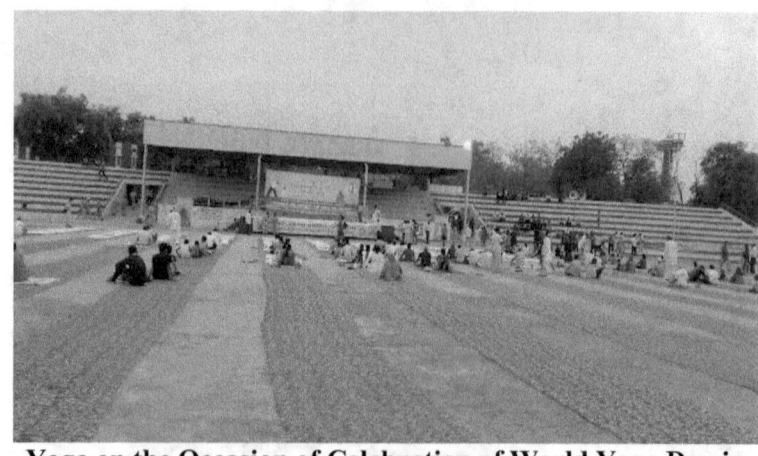

Yoga on the Occasion of Celebration of World Yoga Day in Northern India

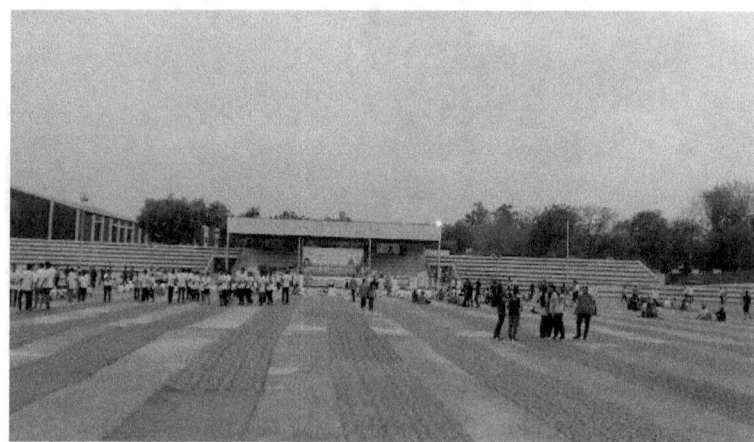

Yoga on the Occasion of Celebration of World Yoga Day in Northern India

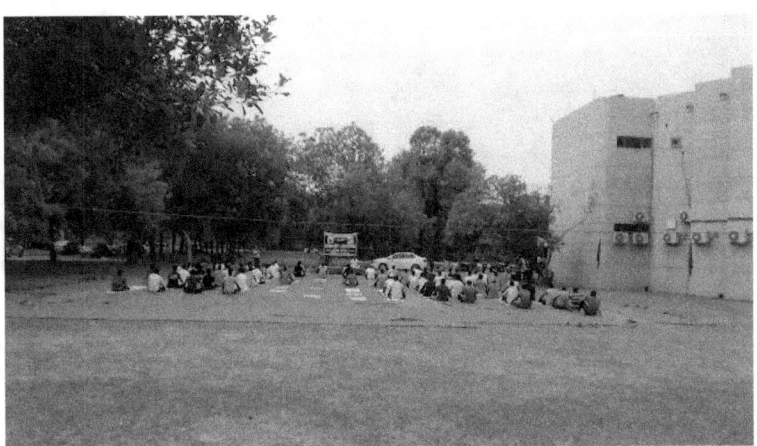

Yoga on the Occasion of Celebration of World Yoga Day in Northern India

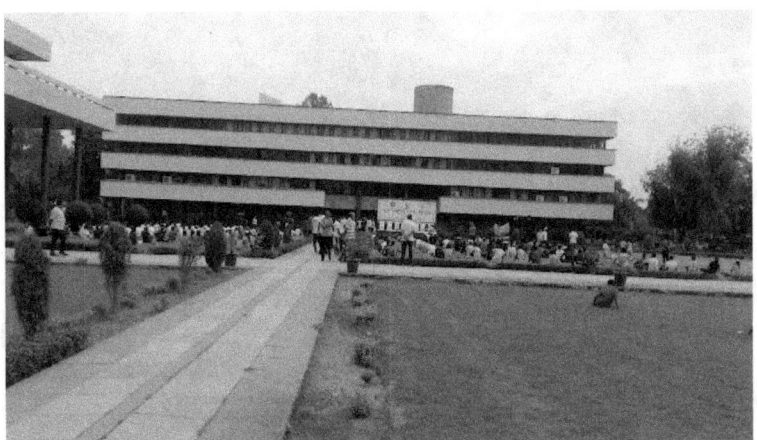

Yoga on the Occasion of Celebration of World Yoga Day in Northern India

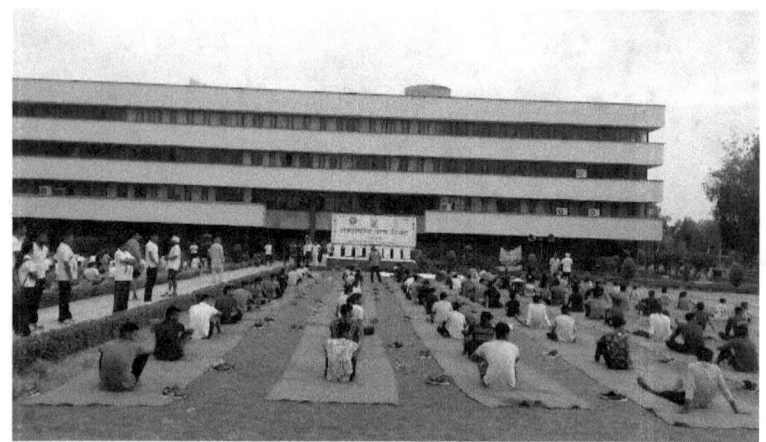

Yoga on the Occasion of Celebration of World Yoga Day in Northern India

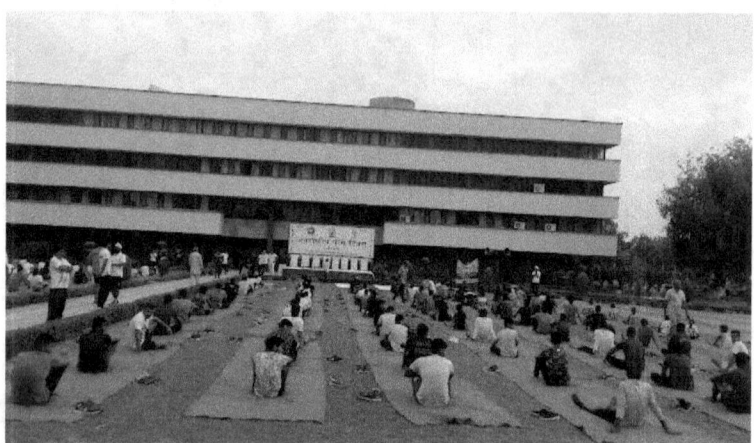

Yoga on the Occasion of Celebration of World Yoga Day in Northern India

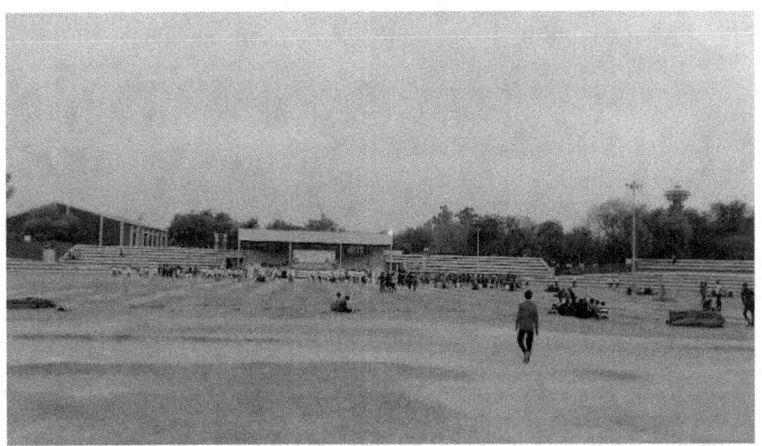

Yoga on the Occasion of Celebration of World Yoga Day in Northern India

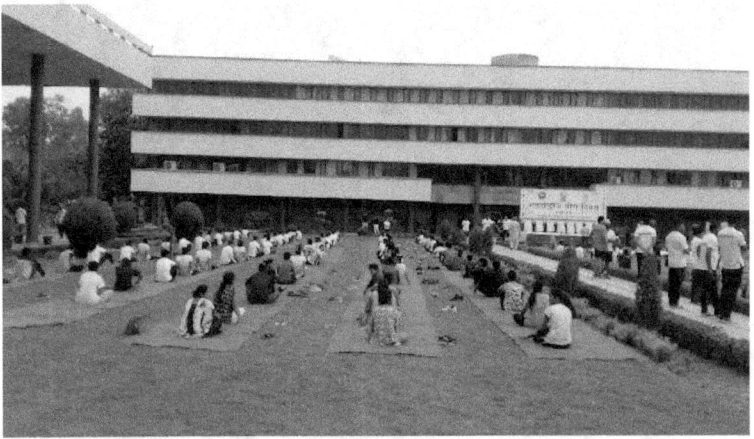

Yoga on the Occasion of Celebration of World Yoga Day in Northern India

22. Religious Person on the Road in Northern India

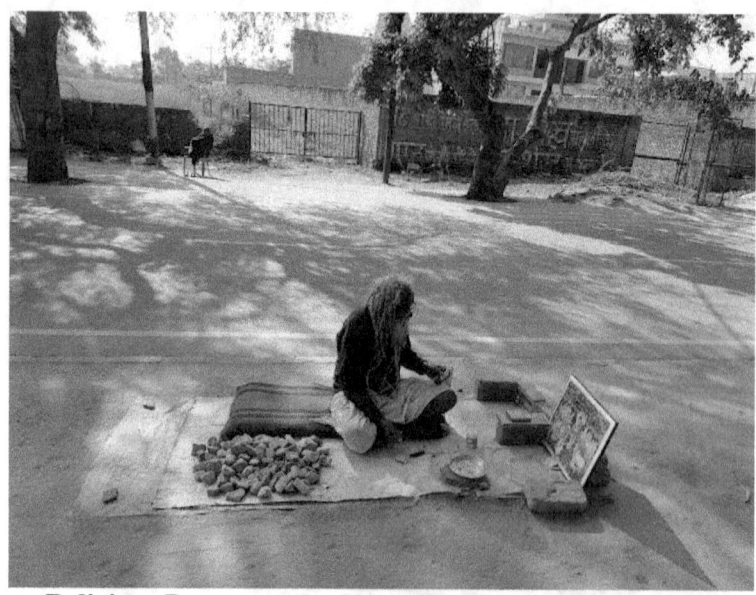

Religious Person on the Side of Road in Northern India

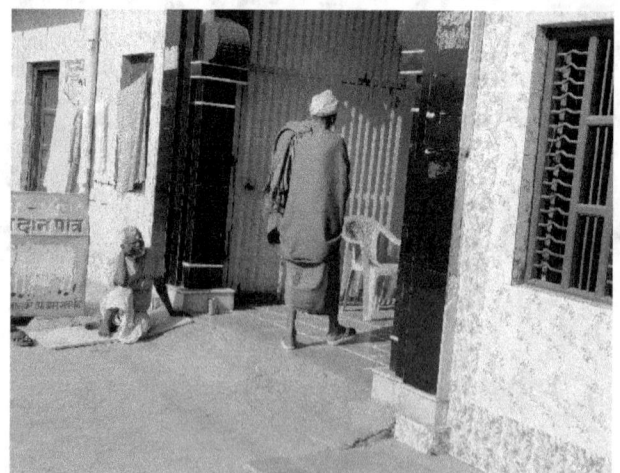

Religious Person on gate of temple in Northern India

23. Couple Travelling on a Bi-cycle in Northern India

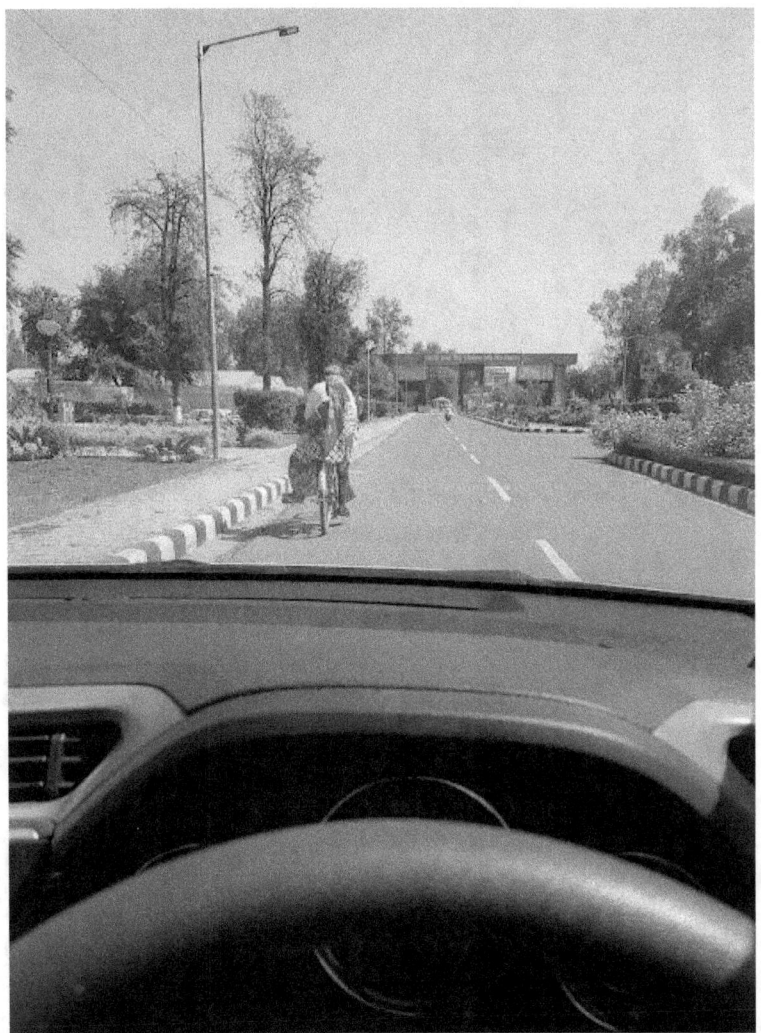

Couple Travelling on a Bi-cycle in Northern India

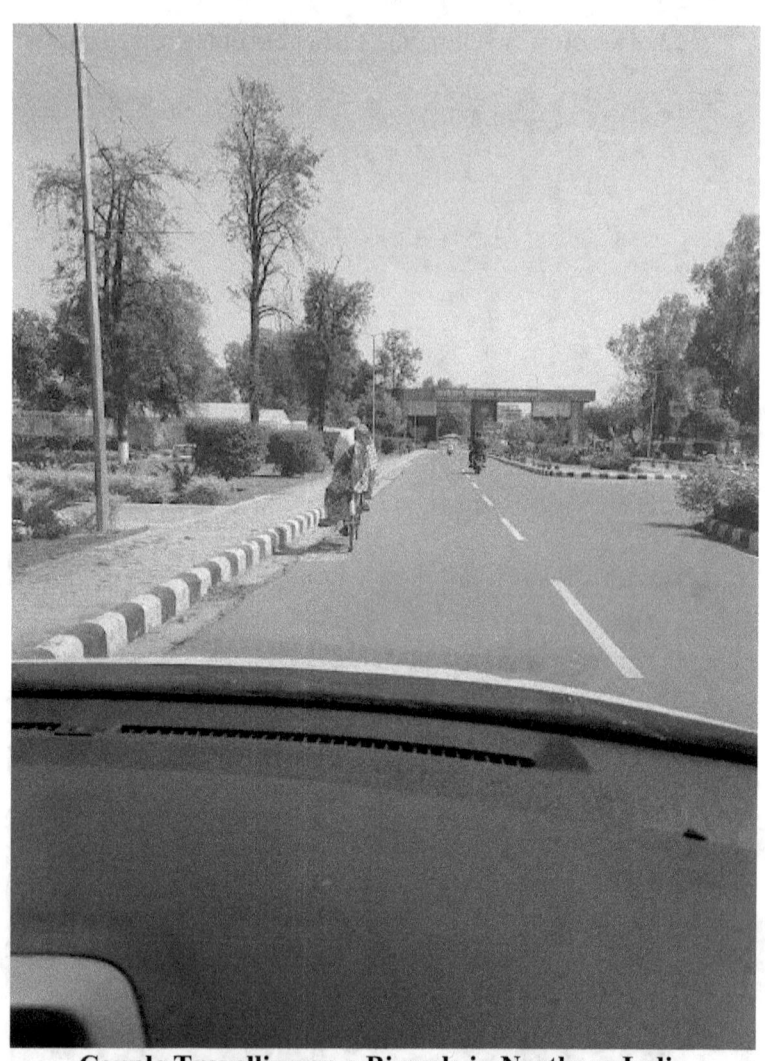
Couple Travelling on a Bi-cycle in Northern India

24. Group of Pigs on their Mission for Search of Food in the Waste on the Side of Road in Northern India

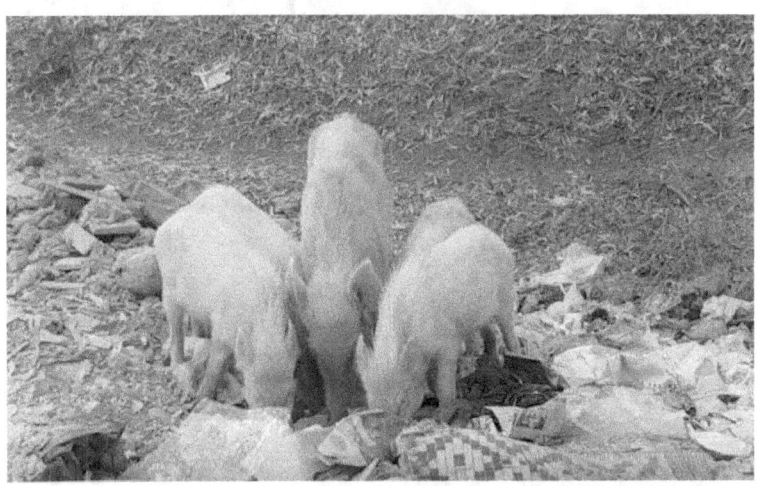

Group of Pigs on their Mission for Search of Food in the Waste on the Side of Road in Northern India

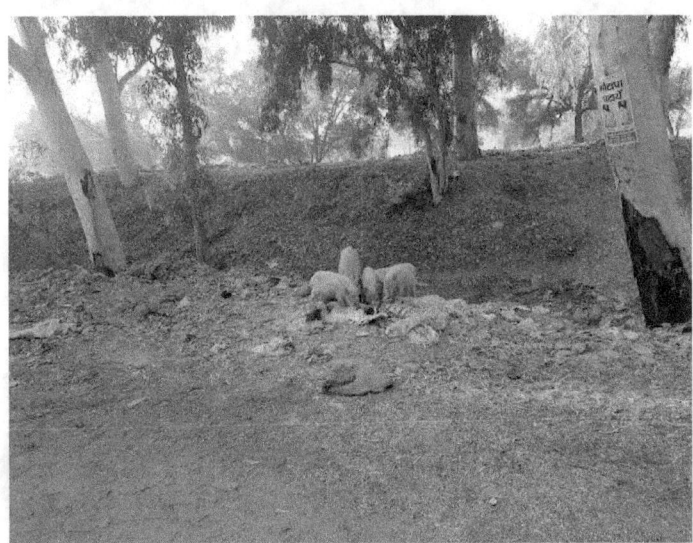

Group of Pigs on their Mission for Search of Food in the Waste on the Side of Road in Northern India

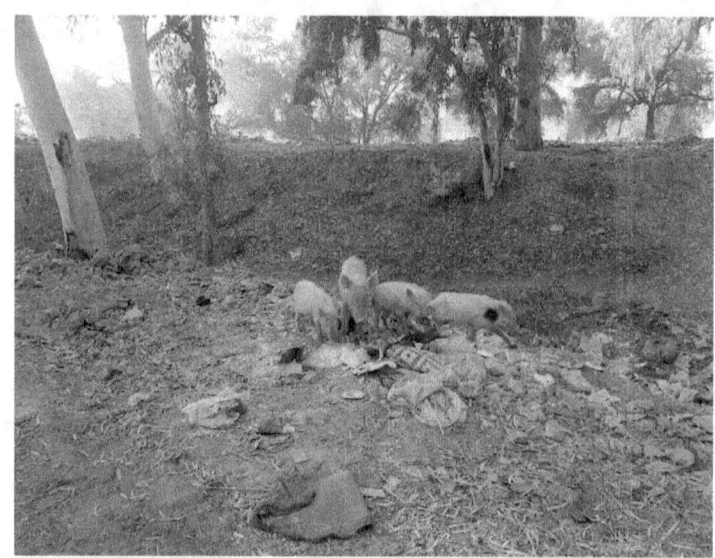

Group of Pigs on their Mission for Search of Food in the Waste on the Side of Road in Northern India

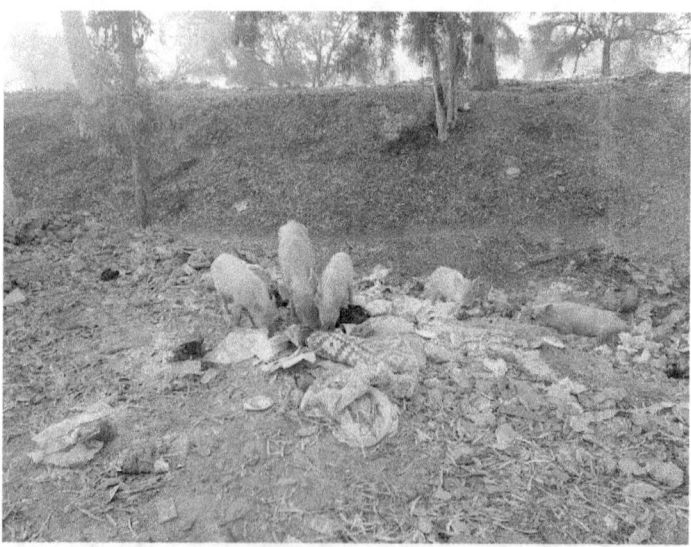

Group of Pigs on their Mission for Search of Food in the Waste on the Side of Road in Northern India

25. Peacock as Indoor Patient in a Veterinary Hospital of Rajasthan in India

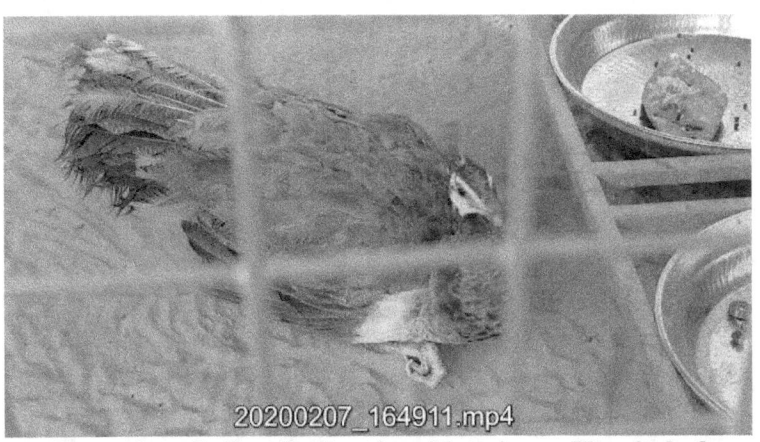

Peacock as Indoor Patient in a Veterinary Hospital of Rajasthan in India

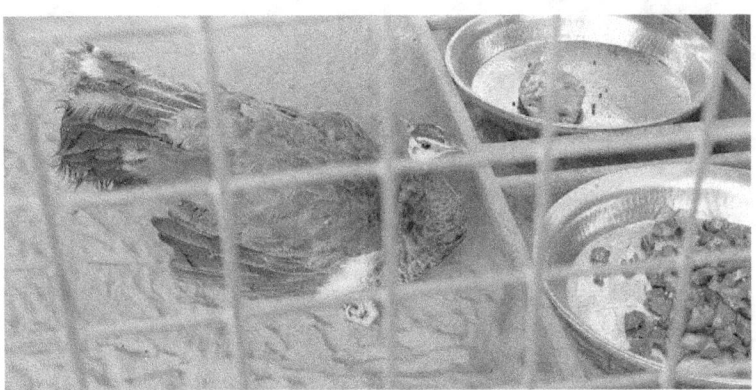

Peacock as Indoor Patient in a Veterinary Hospital of Rajasthan in India

26. Tribal People Moving along with their Animals on the Road in Northern India

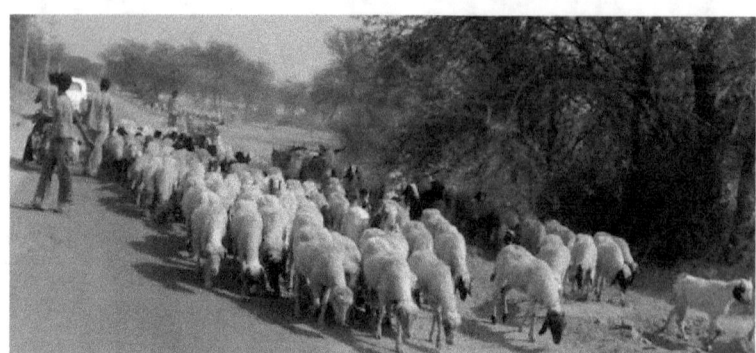

Tribal People Moving along with their Animals on the Road in Northern India

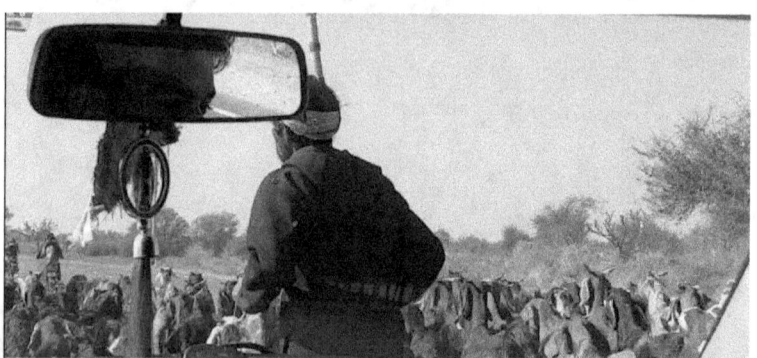

Tribal People Moving along with their Animals on the Road in Northern India

27. Crowd of People on the Public Places in Northern India

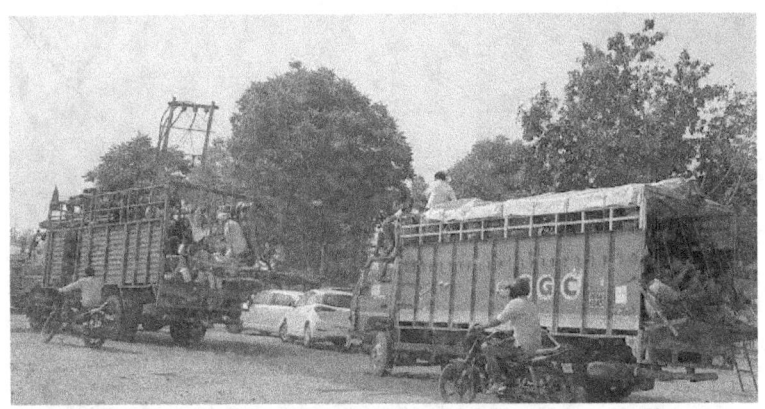

Crowd of People on the Road in Northern India

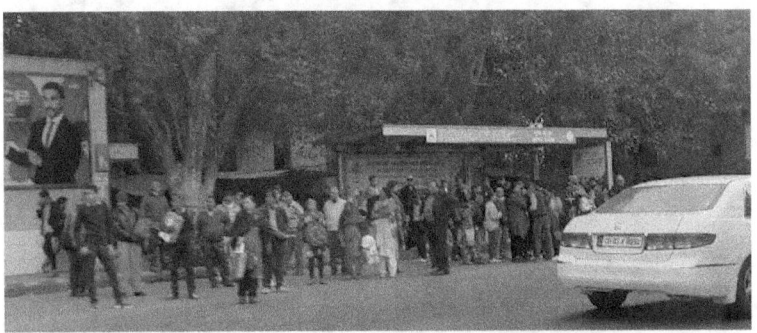

Crowd of People on the Road in Northern India

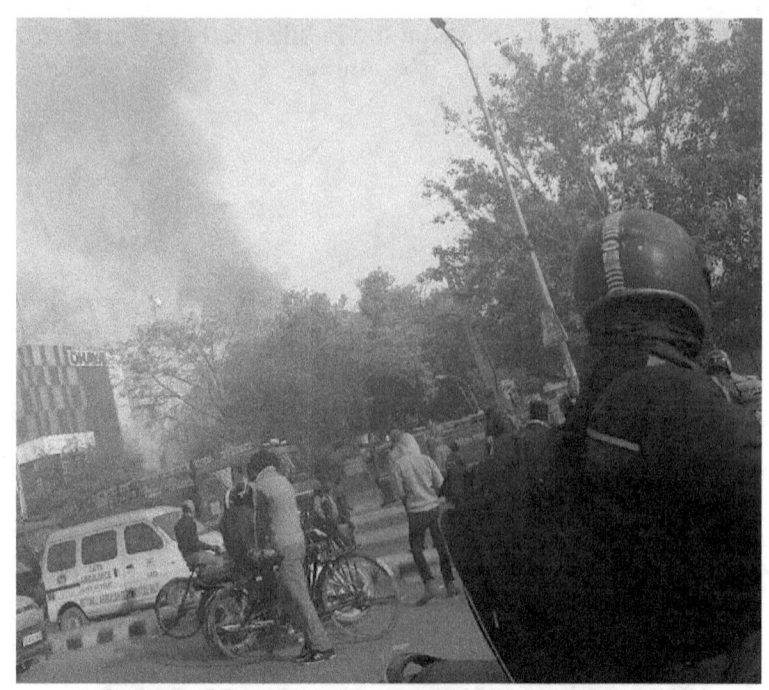
Crowd of People on the Road in Northern India

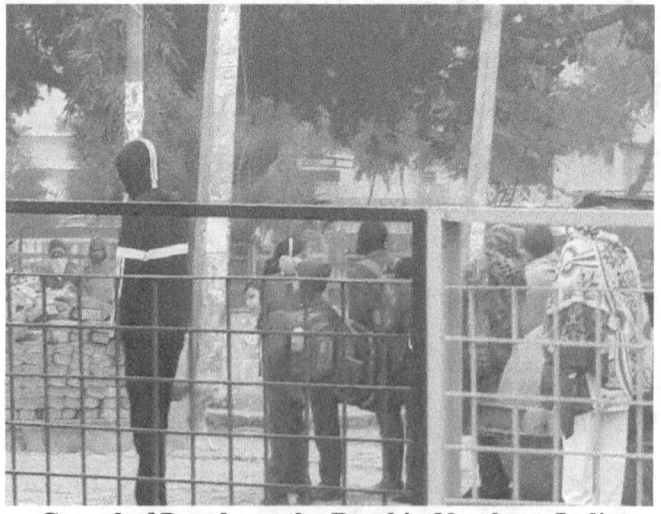
Crowd of People on the Road in Northern India

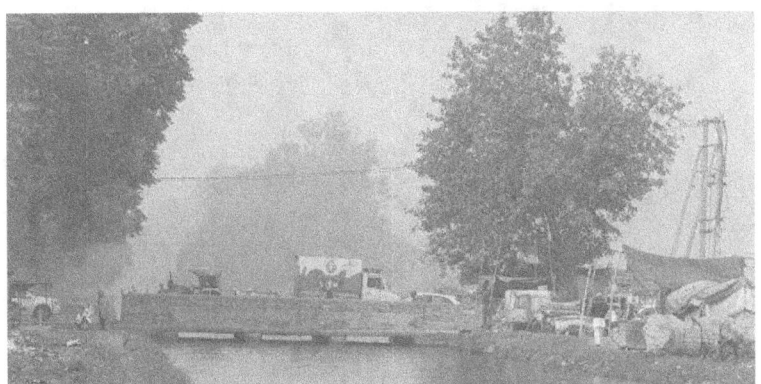

Crowd of People on the Road in Northern India

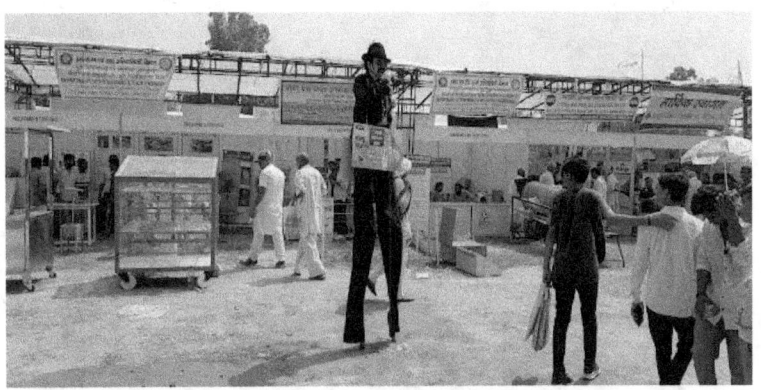

Crowd of People in a Farmers Fair in Northern India

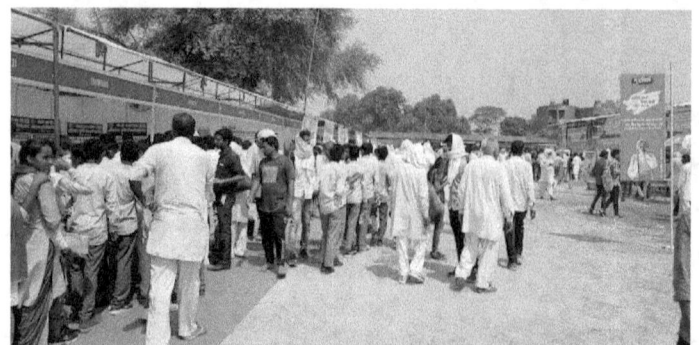

Crowd of People in a Farmers Fair in Northern India

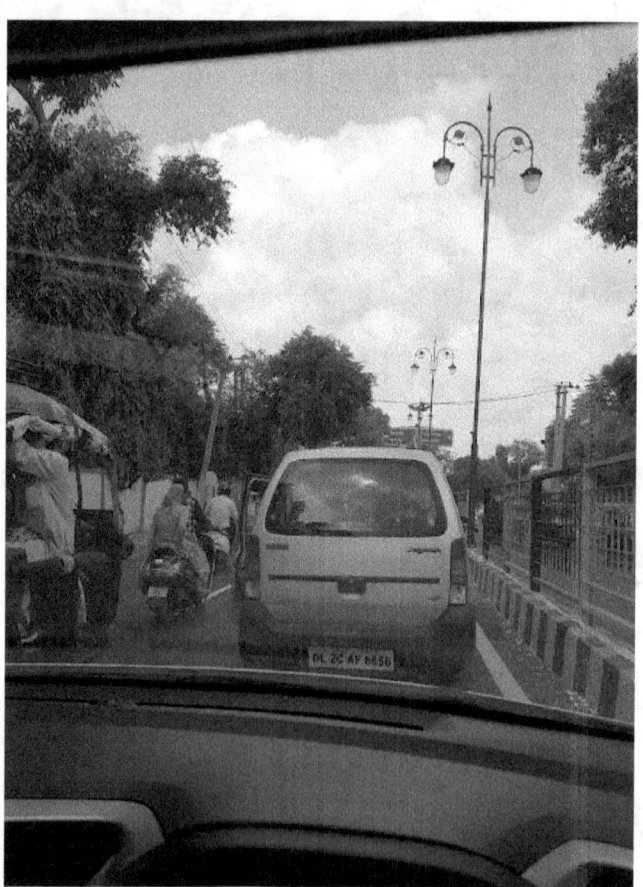

Crowd of People on the Road in Northern India

28. Animals on the Public Place in Northern India

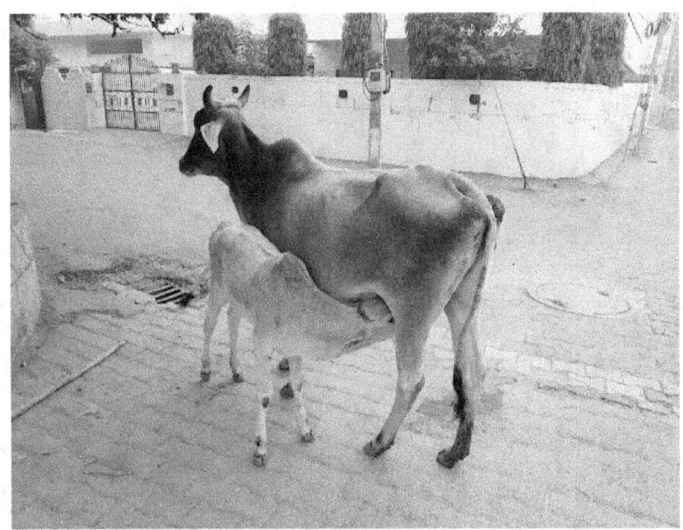

Cow Feeding her Baby on the Public Place in Northern India

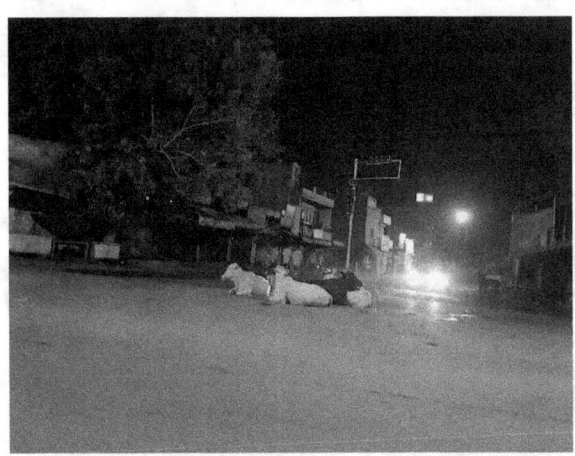

Cows sitting in the Centre of Road in Northern India

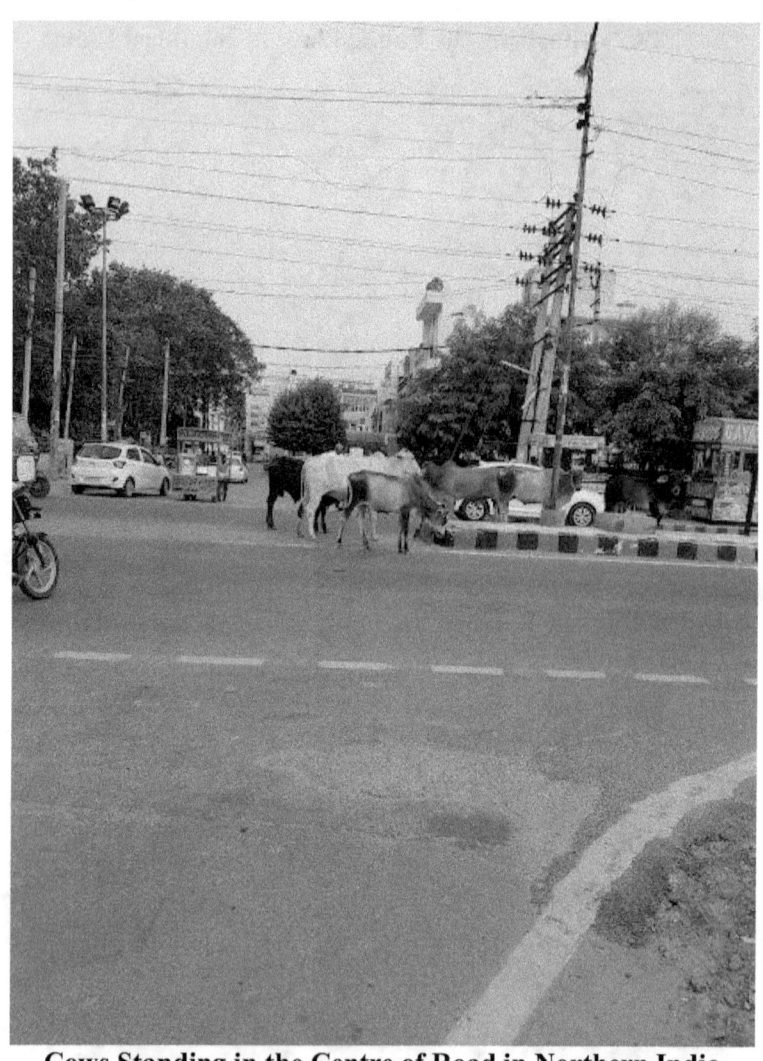
Cows Standing in the Centre of Road in Northern India

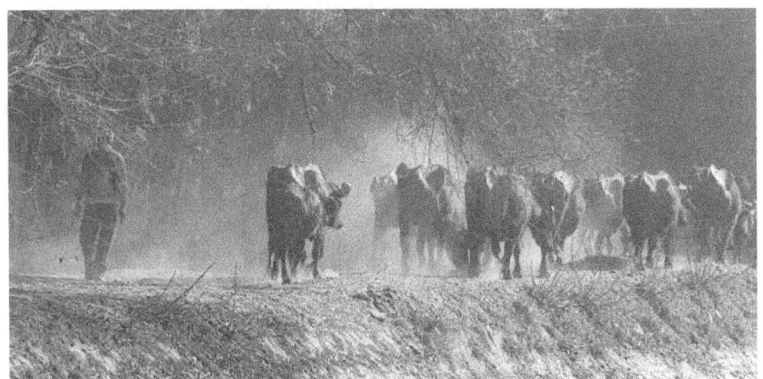

Buffaloes on the ways of Grazing in Northern India

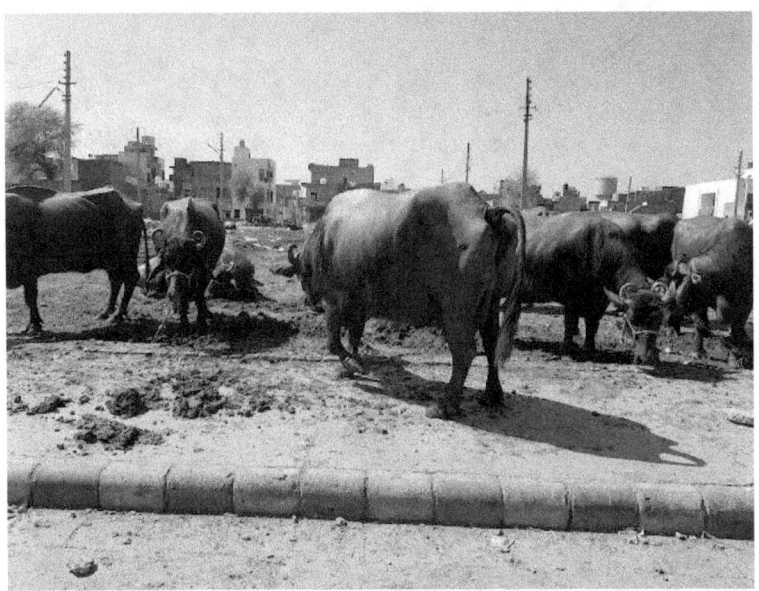

Buffaloes on the Public Place in Northern India

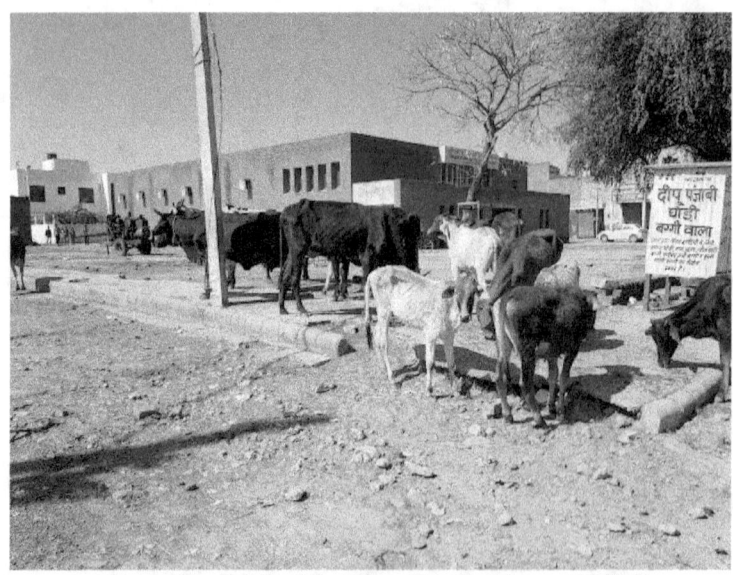

Cows on the Public Place in Northern India

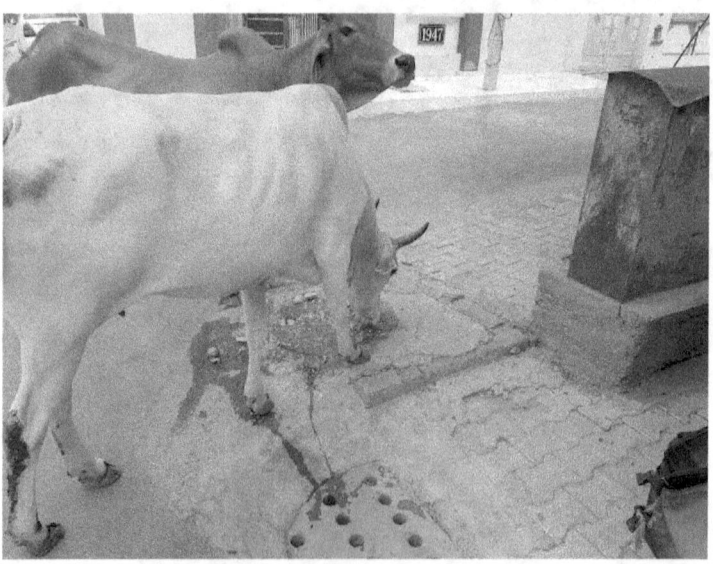

Cows on the Road in Northern India

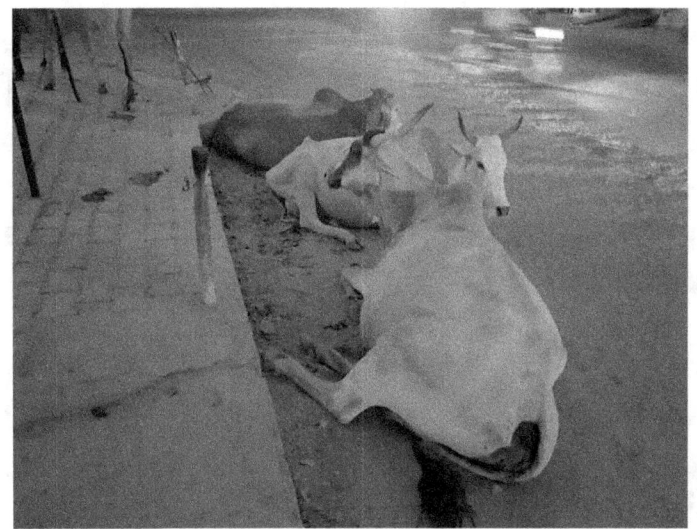

Cows sitting on Road in Northern India

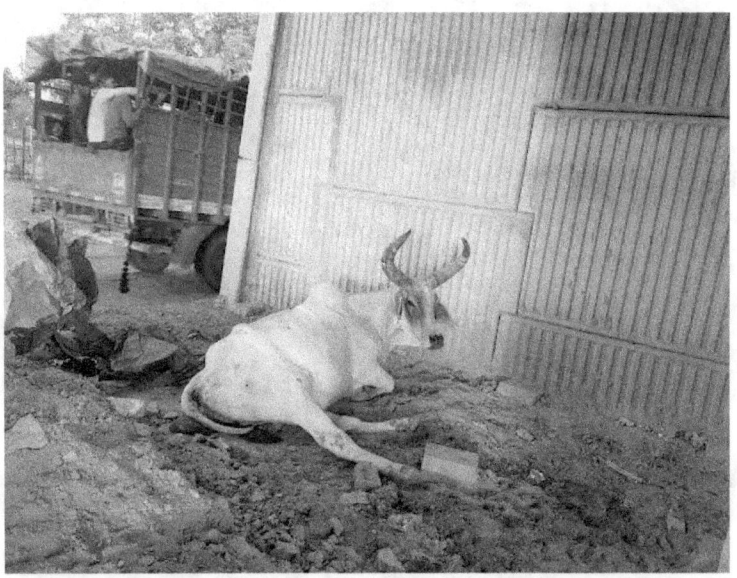

Bull Sitting on the Public Place in Northern India

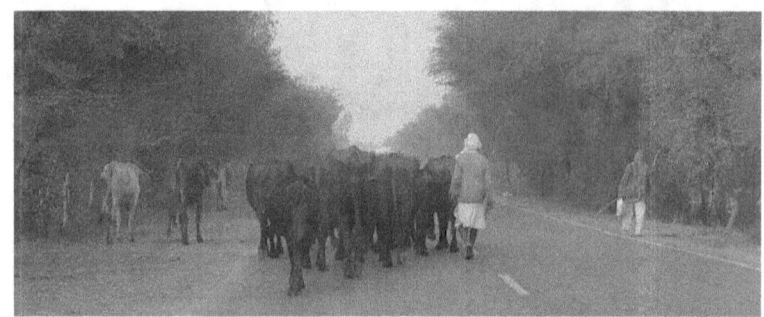

Buffaloes on the ways of Grazing in Northern India

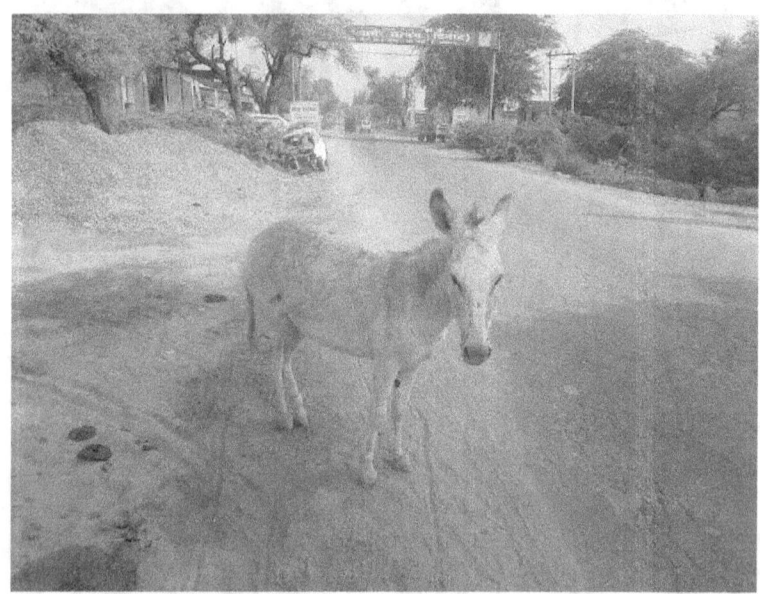

A Rarely Seen Donkey on Road in Northern India

29. Woman Transporting Green Fodder in Northern India

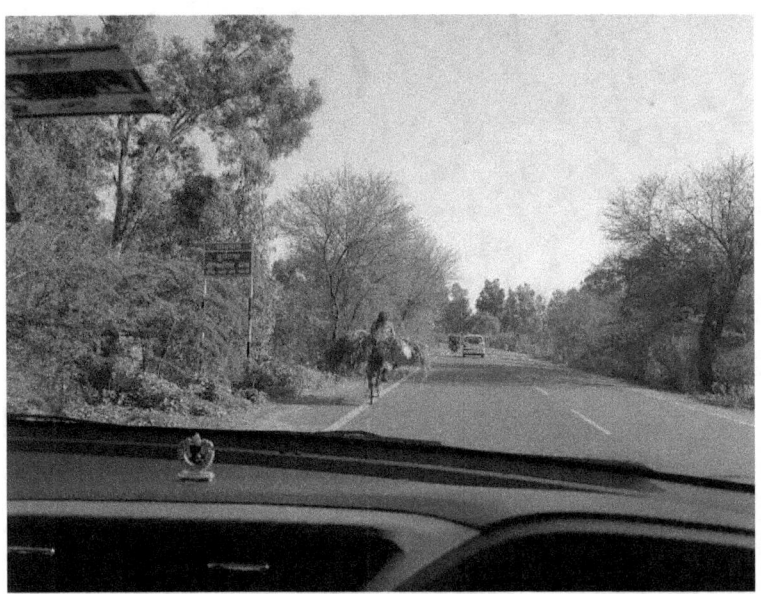

Woman Transporting Green Fodder on a Bi-Cycle

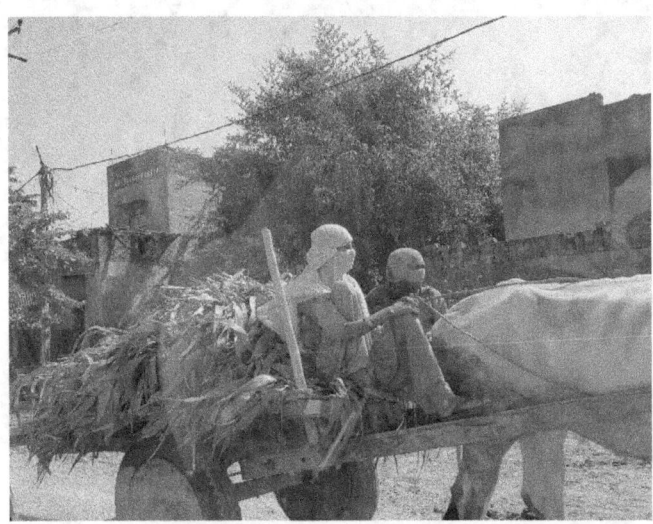

Women Transporting Green Fodder on a Bi-Cycle

30. Beautiful Vulture as an Indoor Patient in Veterinary Hospital of Rajasthan in Northern India

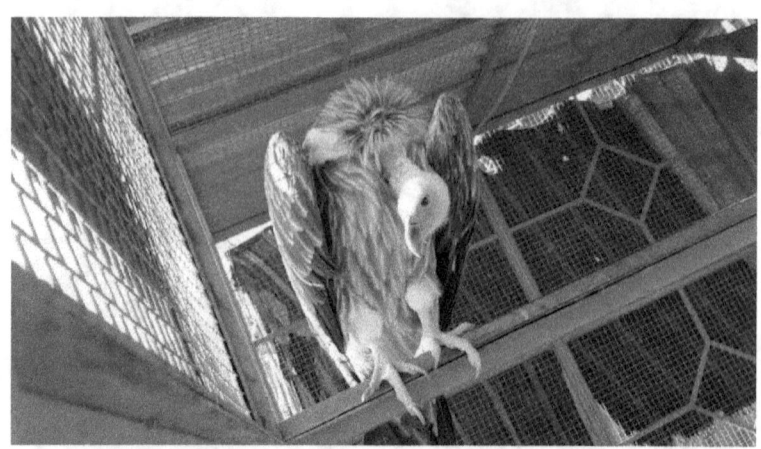

Beautiful Vulture as an Indoor Patient in Veterinary Hospital of Rajasthan in Northern India

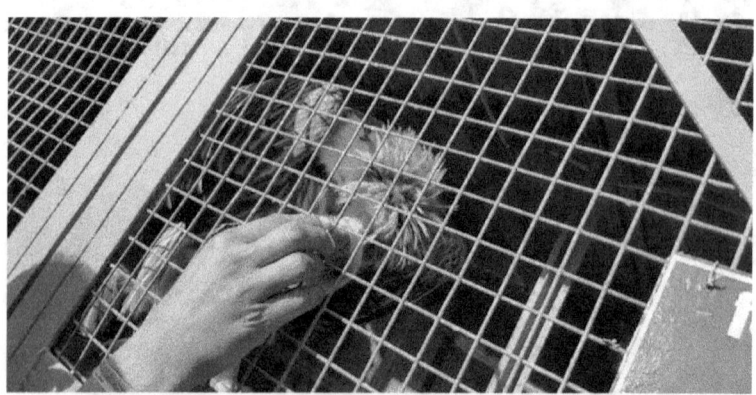

Beautiful Vulture as an Indoor Patient in Veterinary Hospital of Rajasthan in Northern India

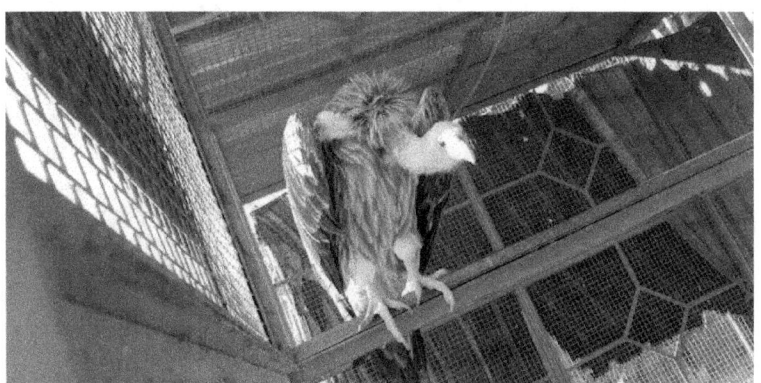

Beautiful Vulture as an Indoor Patient in Veterinary Hospital of Rajasthan in Northern India

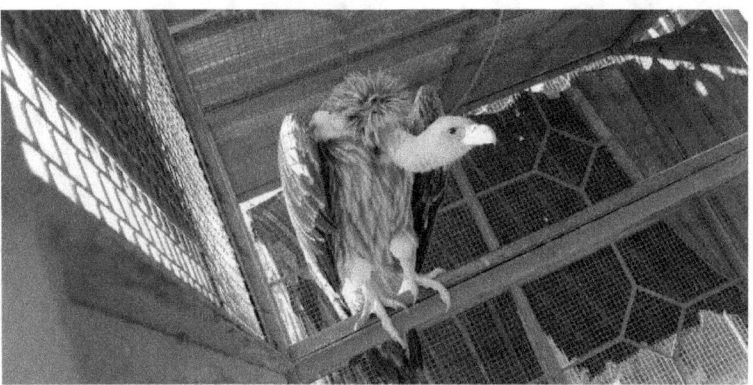

Beautiful Vulture as an Indoor Patient in Veterinary Hospital of Rajasthan in Northern India

31. Struggle of Ants in Transportation of their Food Material in Northern India

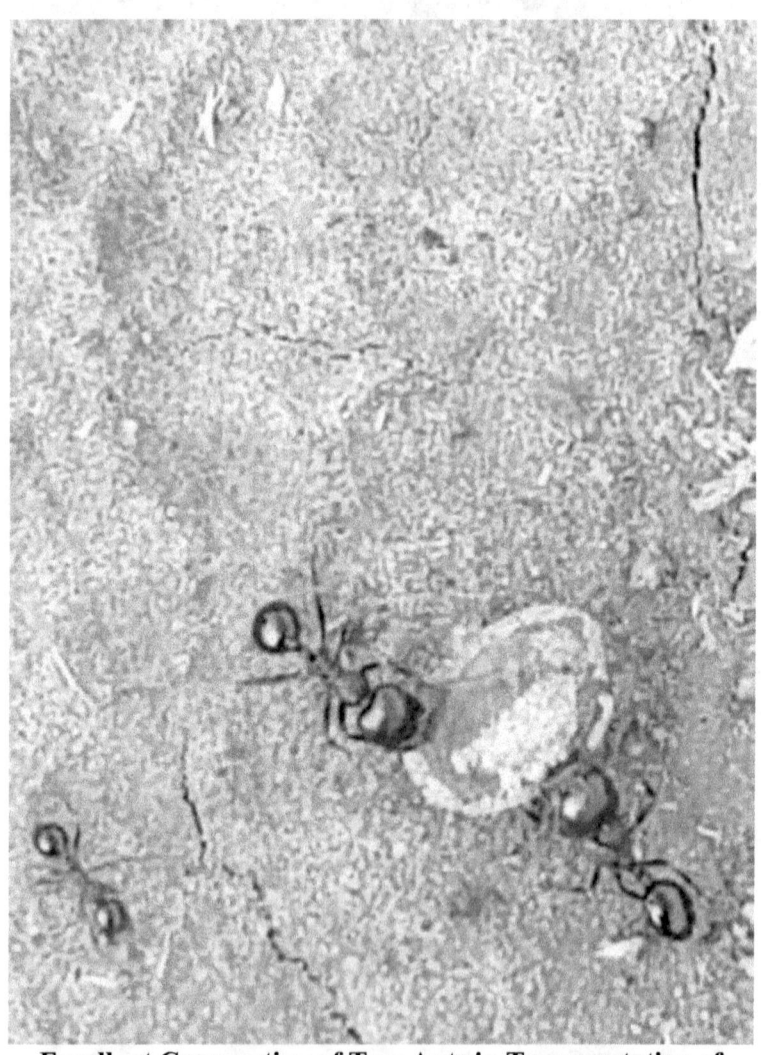

Excellent Cooperation of Two Ants in Transportation of their Food Material

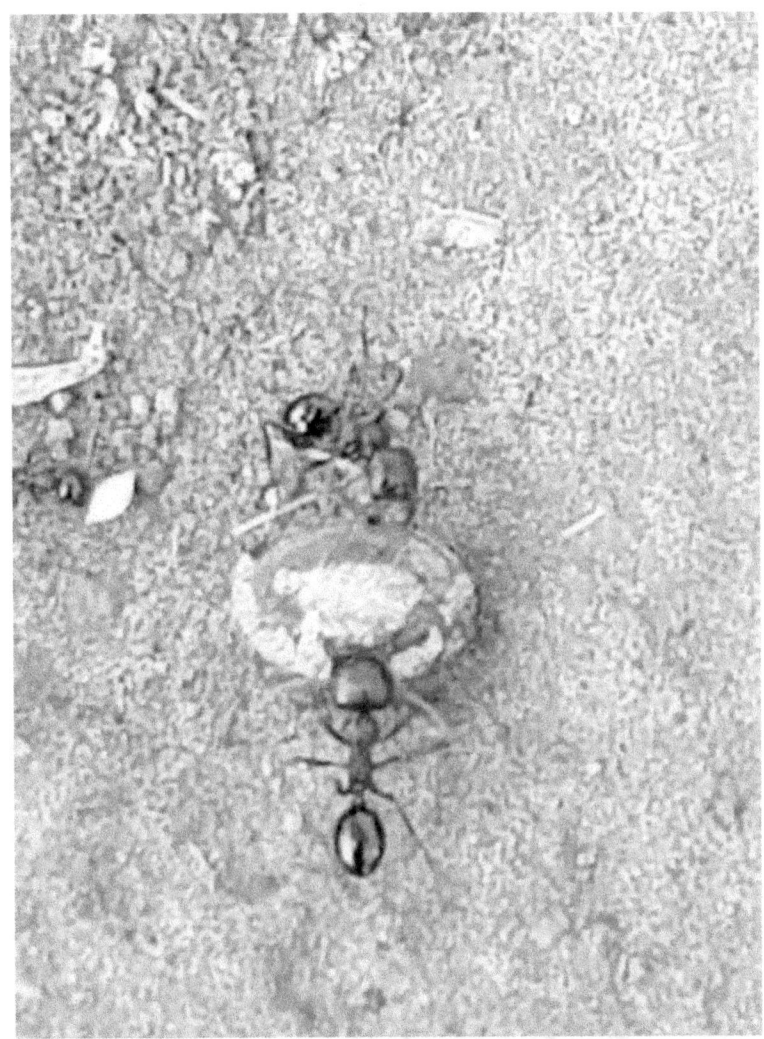

The struggle of Ants in Transportation of their Food Material in Northern India

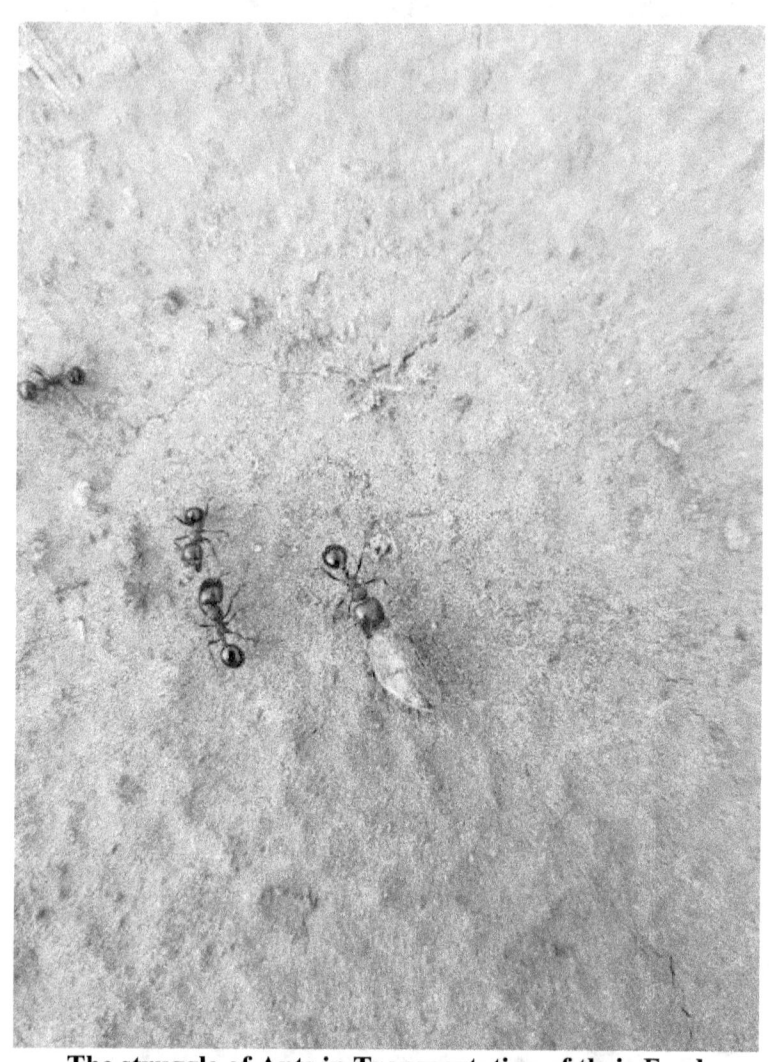

The struggle of Ants in Transportation of their Food
Material in Northern India

32. Cattles with Loss of Legs as Indoor Patient in Veterinary Hospital in a Town of Northern India

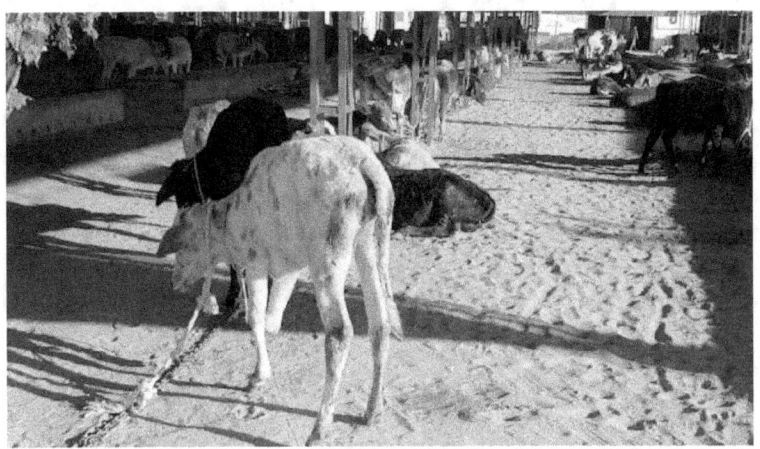

Cattles with Loss of One Leg as Indoor Patient in Veterinary Hospital in a Town of Northern India

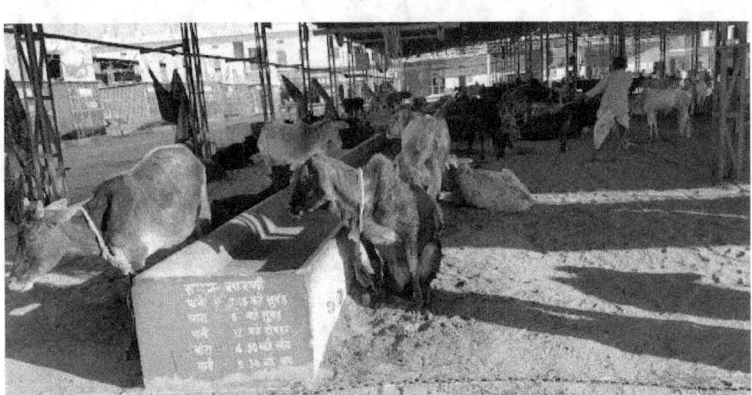

Cattles with Loss of two Legs as Indoor Patient in Veterinary Hospital in a Town of Northern India

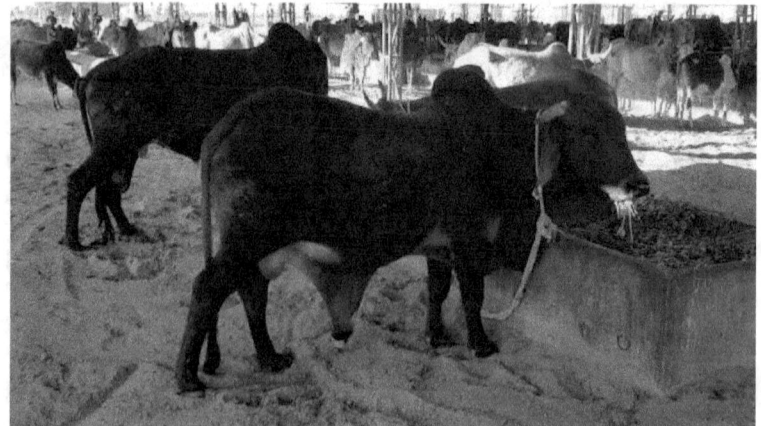

Bull whose Male Organ was destroyed by the Competitor of his Owner as an Indoor Patient in Veterinary Hospital of Rajasthan in India

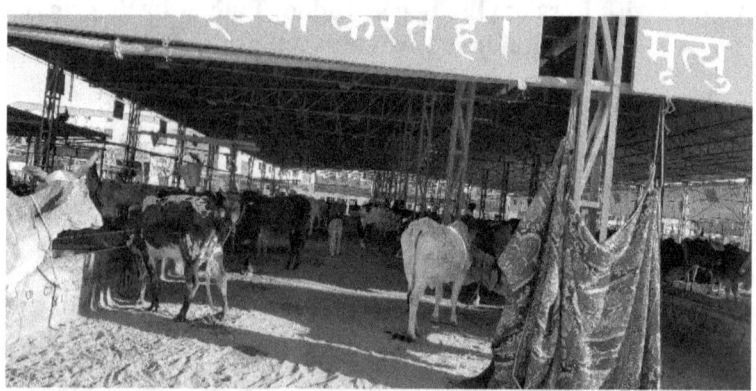

Cattles with Loss of two Legs as Indoor Patient in Veterinary Hospital in a Town of Northern India

33. Swimming and Bathing in Canal Water in Northern India

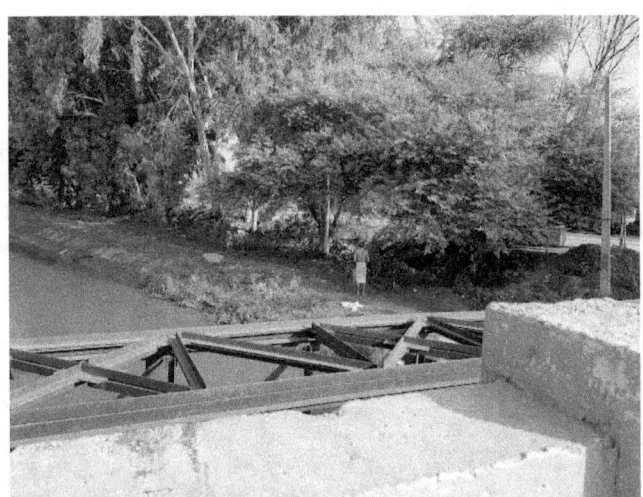

Man after Bathing in Canal Water in Northern India

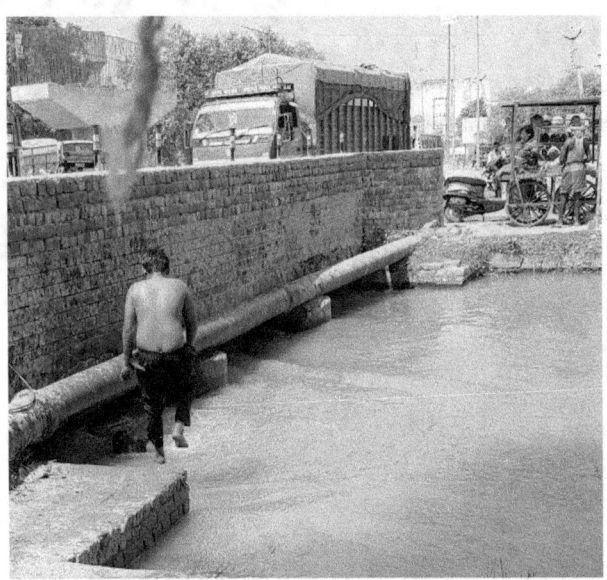

Swimming and Bathing in Canal Water in Northern India

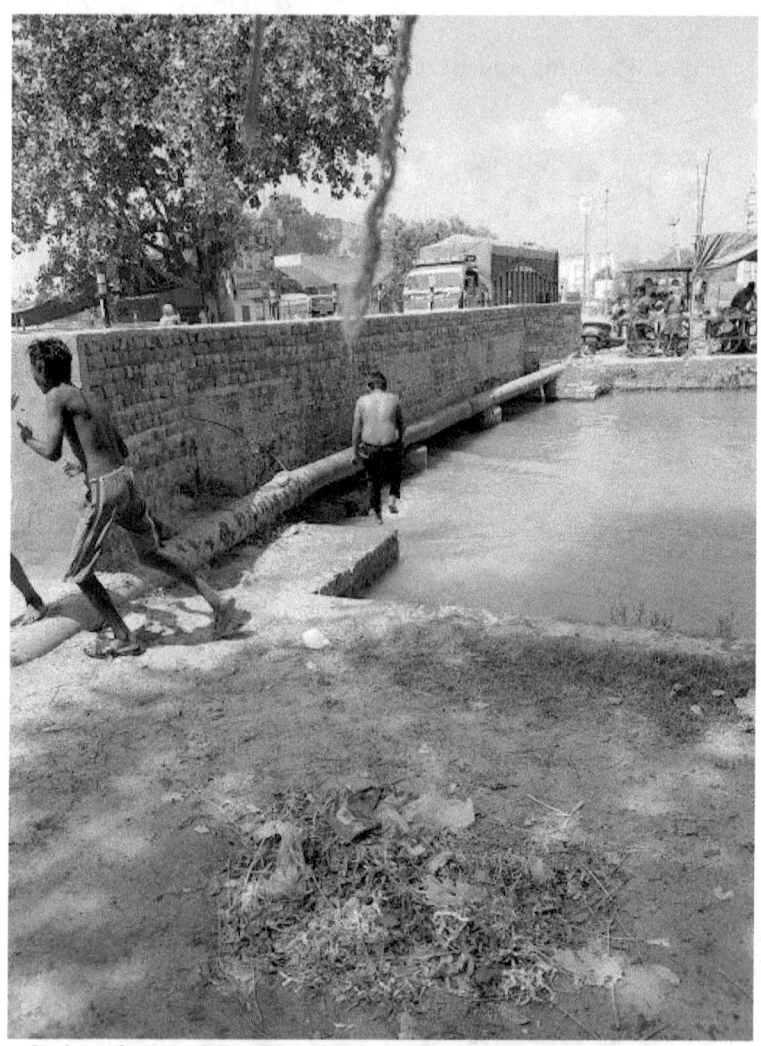

Swimming and Bathing in Canal Water in Northern India

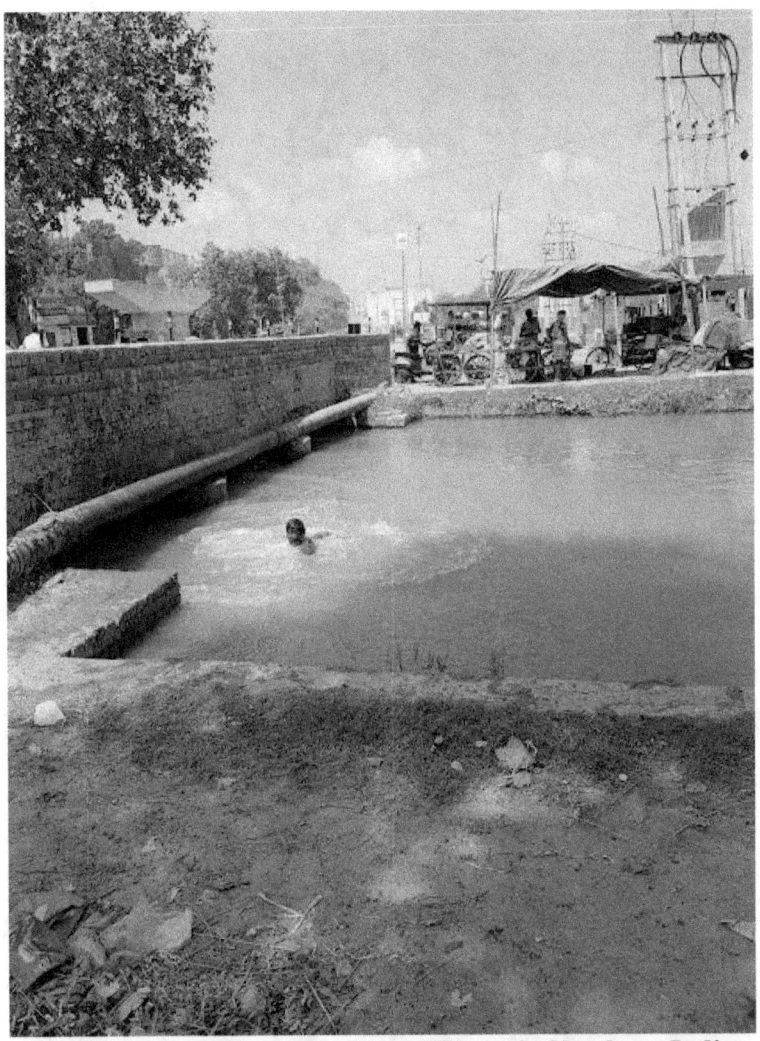

Swimming and Bathing in Canal Water in Northern India

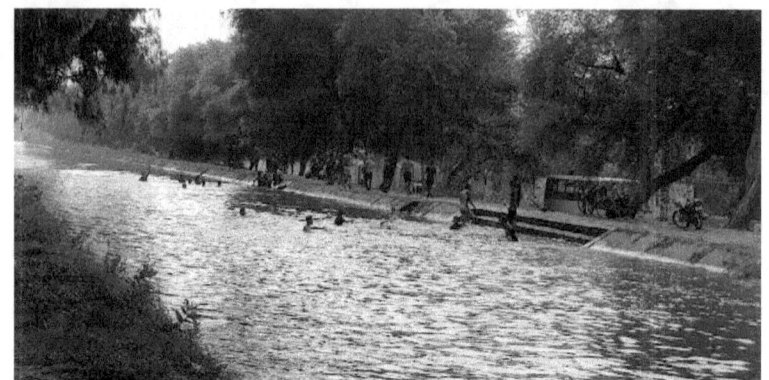

Swimming and Bathing in Canal Water in Northern India

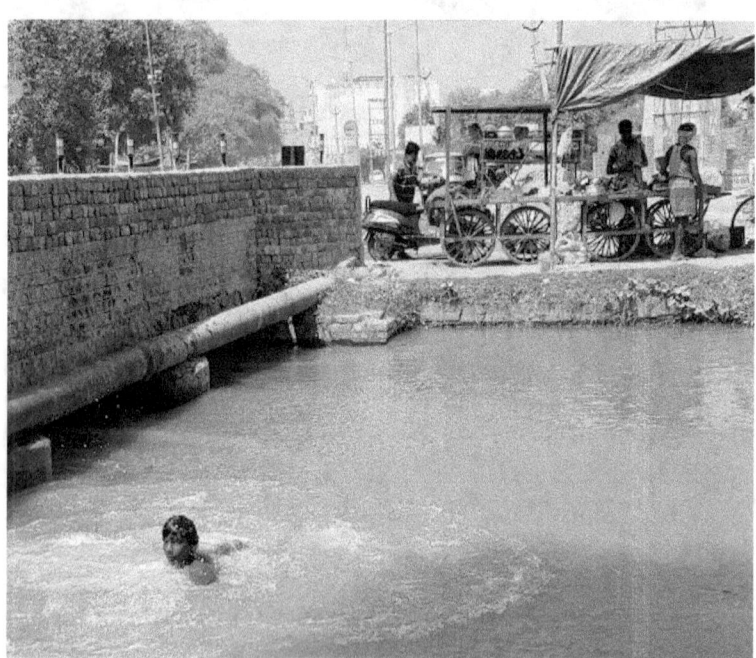

Swimming and Bathing in Canal Water in Northern India

34. Struggle for Transporting Heavy Loads on Human Operated Tricycle/Bi-cycle in a Town of Northern India

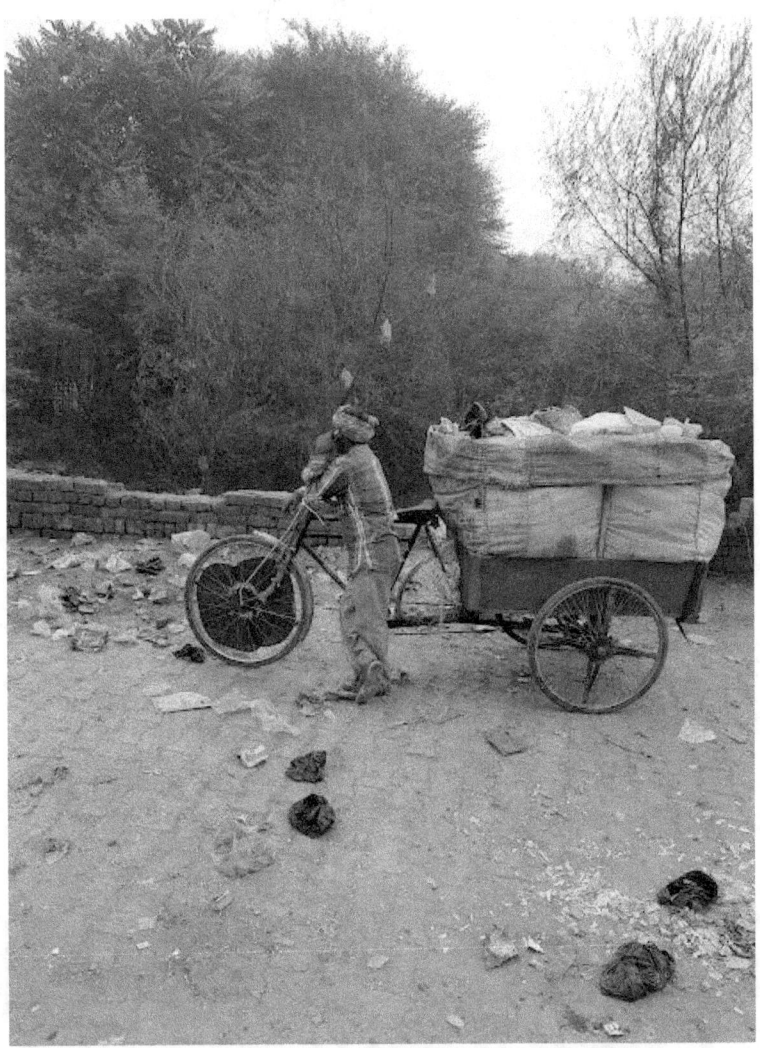

Struggle for Transporting Heavy Loads on Human Operated Tricycle in a Town of Northern India

Struggle for Transporting Heavy Loads on Human Operated Tricycle in a Town of Northern India

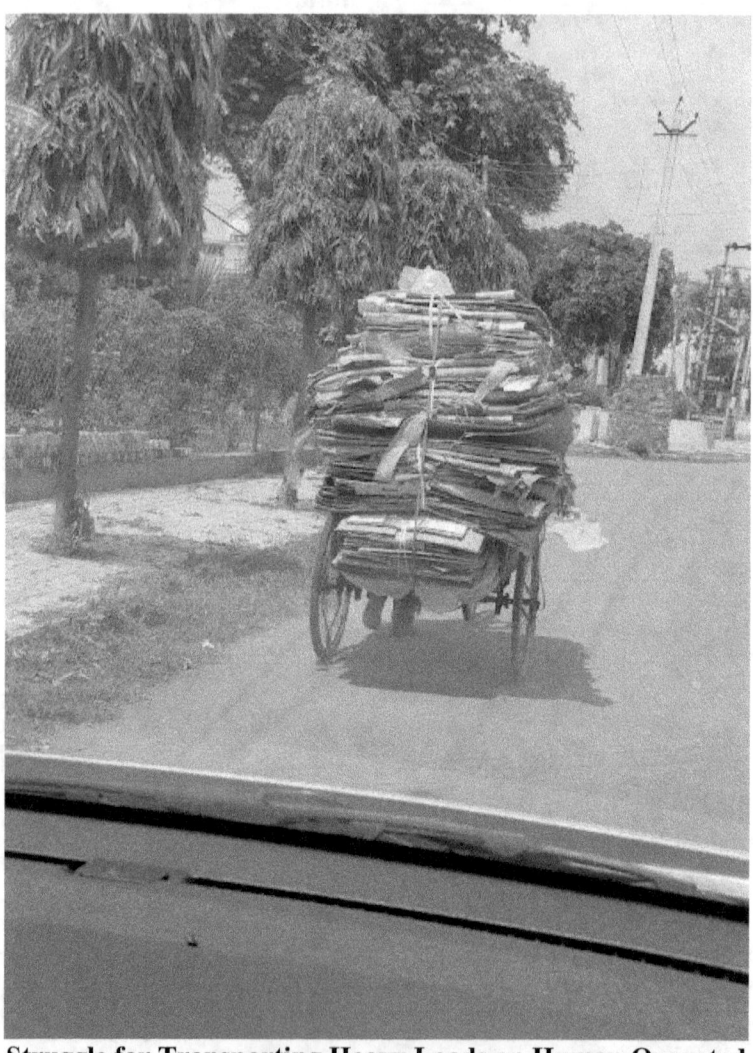

Struggle for Transporting Heavy Loads on Human Operated Tricycle in a Town of Northern India

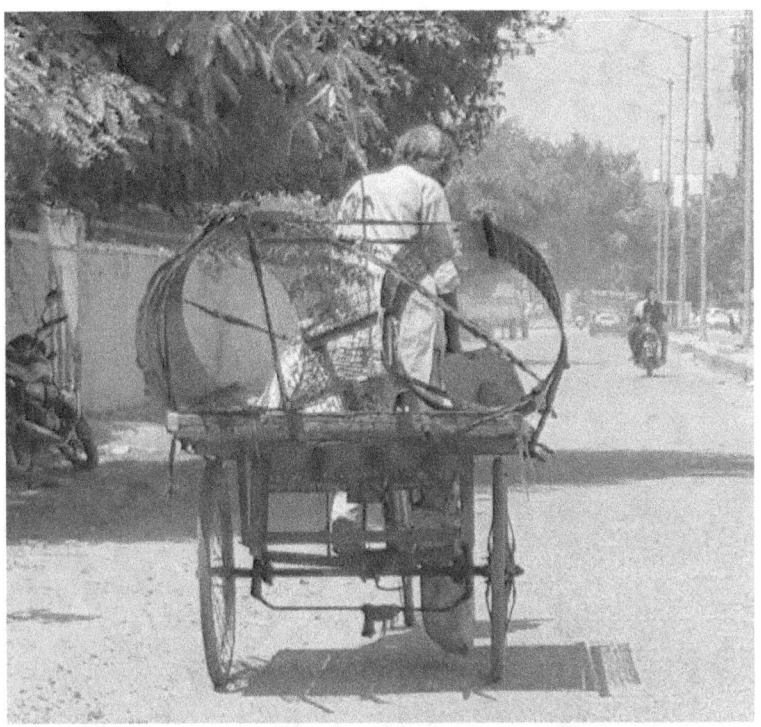

Struggle for Transporting Heavy Loads on Human Operated Tricycle in a Town of Northern India

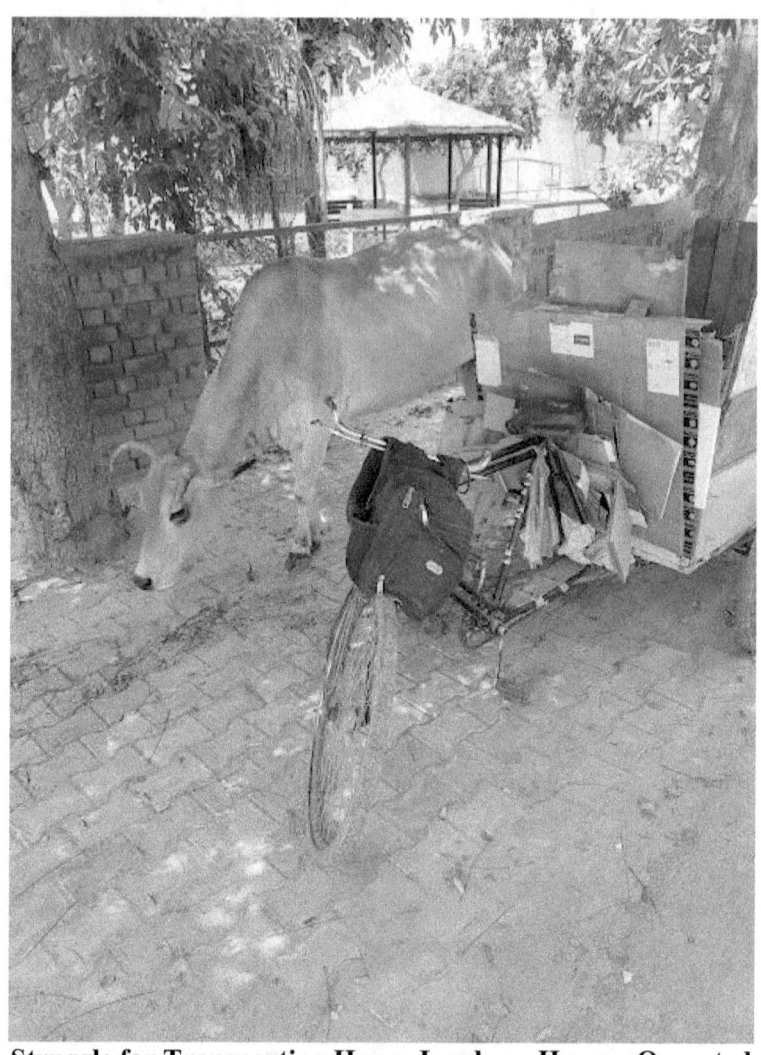

Struggle for Transporting Heavy Loads on Human Operated Tricycle in a Town of Northern India

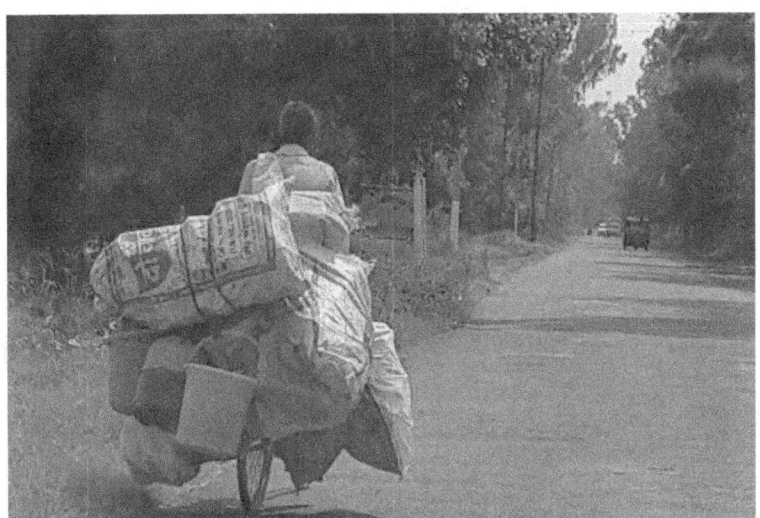

Struggle for Transporting Heavy Loads on Human Operated Bi-cycle in a Town of Northern India

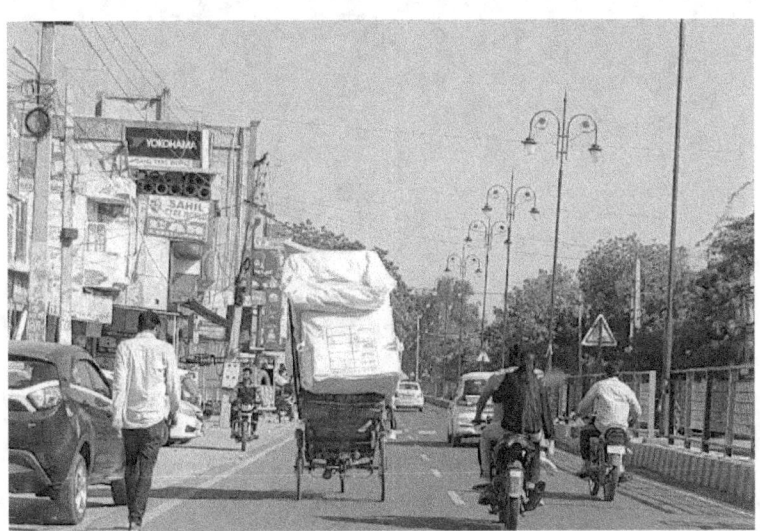

Struggle for Transporting Heavy Loads on Human Operated Tricycle in a Town of Northern India

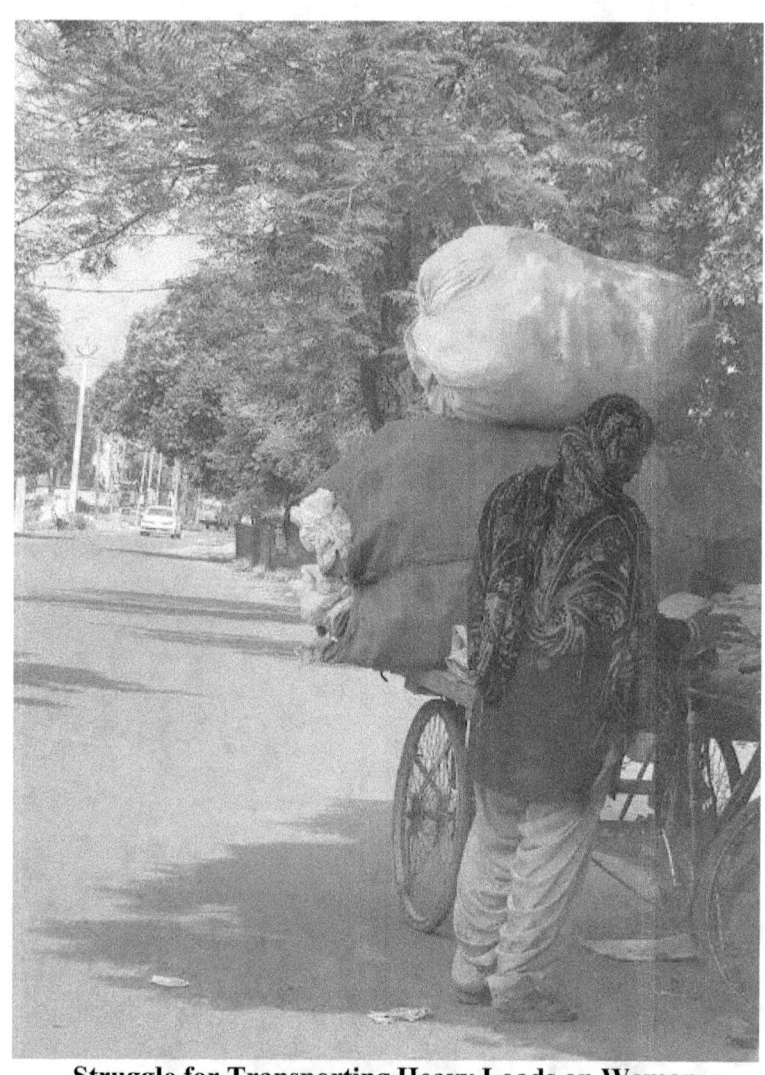

Struggle for Transporting Heavy Loads on Woman Operated Tricycle in a Town of Northern India

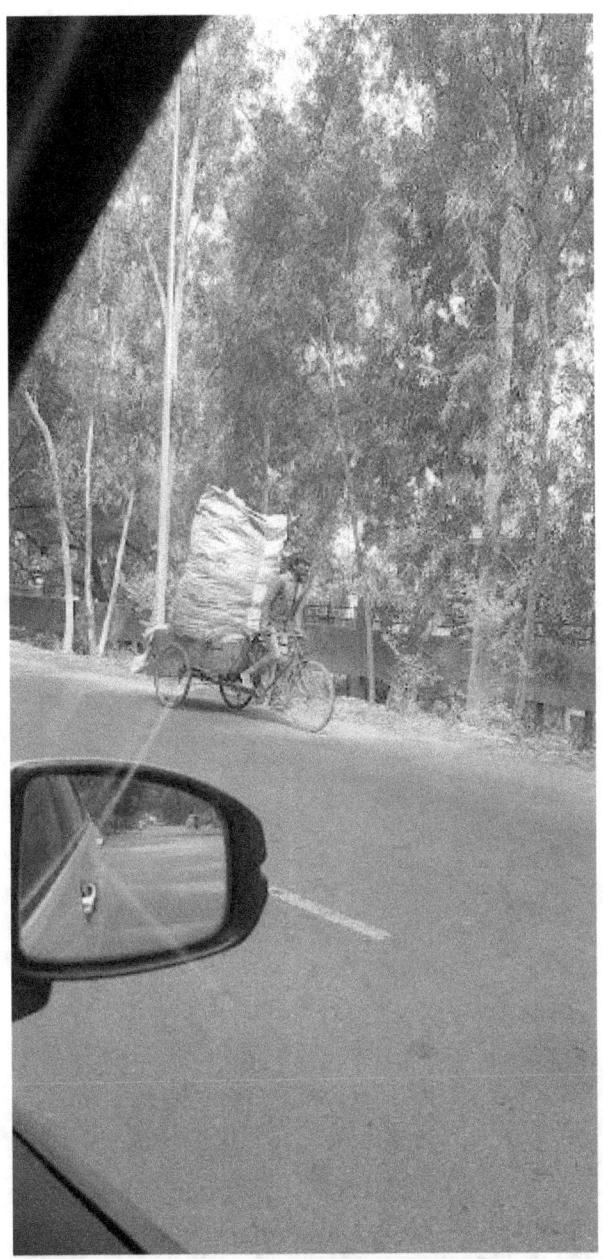

Struggle for Transporting Heavy Loads on Human Operated Tricycle in a Town of Northern India

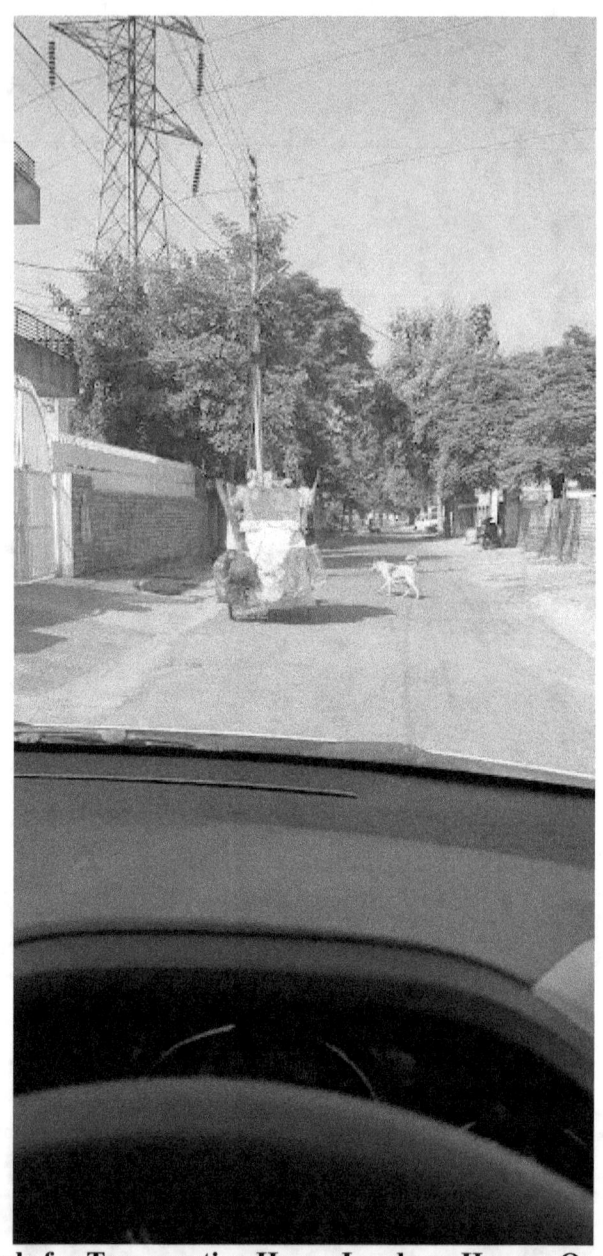

Struggle for Transporting Heavy Loads on Human Operated Tricycle in a Town of Northern India

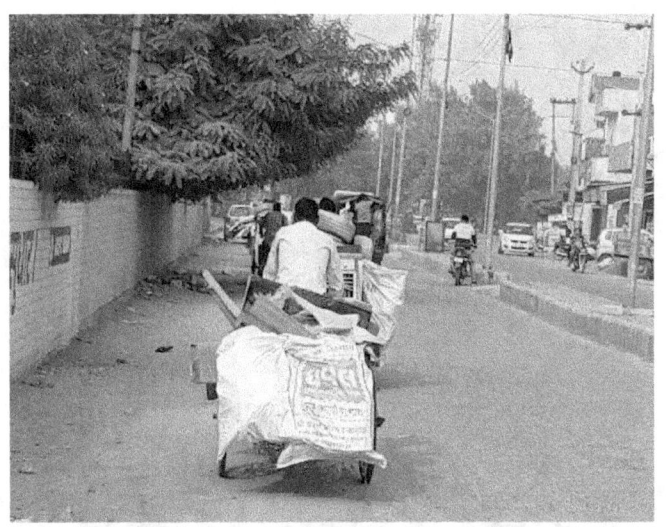

Struggle for Transporting Heavy Loads on Human Operated Tricycle in a Town of Northern India

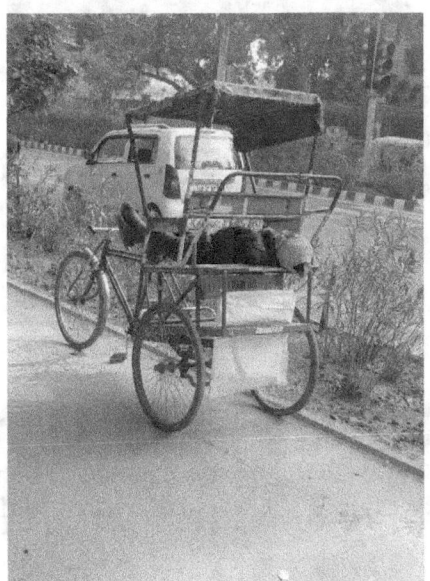

Struggle: Tricycle operator having a sleep on Tricycle in a Town of Northern India

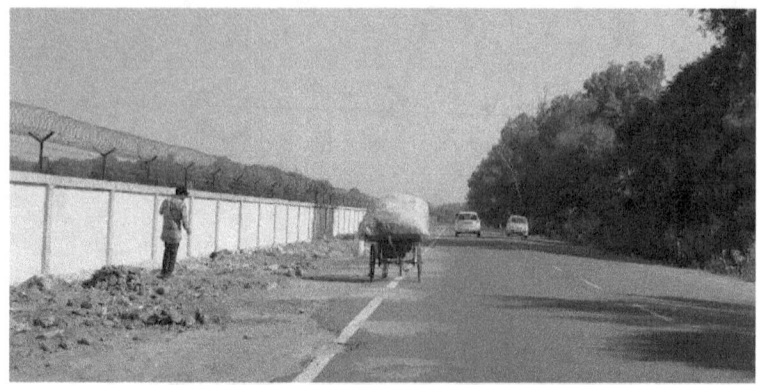

Struggle for Transporting Heavy Loads on Human Operated Tricycle in a Town of Northern India

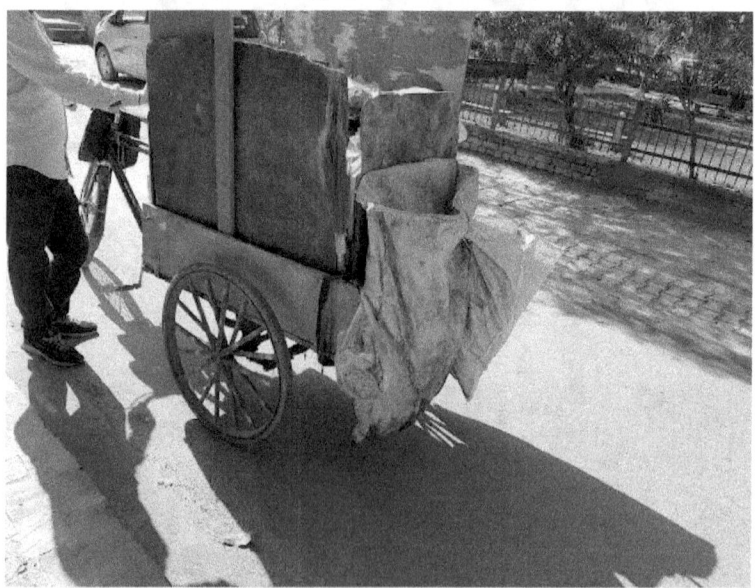

Struggle for Transporting Heavy Loads on Human Operated Tricycle in a Town of Northern India

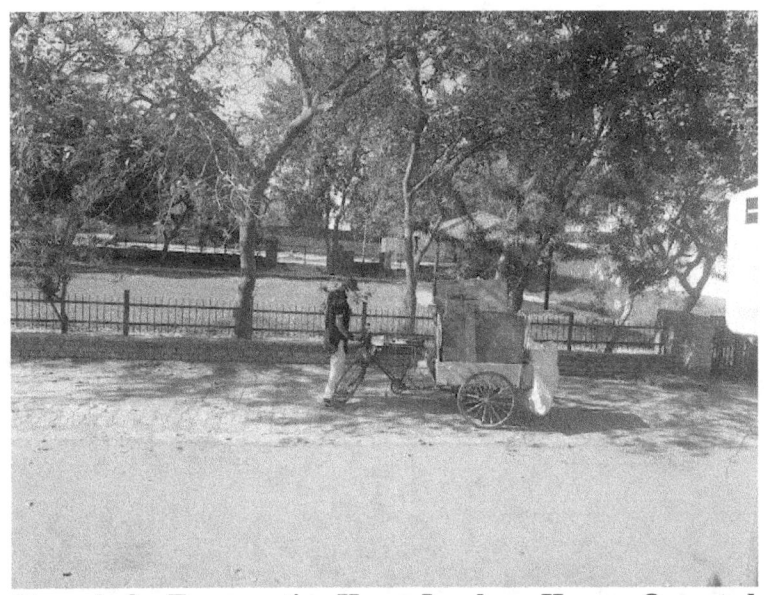

Struggle for Transporting Heavy Loads on Human Operated Tricycle in a Town of Northern India

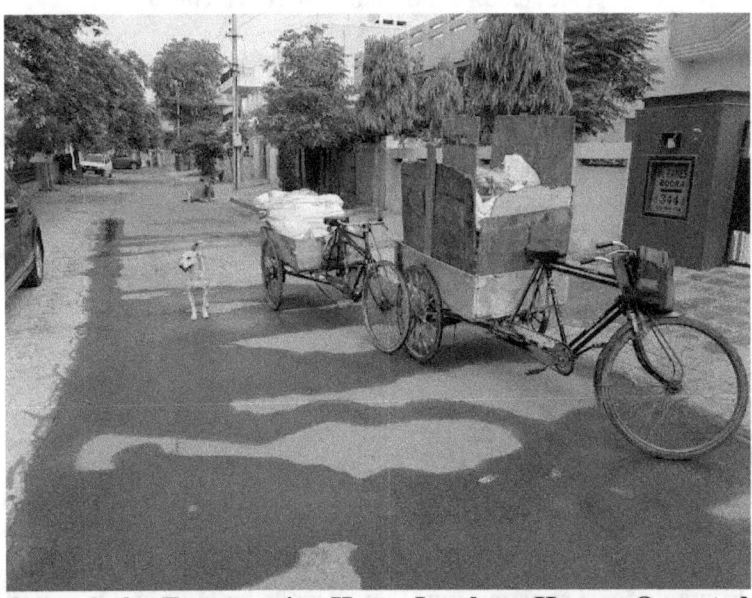

Struggle for Transporting Heavy Loads on Human Operated Tricycle in a Town of Northern India

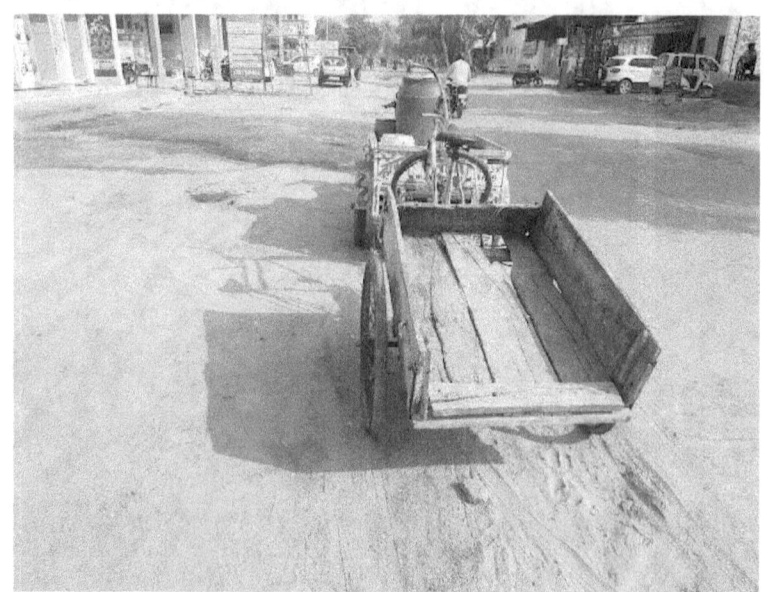

Struggle for Transporting Heavy Loads on Human Operated Tricycle in a Town of Northern India

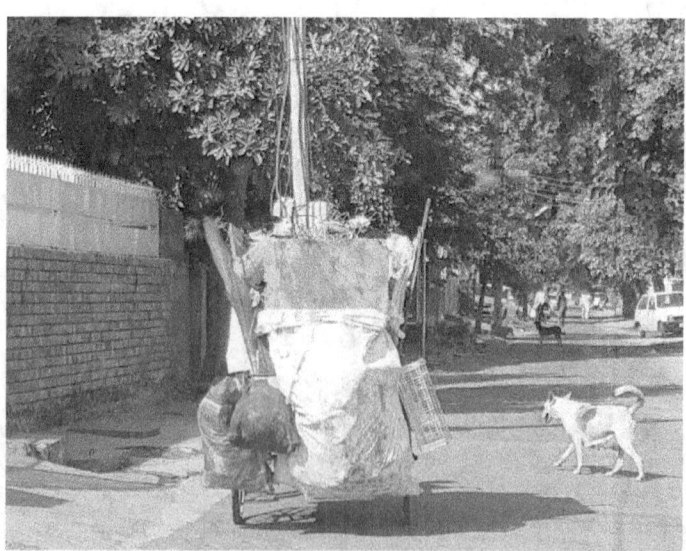

Struggle for Transporting Heavy Loads on Human Operated Tricycle in a Town of Northern India

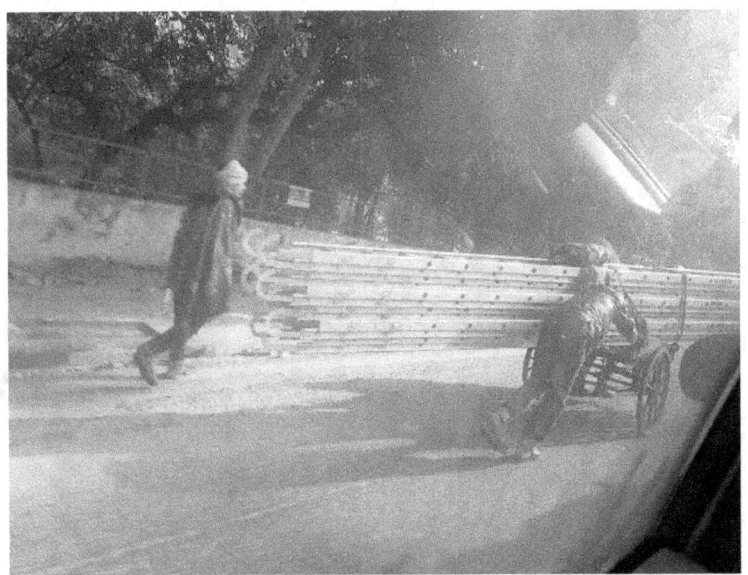

Large Size with Heavy Load on Human Operated Tricycle in Northern India

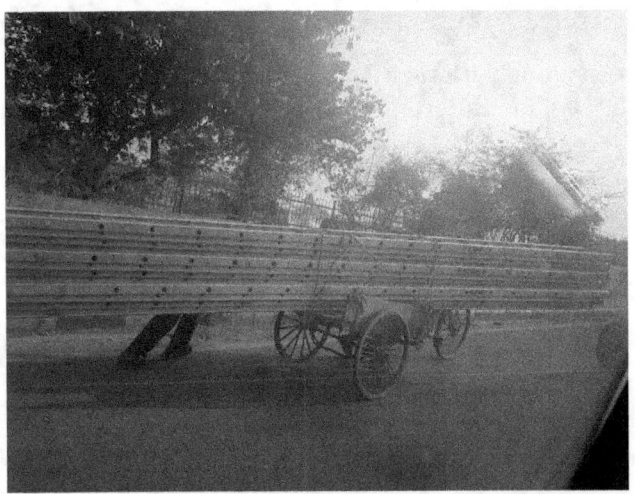

Large Size with Heavy Load on Human Operated Tricycle in Northern India

35. Women along with their Babies Begging from Door to Door with Song for Entertainment in a Town of Northern India

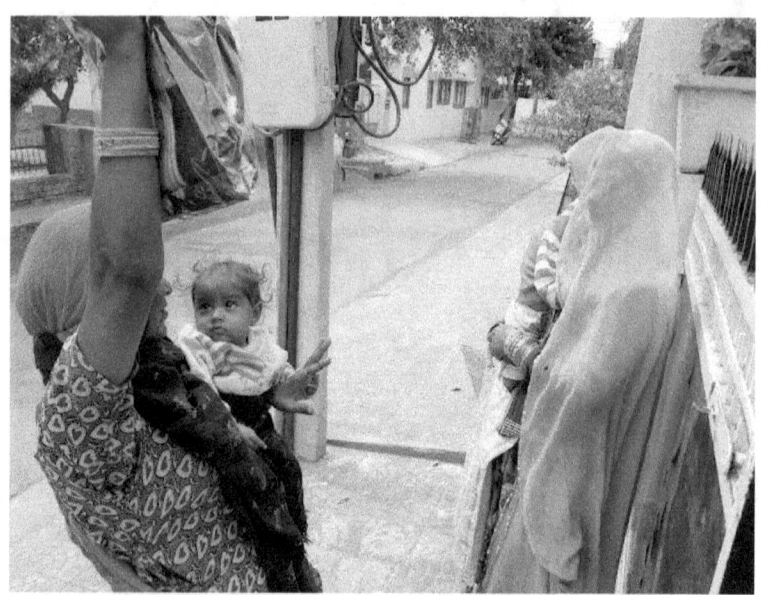

Women along with their Babies Begging from Door to Door with Song for Entertainment in a Town of Northern India

36. People Travelling by Different Vehicles on the Roads at Red Light Stoppage in Northern India

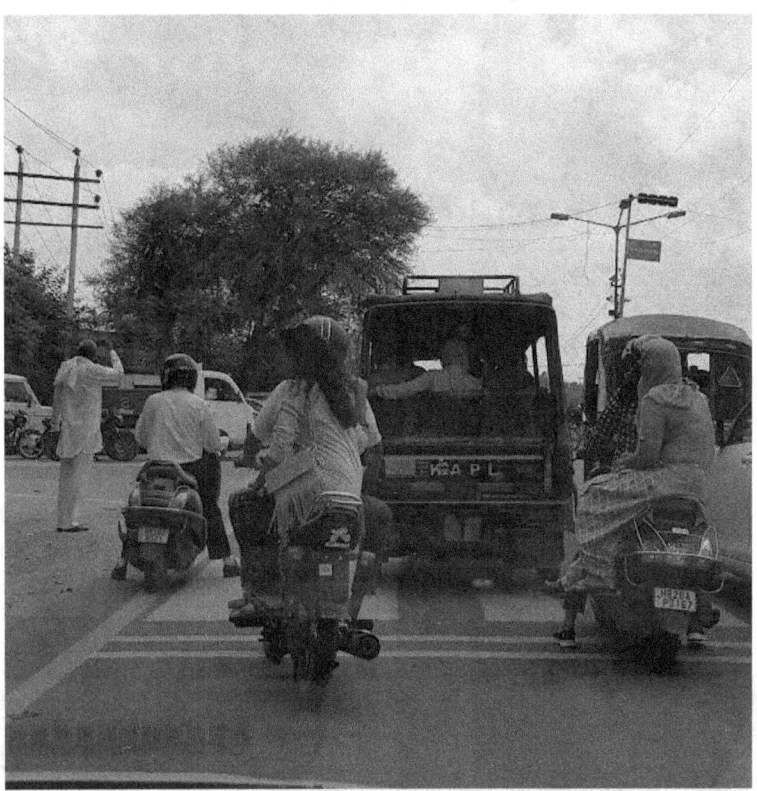

People Travelling by Different Vehicles on the Roads at Red Light Stoppage in Northern India

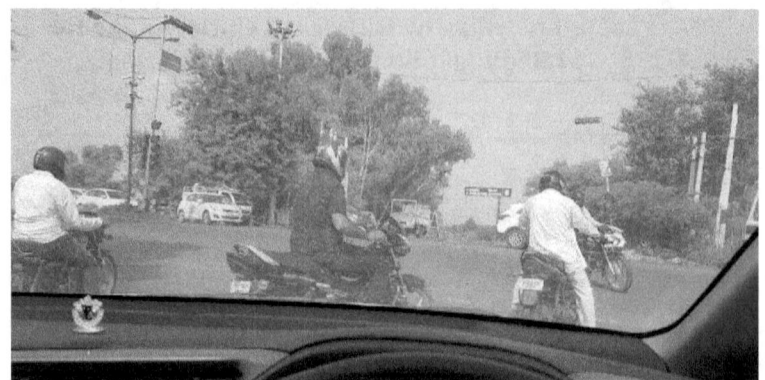

People Travelling by Motor Bike crossing the Roads at Red Light Stoppage in Northern India

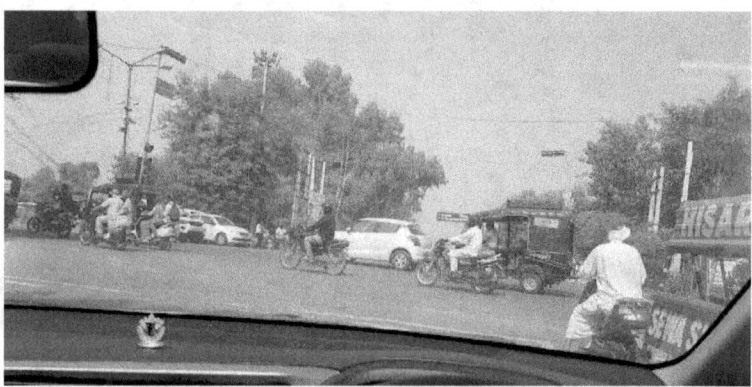

People Travelling by Different Vehicles crossing the Roads at Red Light Stoppage in Northern India

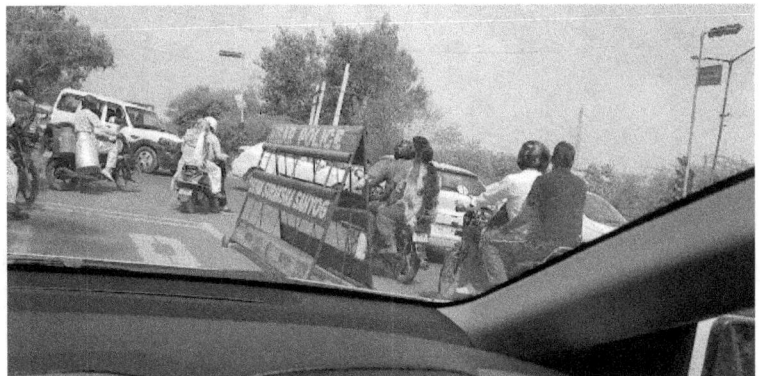

People Travelling by Different Vehicles crossing the Roads at Red Light Stoppage in Northern India

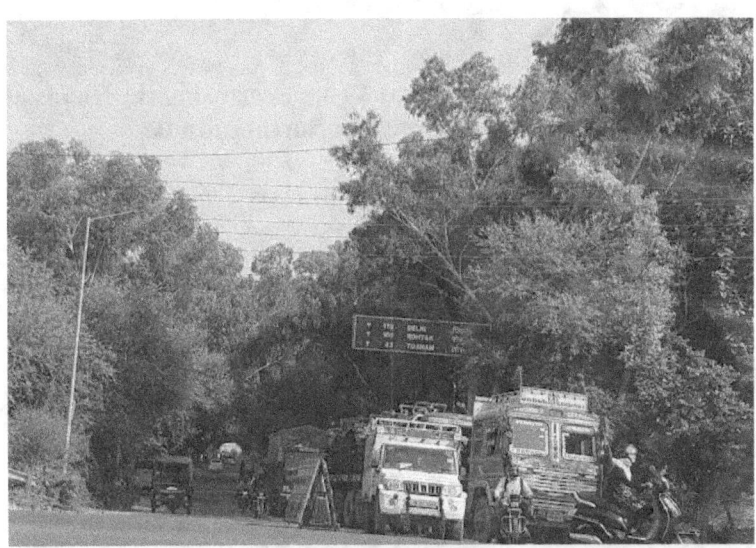

People Travelling by Different Vehicles on the Roads at Red Light Stoppage in Northern India

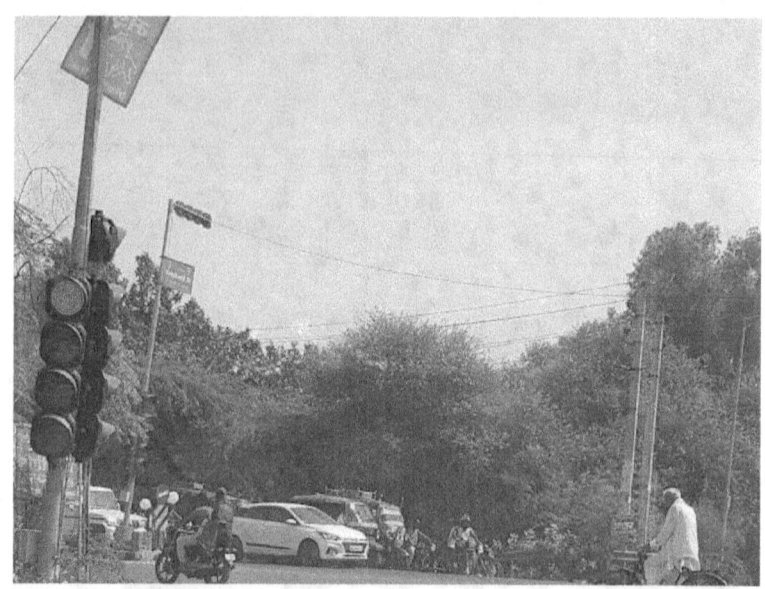

People Travelling by Different Vehicles crossing the Roads at Red Light Stoppage in Northern India

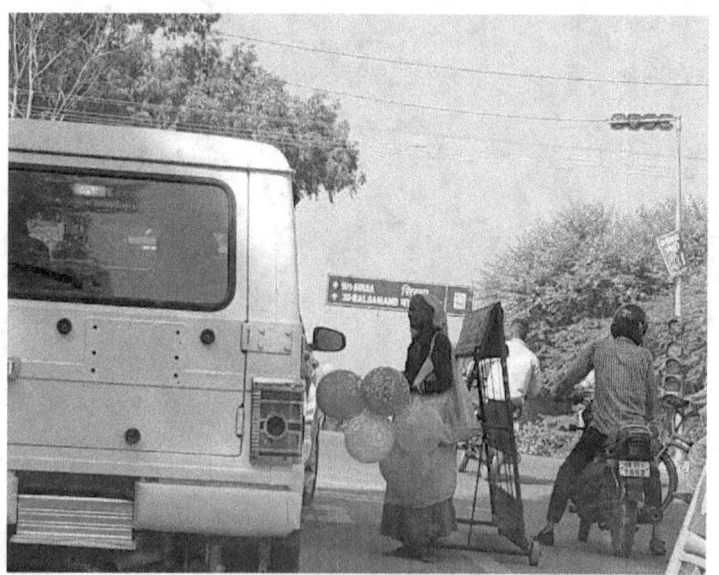

Woman Selling Balloons on the Roads at Red Light Stoppage in Northern India

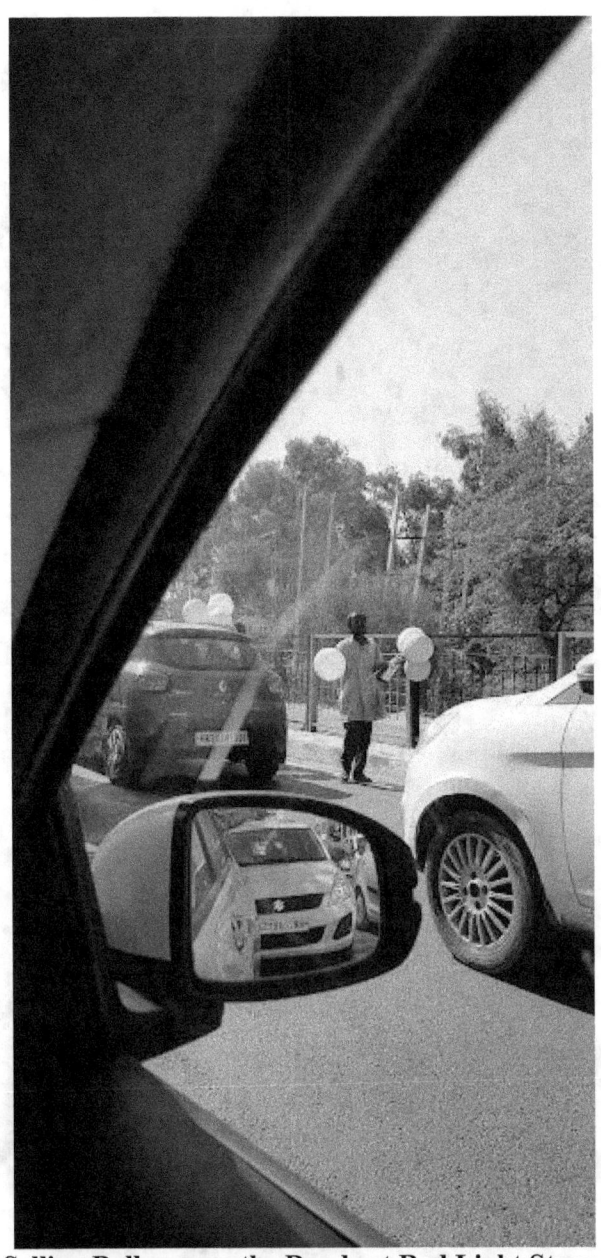

Man Selling Balloons on the Roads at Red Light Stoppage in Northern India

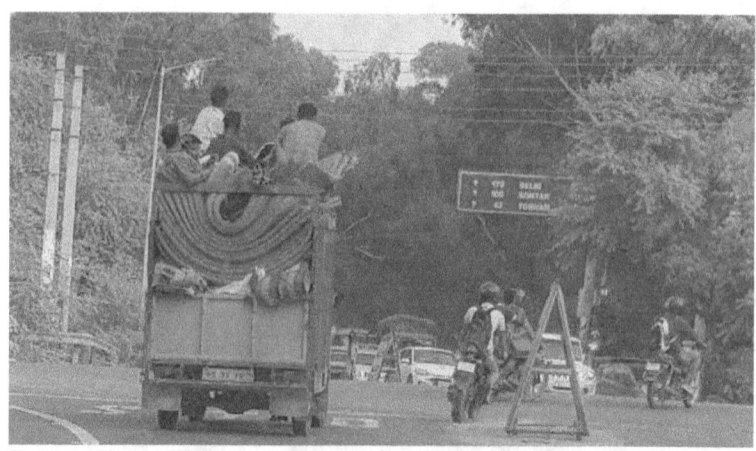

People Travelling by Different Vehicles crossing the Roads at Red Light Stoppage in Northern India

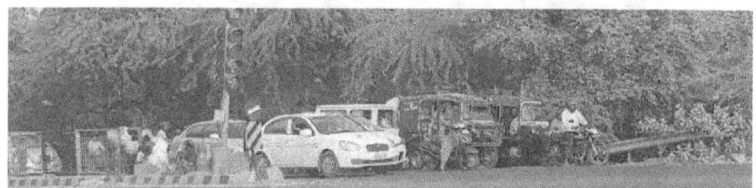

People Travelling by Different Vehicles on the Roads at Red Light Stoppage in Northern India

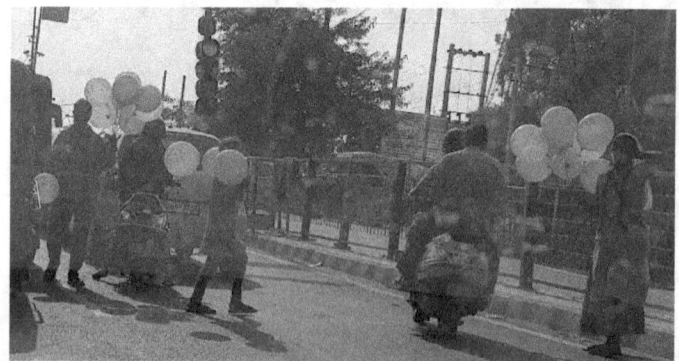

Man, Woman and Children Selling Balloons on the Roads at Red Light Stoppage in Northern India

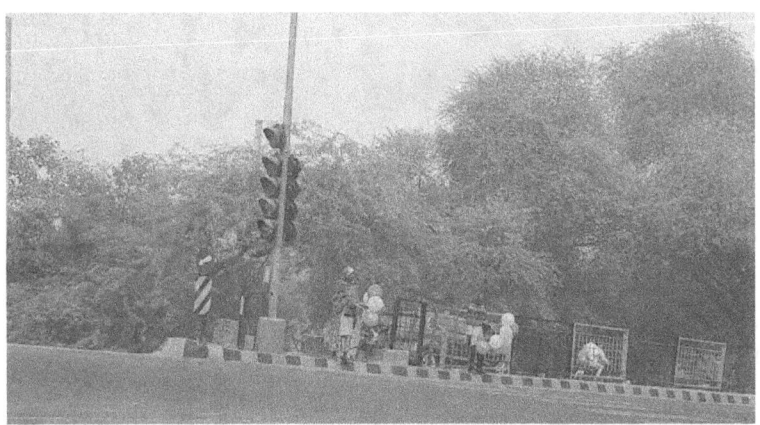

Man, Woman and Children Selling Balloons on the Roads at Red Light Stoppage in Northern India

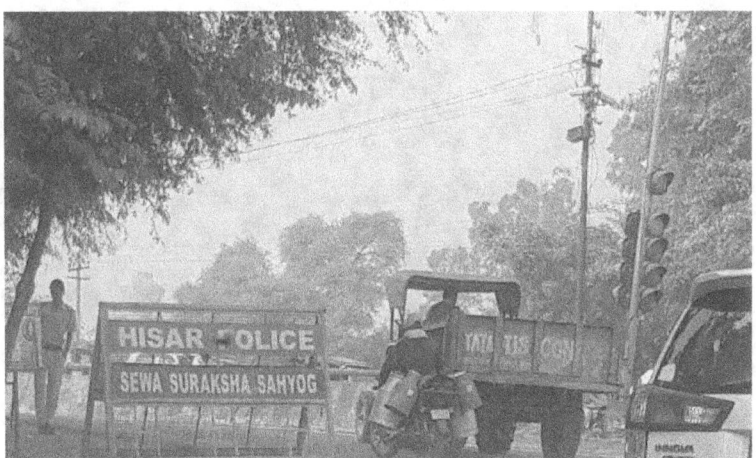

People Travelling by Different Vehicles crossing the Roads at Red Light Stoppage in Northern India

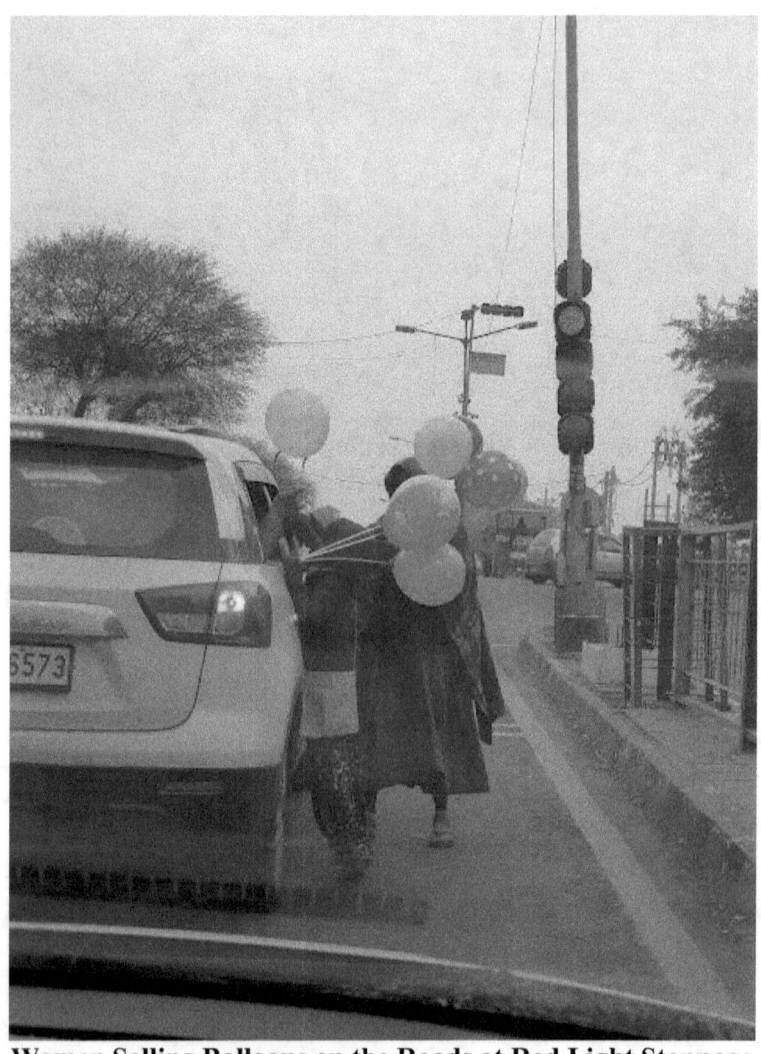

Women Selling Balloons on the Roads at Red Light Stoppage in Northern India

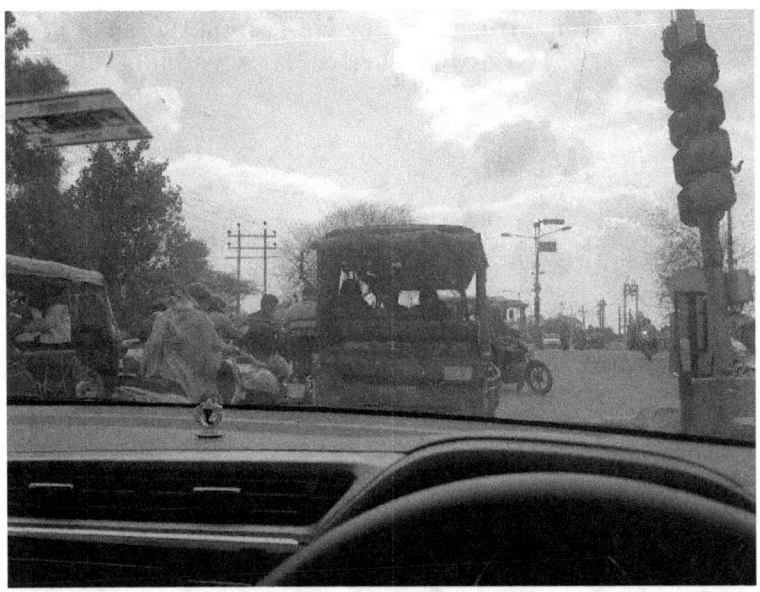

People Travelling by Different Vehicles on the Roads at Red Light Stoppage in Northern India

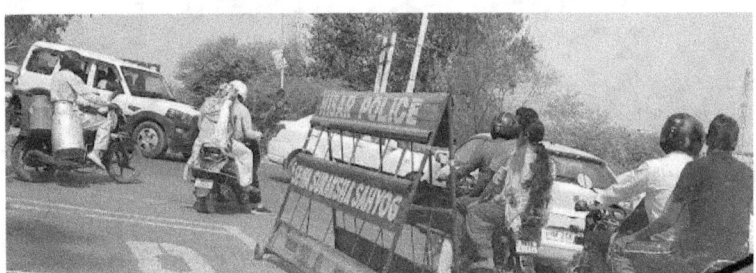

People Travelling by Different Vehicles on the Roads at Red Light Stoppage in Northern India

37. Amazing Struggle of Bug for Transportation of Food Grain in a Park of Northern India

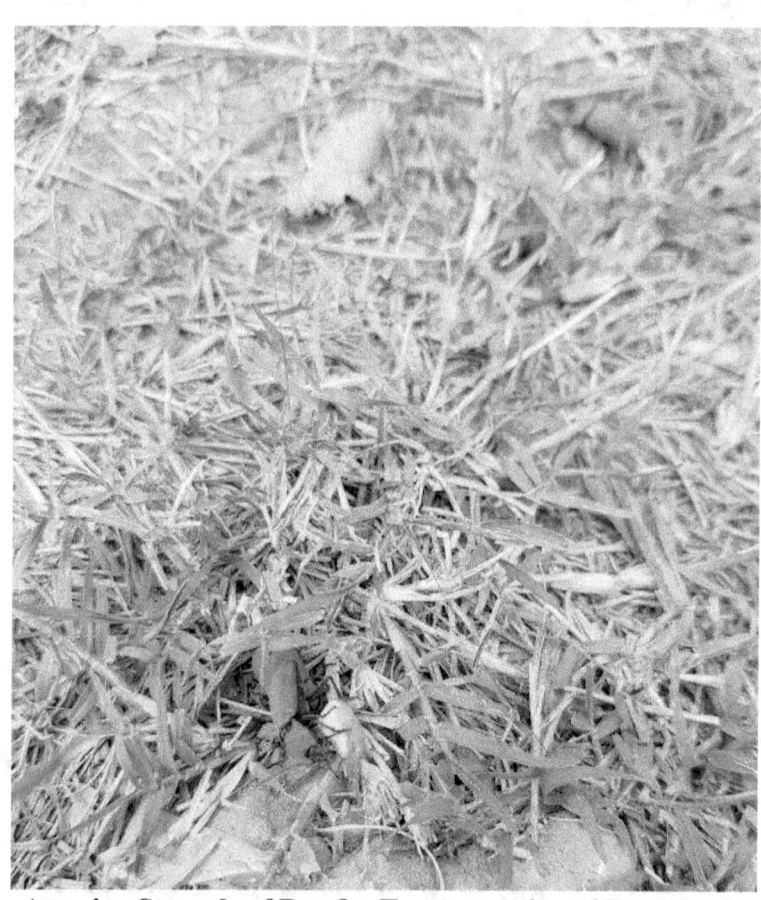

Amazing Struggle of Bug for Transportation of Food Grain in a Park of Northern India

38. Saints Moving Door to Door for Begging with Entertainment in a Town of Northern India

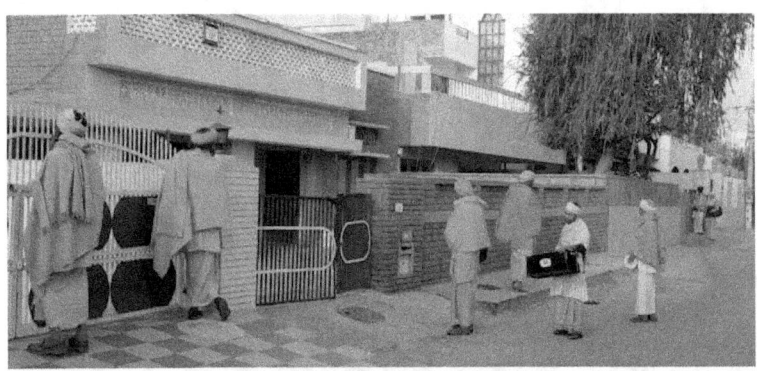

Saints Moving Door to Door for Begging with Entertainment in a City of Northern India

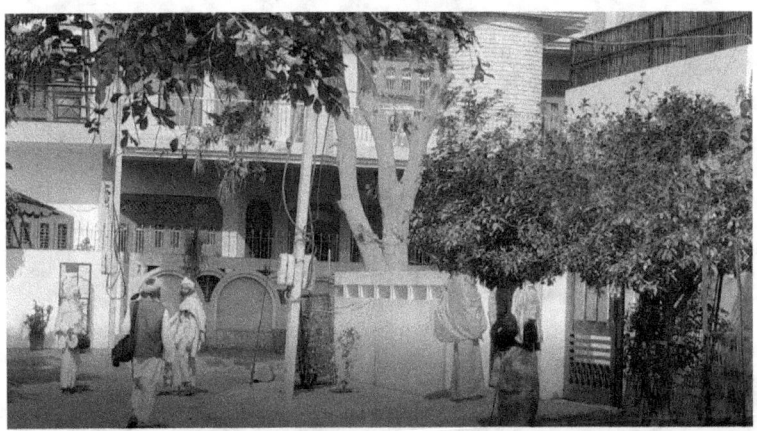

Saints Moving Door to Door for Begging with Entertainment in a City of Northern India

39. Driving Motor Bike Ignoring Driving Rules in Northern India

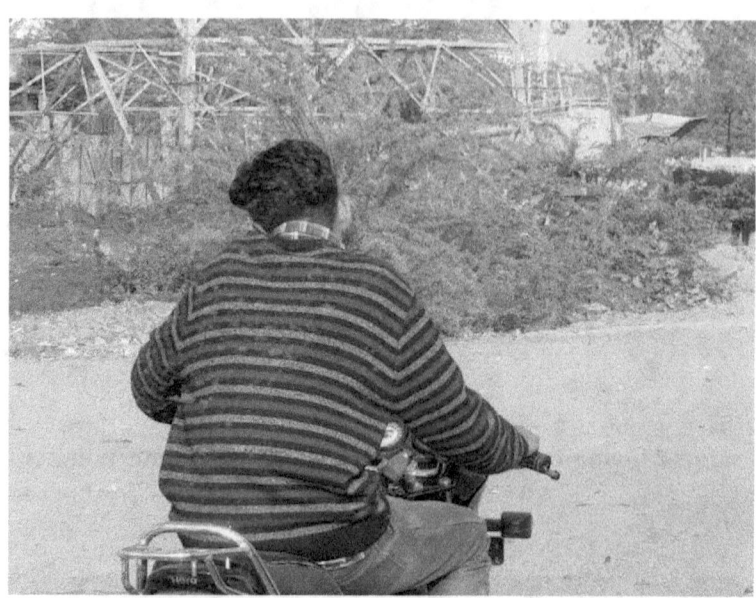

Young Boy Busy on Mobile Talking with full Focus while Driving Motor Bike without Helmet in Northern India

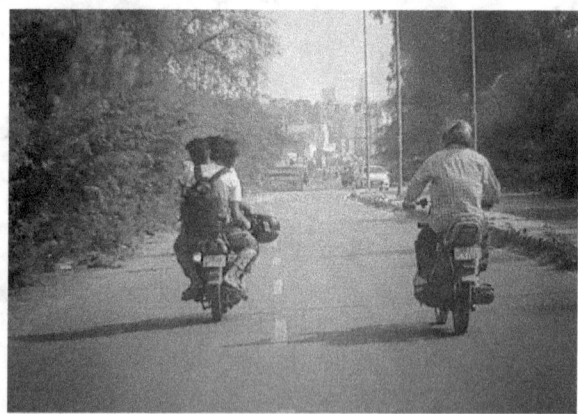

Driving of Motor Bike by keeping Helmet in the hand of Co-Passenger in Northern India

40. Celebration of Worship on the Bank of a Canal in Northern India

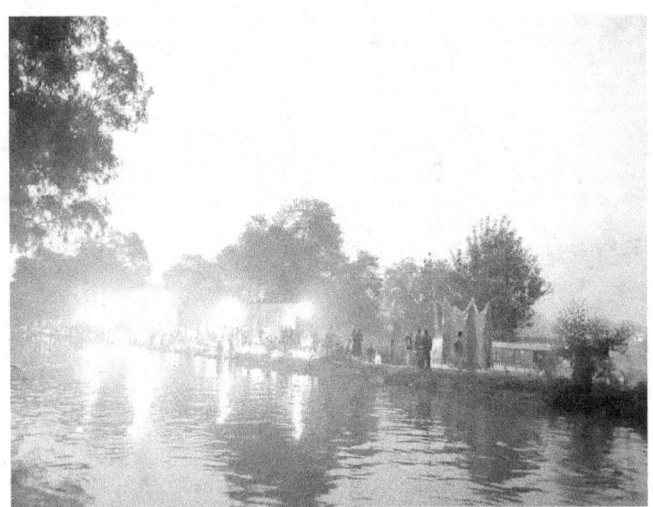

Celebration of Worship on the Bank of a Canal in Northern India

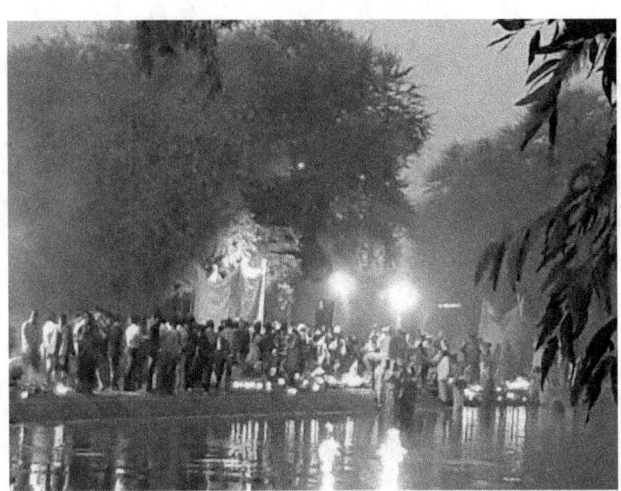

Celebration of Worship on the Bank of a Canal in Northern India

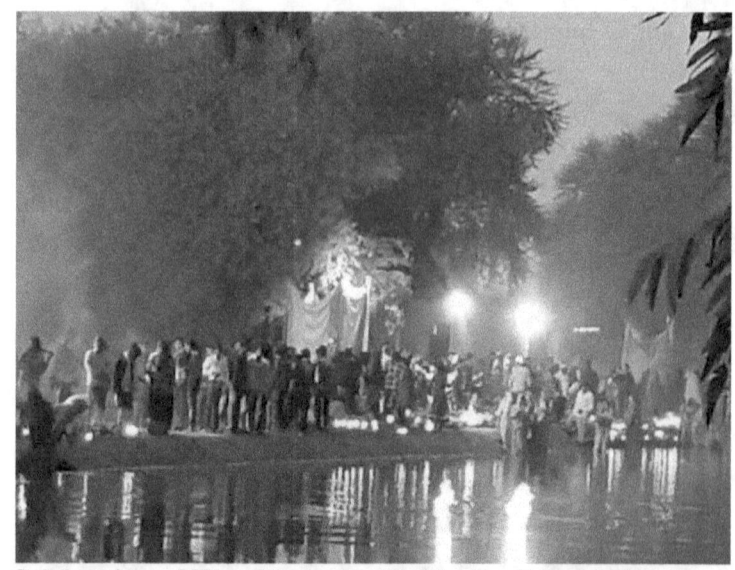

Celebration of Worship on the Bank of a Canal in Northern India

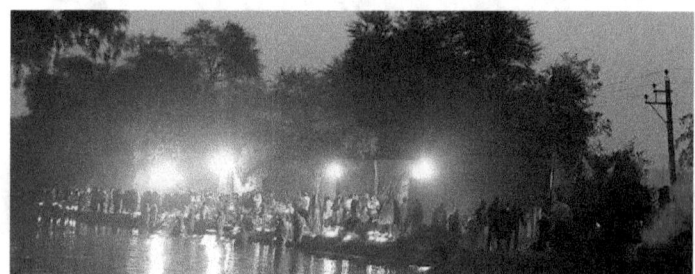

Celebration of Worship on the Bank of a Canal in Northern India

41. Farming Community Women for Transporting Farm Produce on their Head in Northern India
Work is Worship for farmers of India

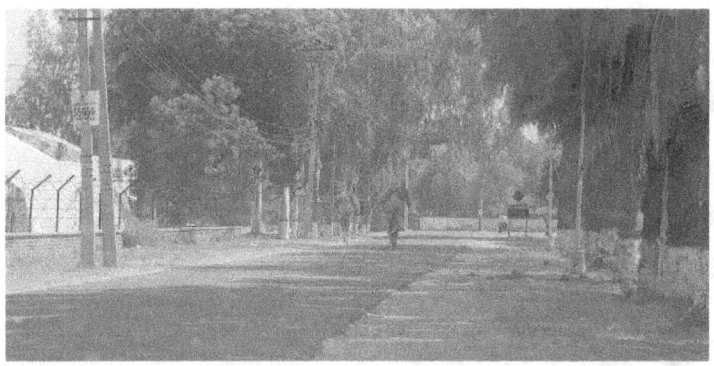

Farming Community Women Transporting Green Fodder on their Head in Northern India

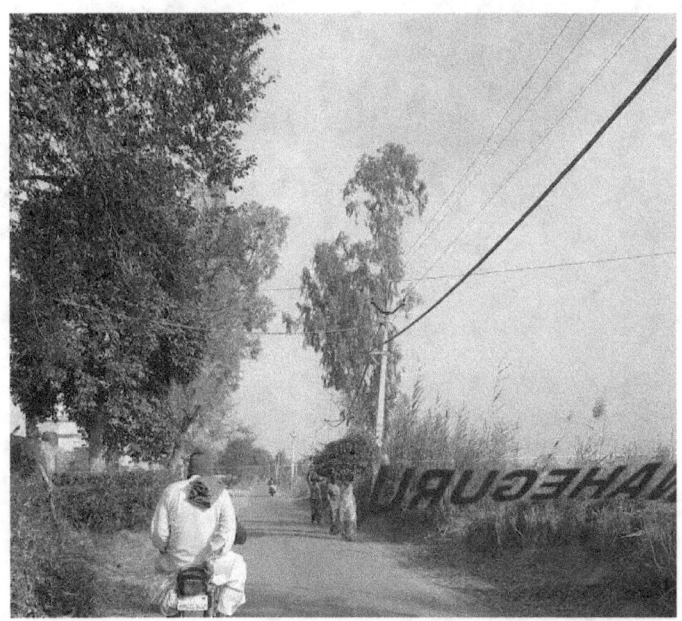

Farming Community Women Transporting Farm Produce on their Head in Northern India

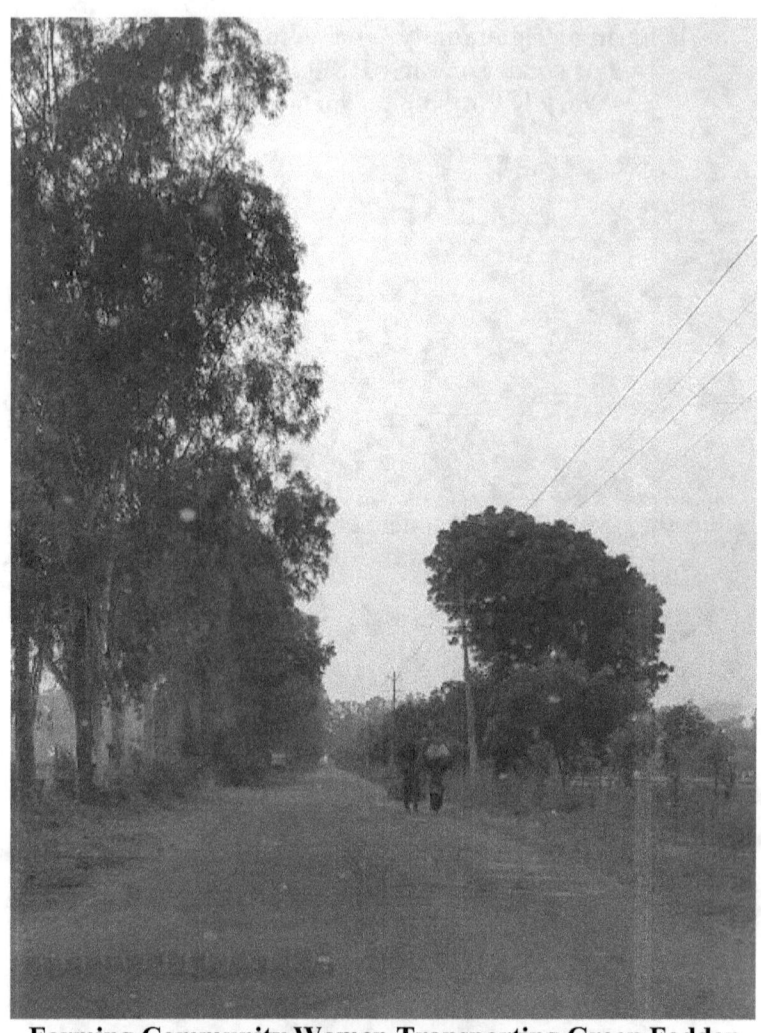

Farming Community Women Transporting Green Fodder on their Head in Northern India

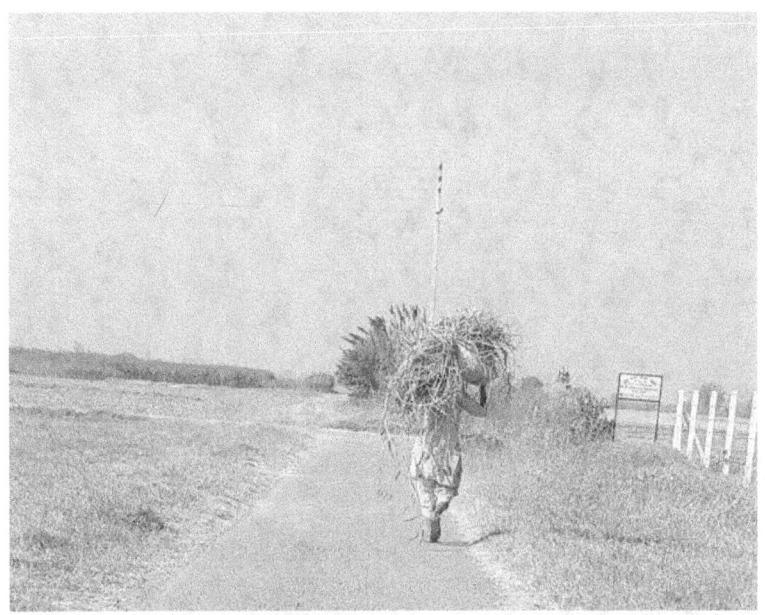

Farming Community Women Transporting Farm Produce on their Head in Northern India

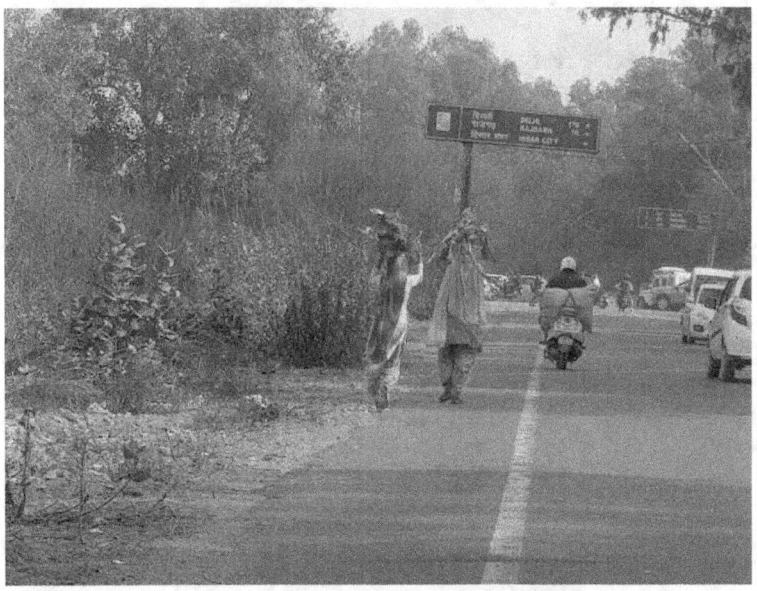

Farming Community Women Transporting Farm Produce on their Head in Northern India

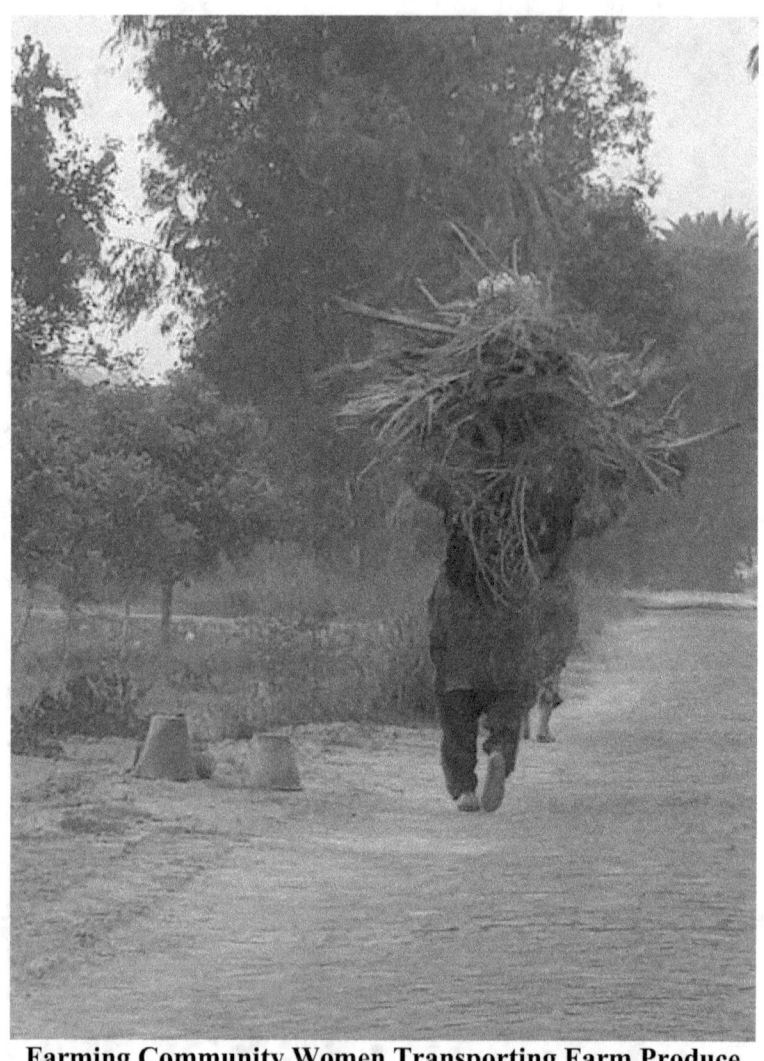

Farming Community Women Transporting Farm Produce on their Head in Northern India

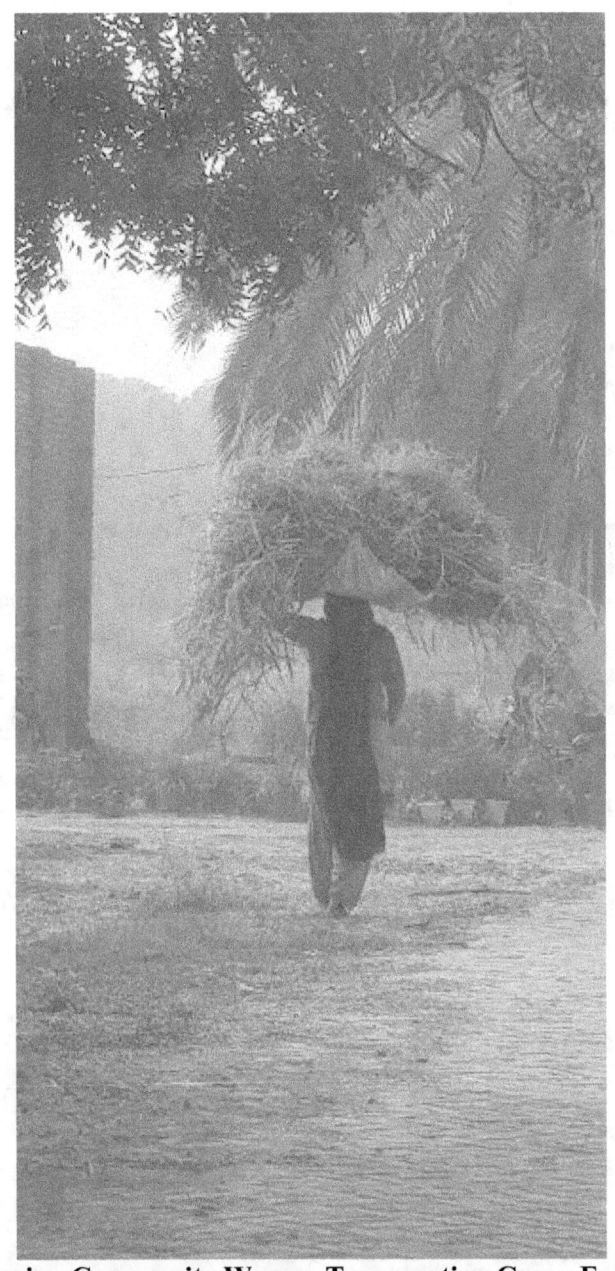

Farming Community Women Transporting Green Fodder on their Head in Northern India

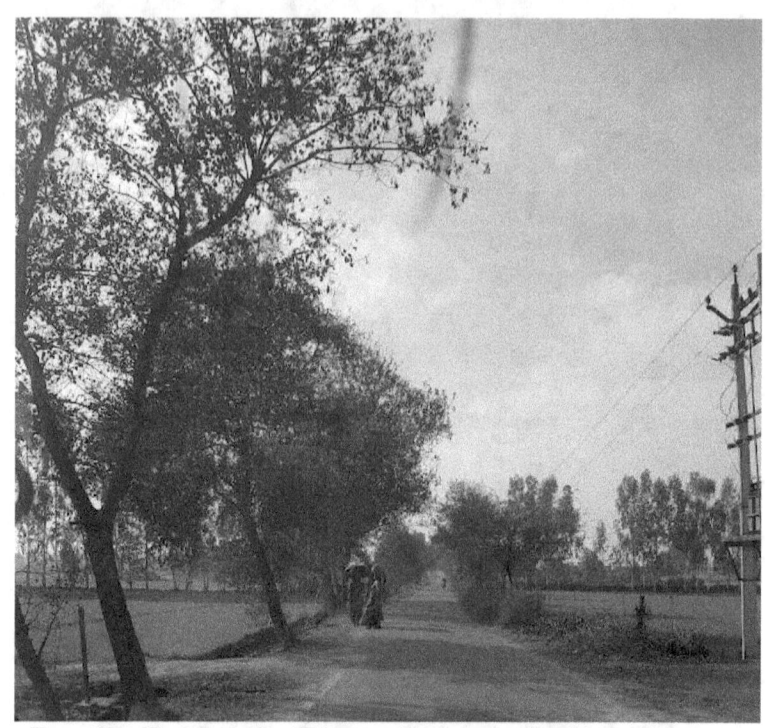

Farming Community Women Transporting Farm Produce on their Head in Northern India

42. Farmers Transporting Farm Produce by Driving Animal Cart in Northern India

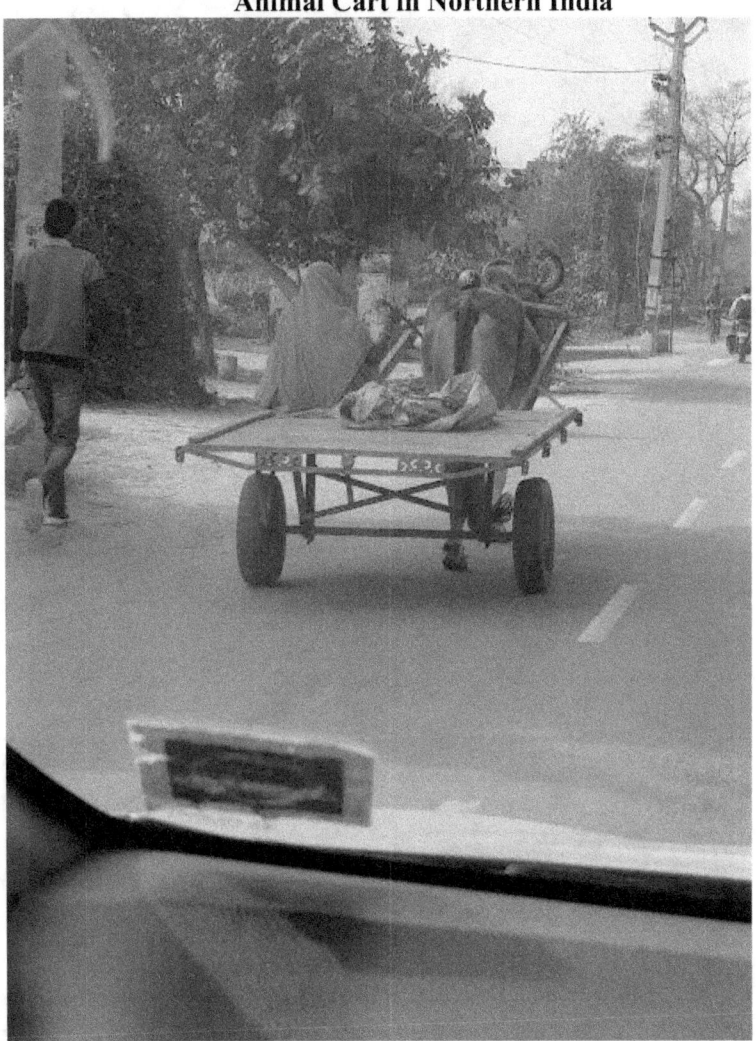

Woman Farmer Driving Animal Cart for Transporting Farm Produce

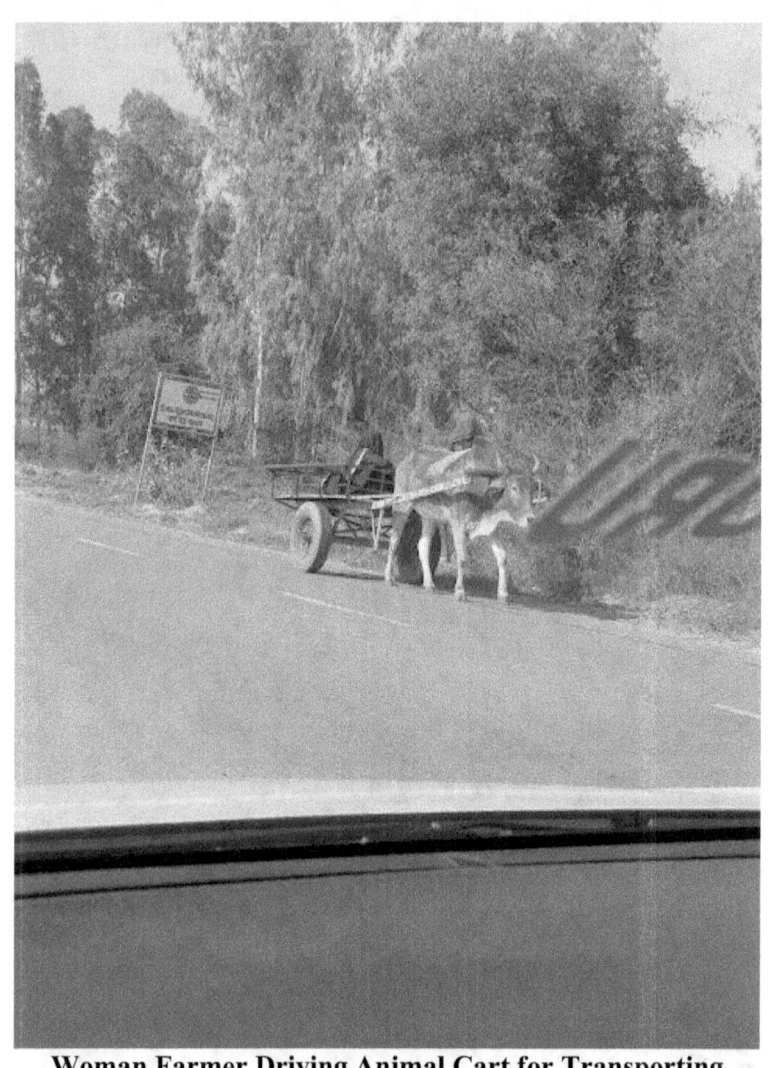

Woman Farmer Driving Animal Cart for Transporting Farm Produce

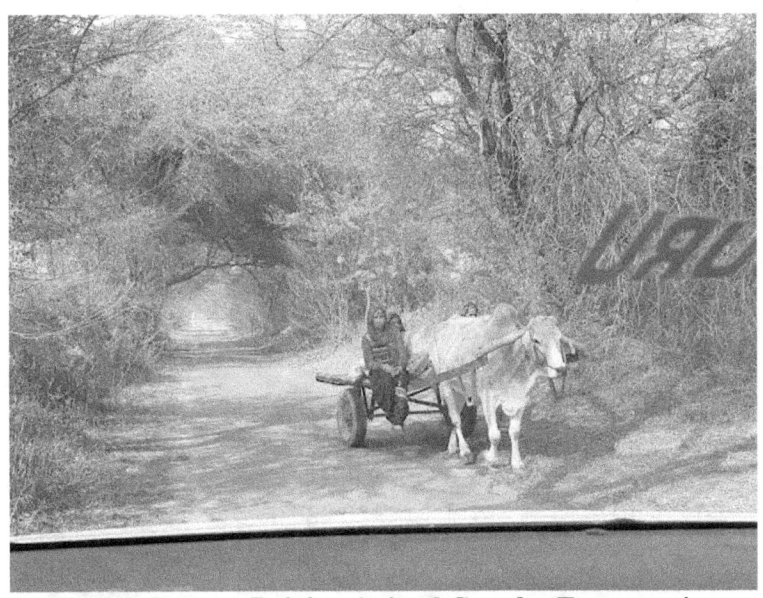

Woman Farmer Driving Animal Cart for Transporting Farm Produce

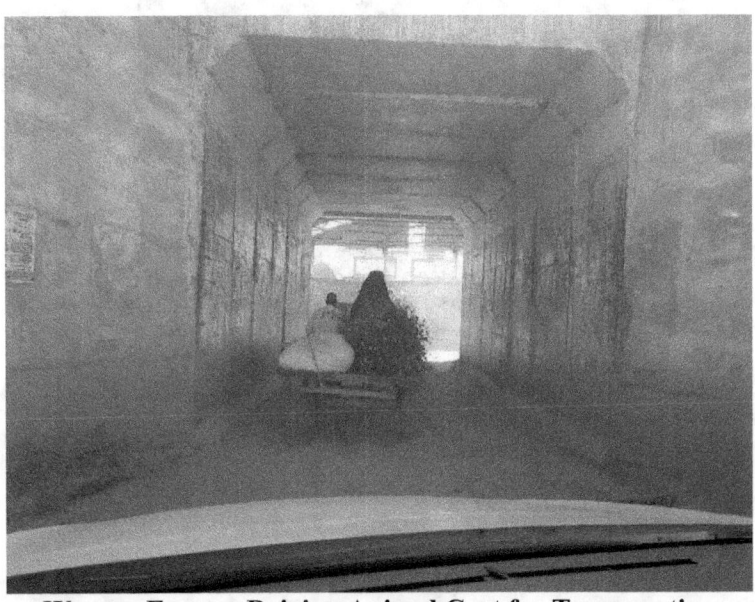

Woman Farmer Driving Animal Cart for Transporting Farm Produce

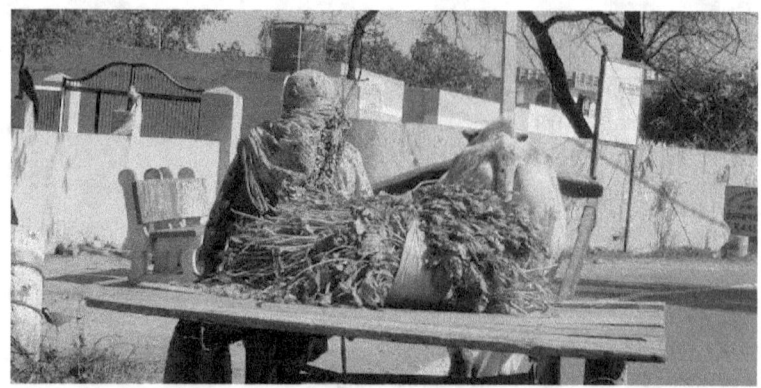

Woman Farmer Driving Animal Cart for Transporting Farm Produce

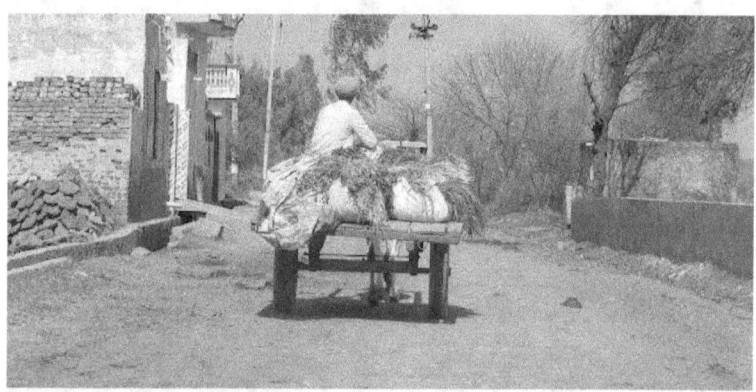

Transportation of Green Fodder on Animal Operated Vehicle in Northern India where Animal Controlled by Man Farmer

43. Overloaded Two Wheelers on the Roads in Northern India

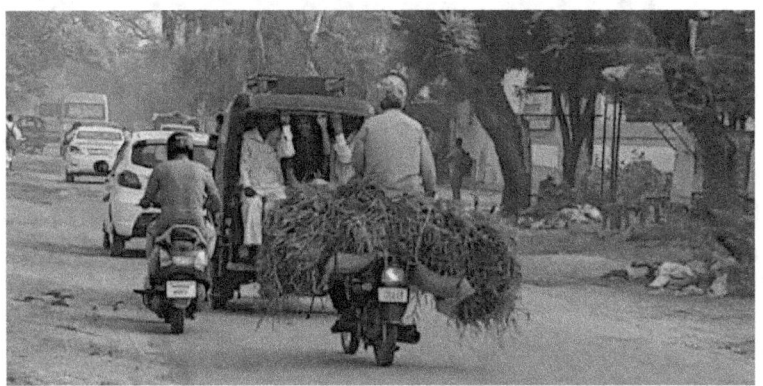

Transportation of Fodder on Two-Wheeler

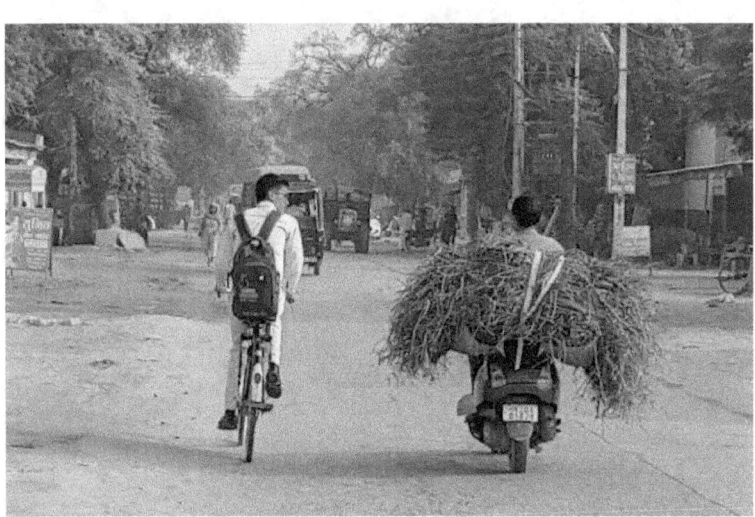

Transportation of Fodder on Two-Wheeler

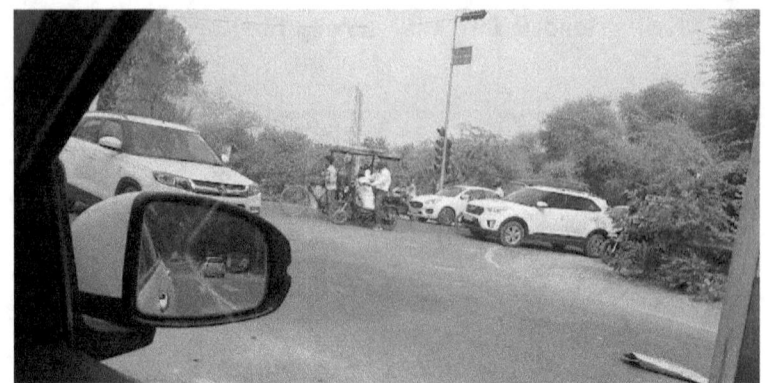

Transportation of Overloaded luggage on Two-Wheeler

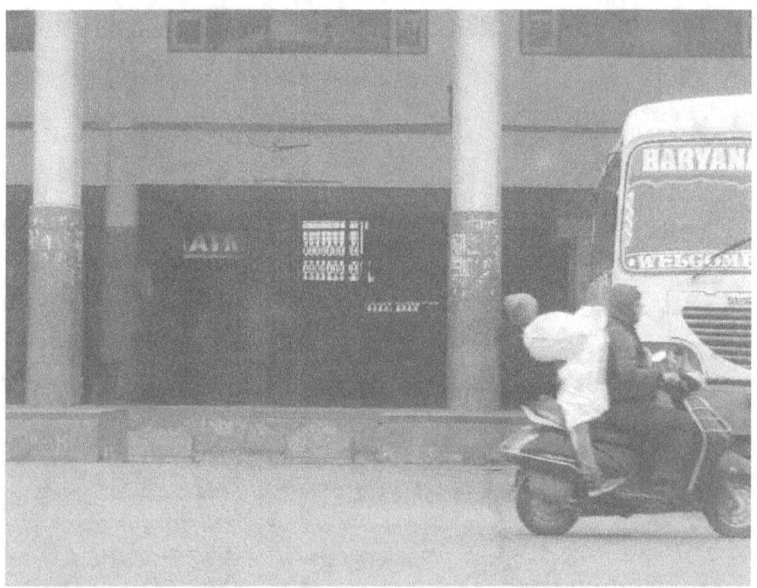

Transportation of Overloaded luggage on Two-Wheeler

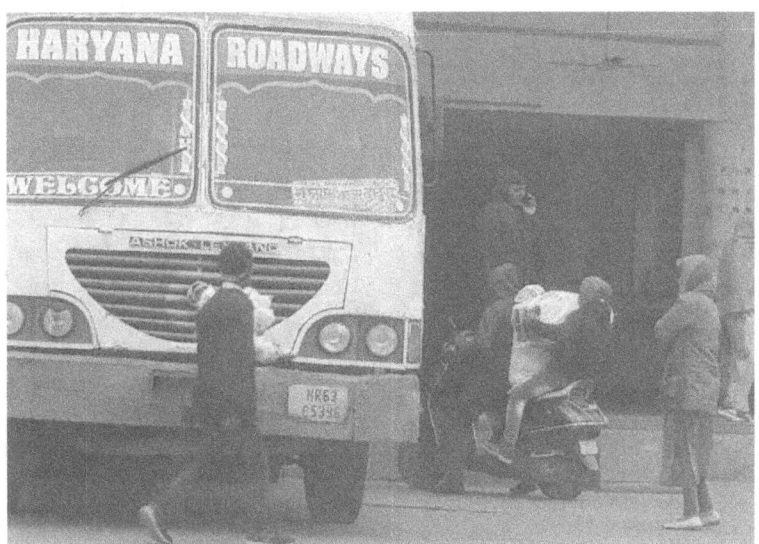

Transportation of Overloaded luggage on Two-Wheeler

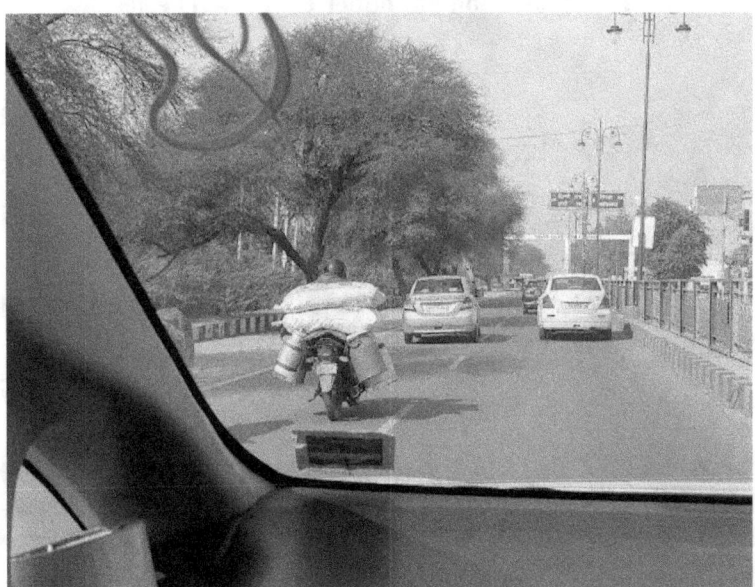

Transportation of Overloaded luggage on Two-Wheeler

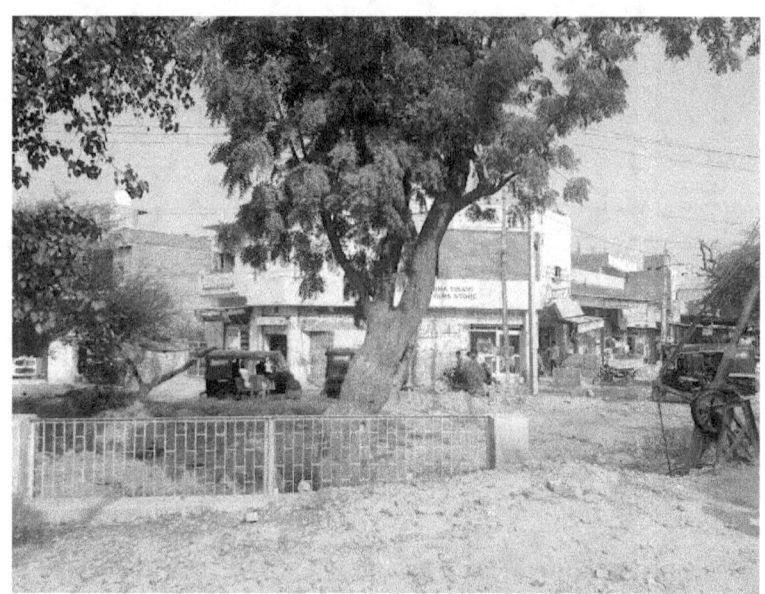

Transportation of Fodder on Two-Wheeler

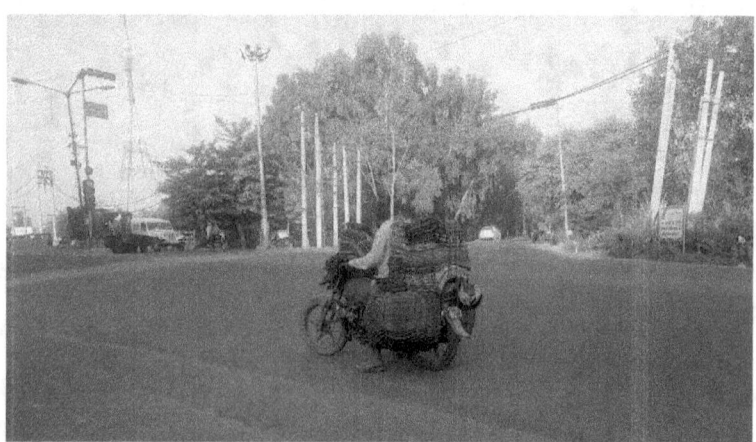

Amazing Transportation of Overloaded clothes on Two-Wheeler

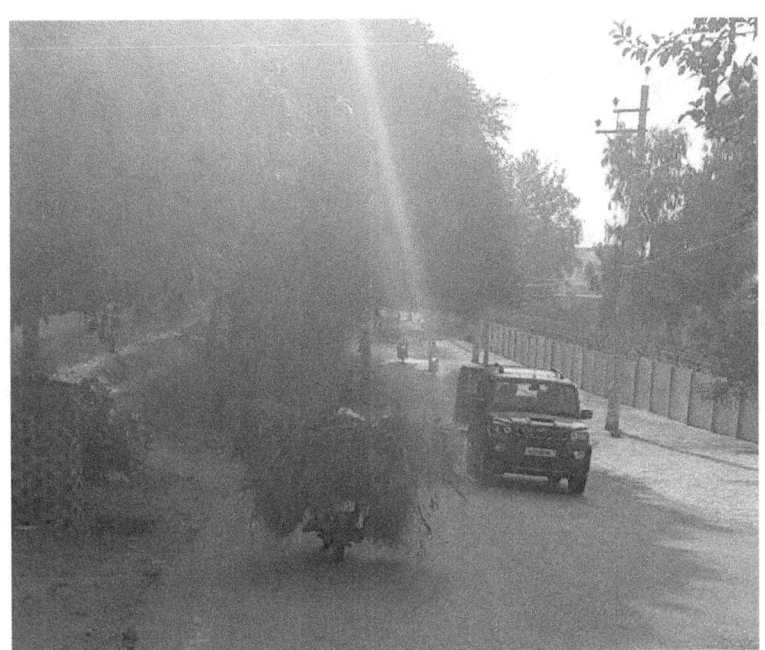

Transportation of Fodder on Two-Wheeler

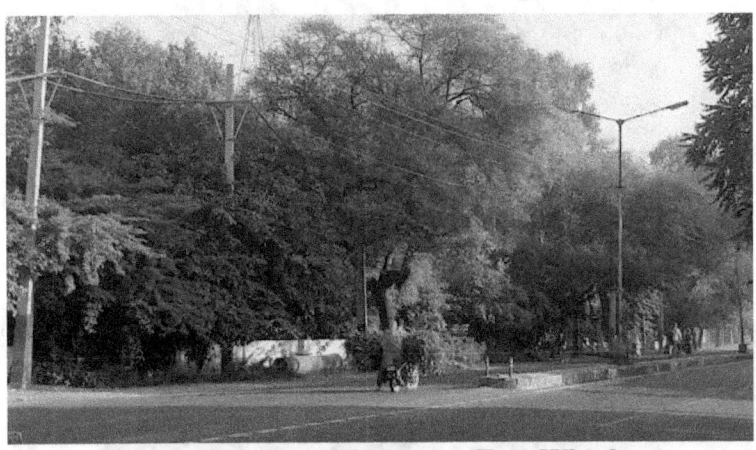

Transportation of Fodder on Two-Wheeler

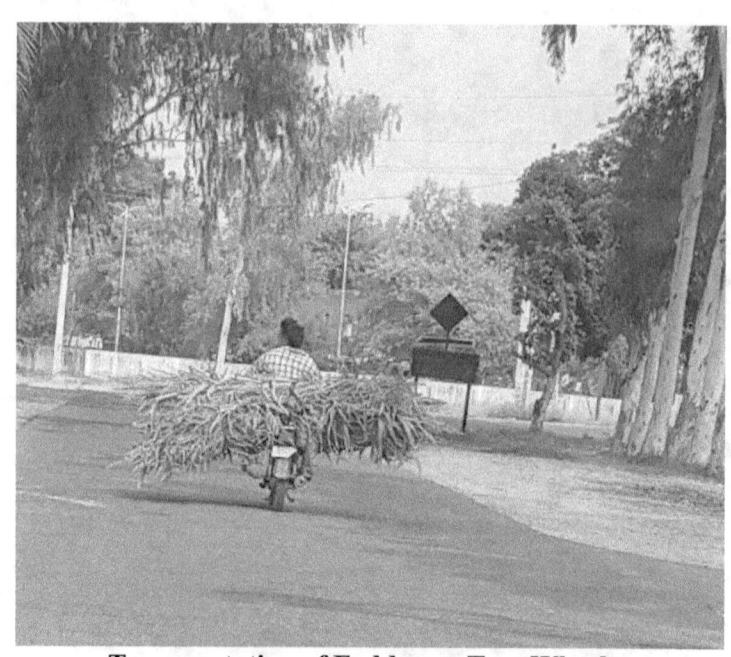

Transportation of Fodder on Two-Wheeler

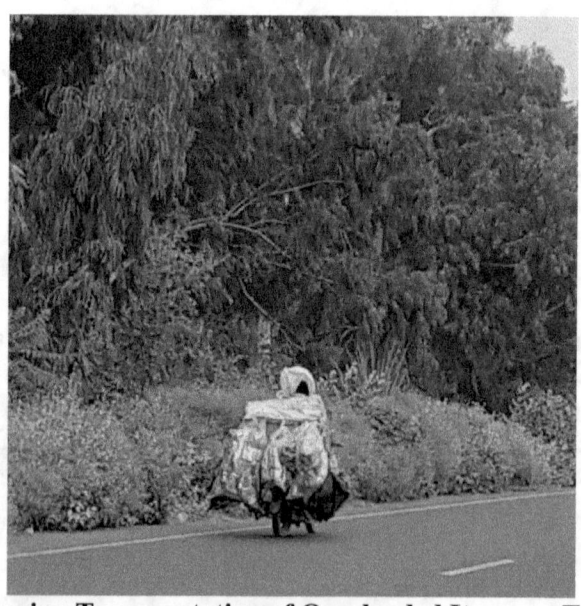

Amazing Transportation of Overloaded Items on Two-Wheeler

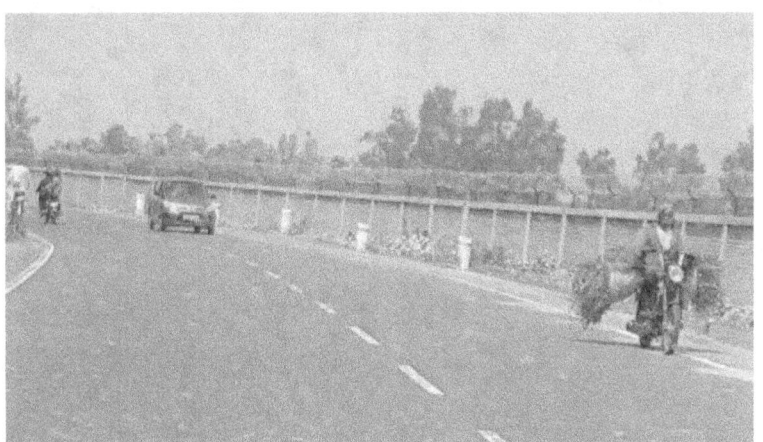

Transportation of Fodder on Two-Wheeler

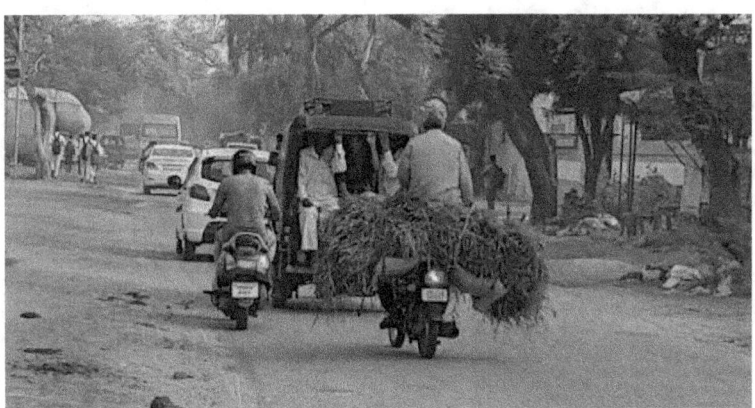

Transportation of Fodder on Two-Wheeler

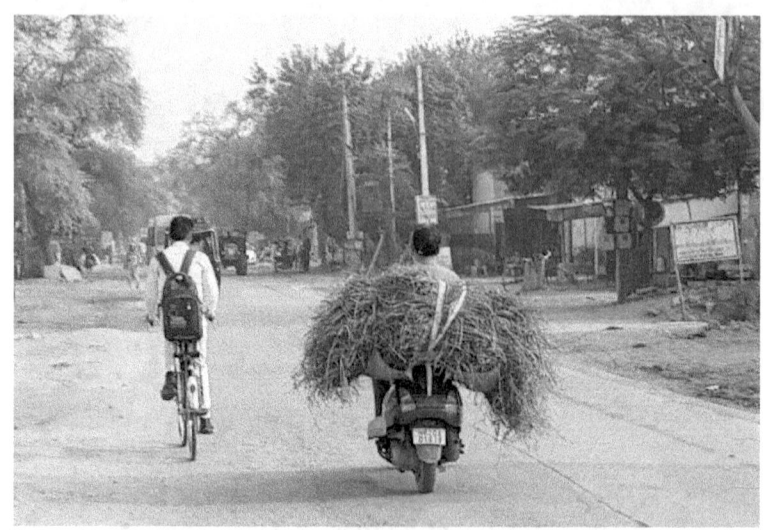

Transportation of Fodder on Two-Wheeler

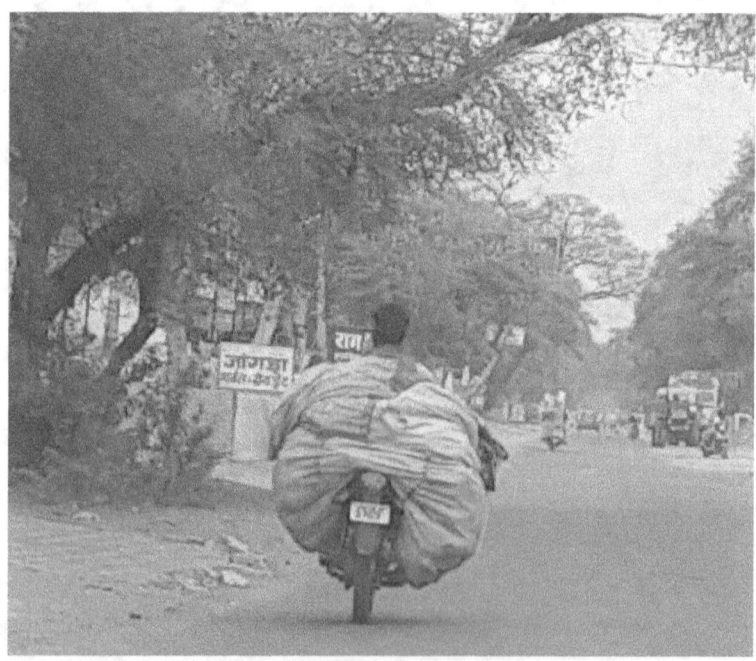

Transportation of Waste material on Two-Wheeler

44. Overloaded Four-Wheeler Vehicles on the Roads in Northern India

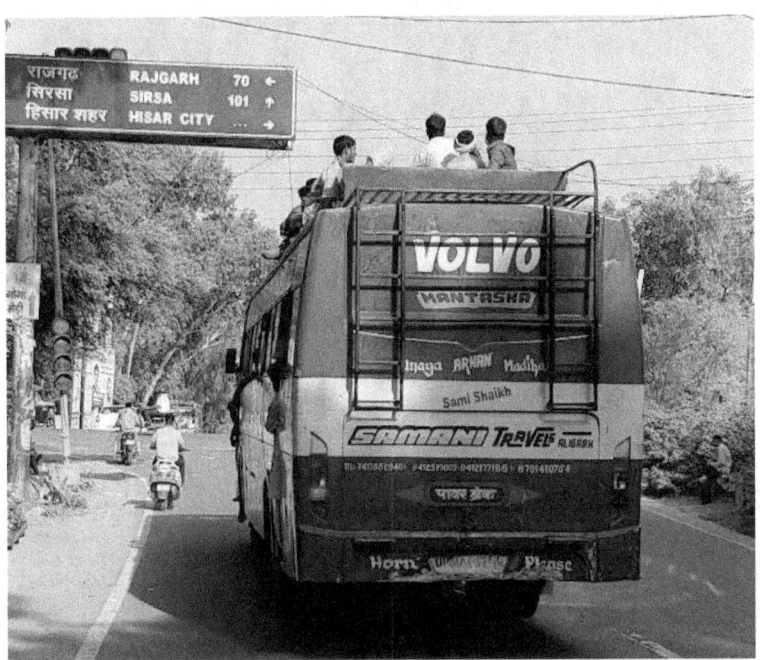

Overloaded Passengers in a Bus

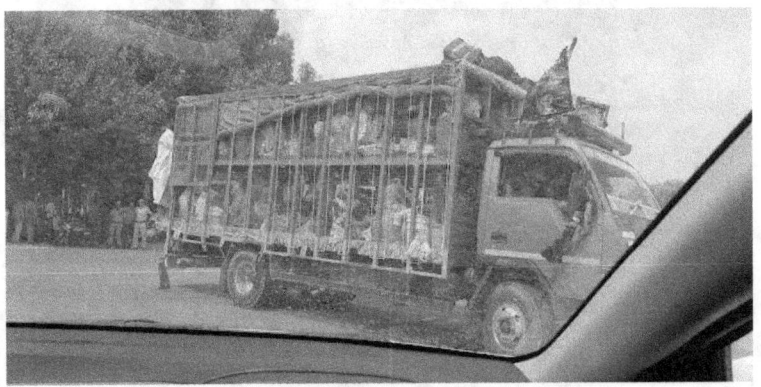

Overloaded Passengers in a Truck

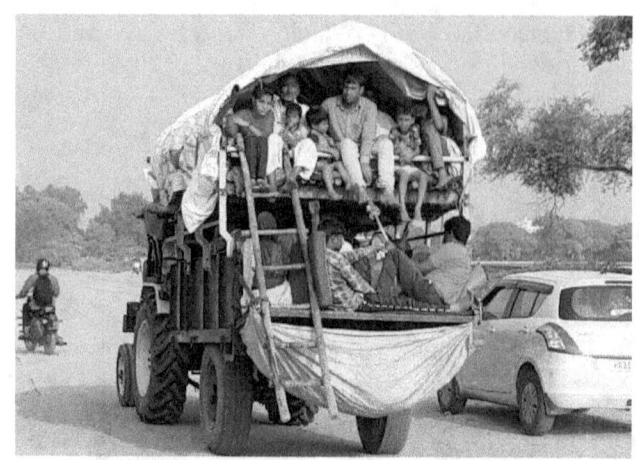

Overloaded Passengers in a Truck

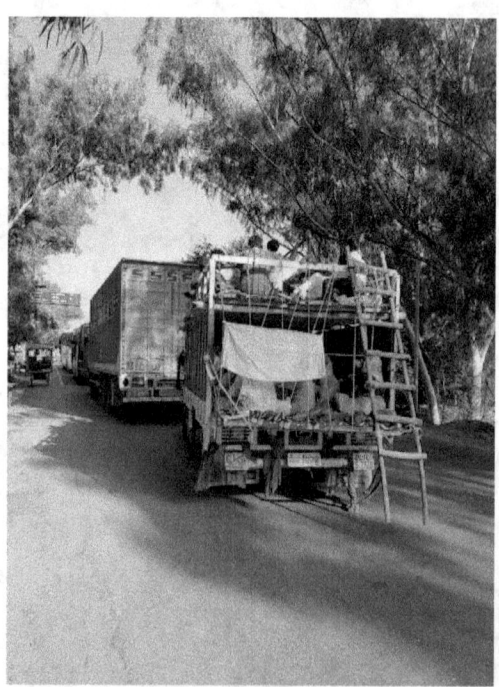

Overloaded Passengers in a Truck

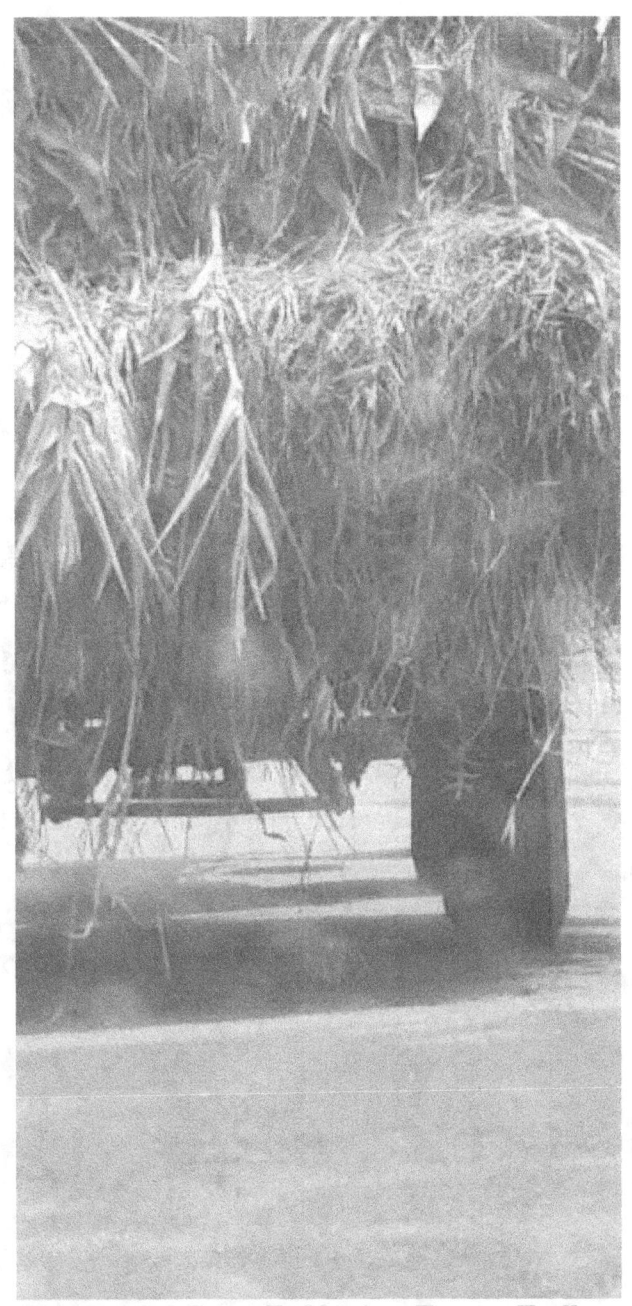

Overloaded Green Fodder in a Tractor Trolley

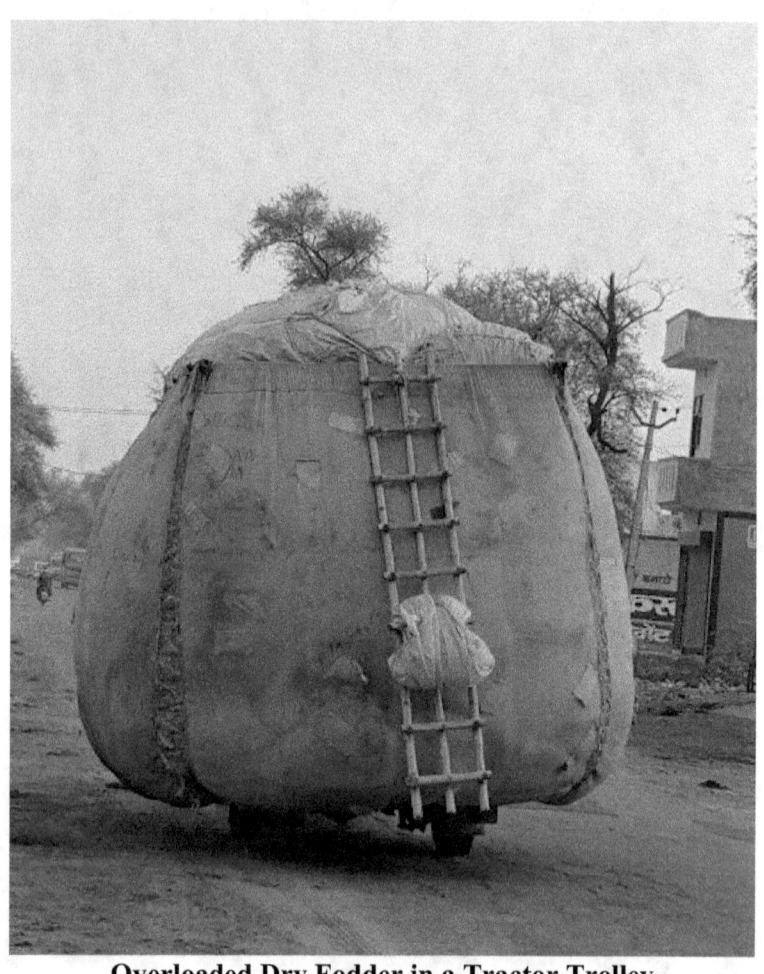

Overloaded Dry Fodder in a Tractor Trolley

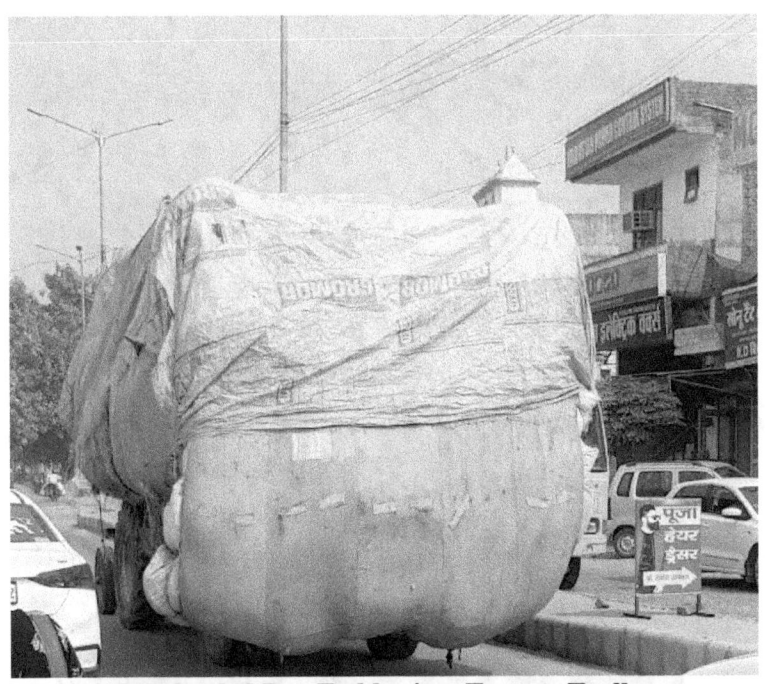

Overloaded Dry Fodder in a Tractor Trolley

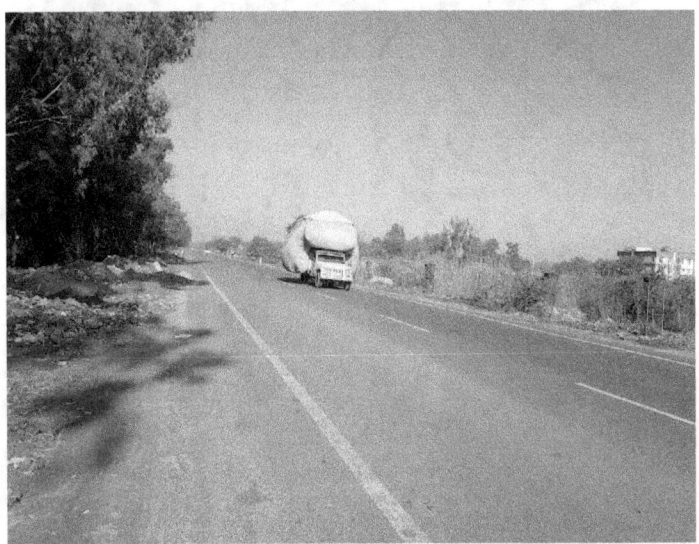

Overloaded Dry Fodder in a Mini Truck

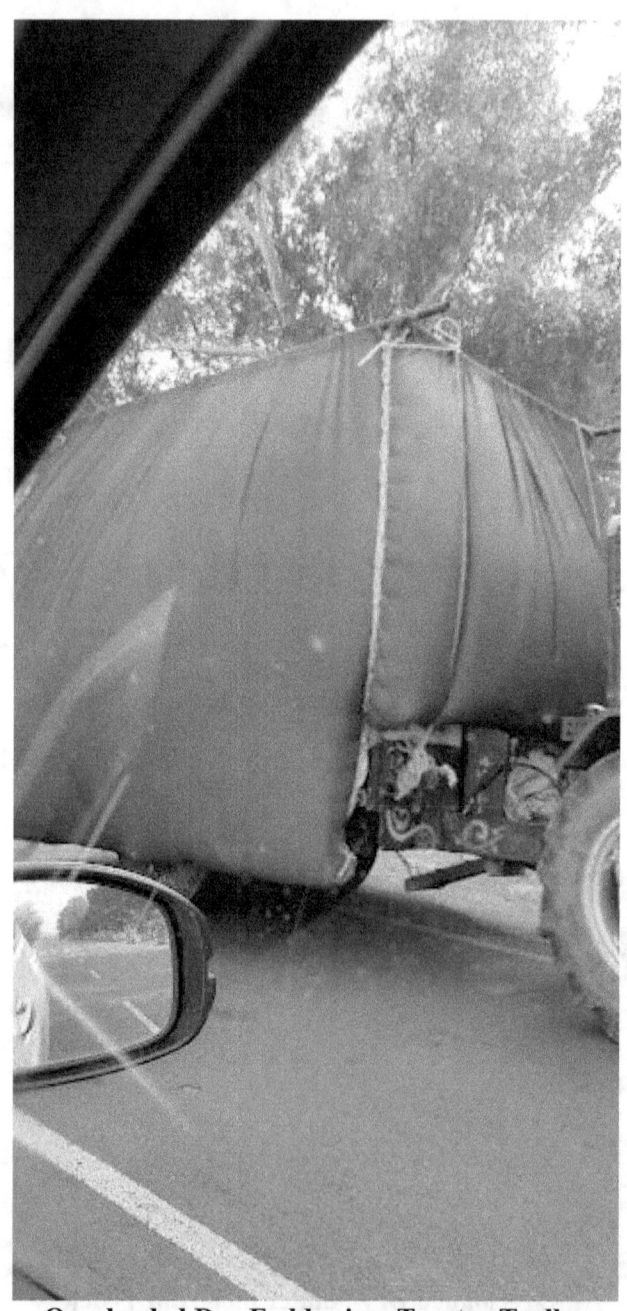

Overloaded Dry Fodder in a Tractor Trolley

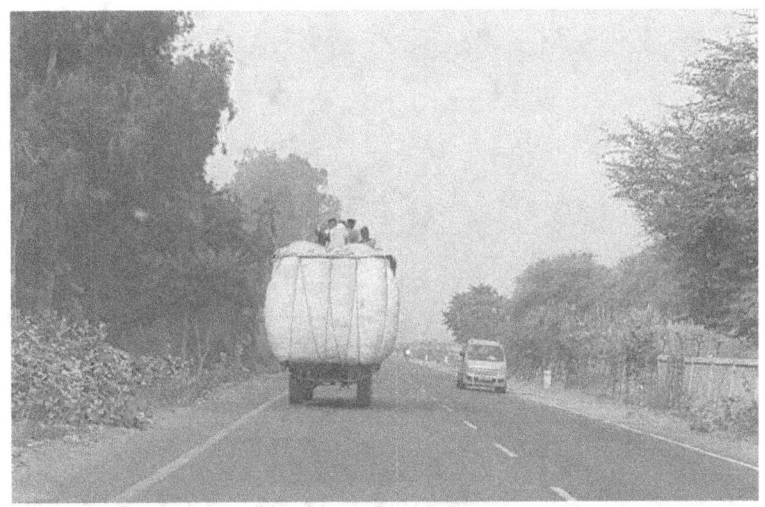

Overloaded Dry Fodder in a Tractor Trolley

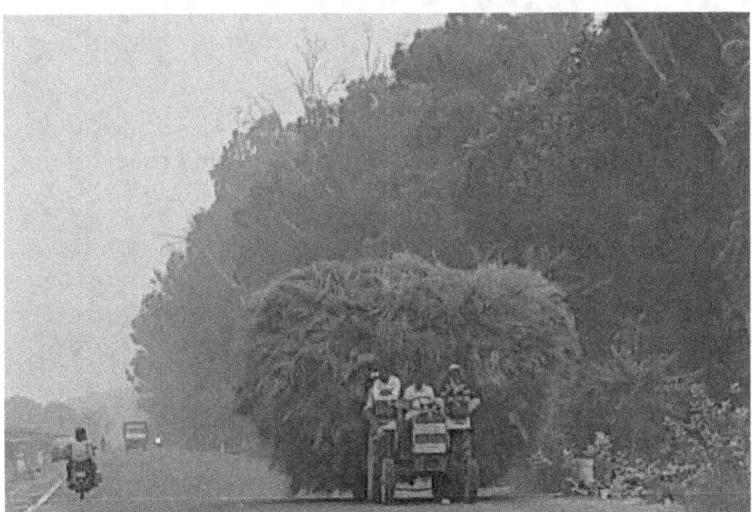

Overloaded Dry Fodder in a Tractor Trolley

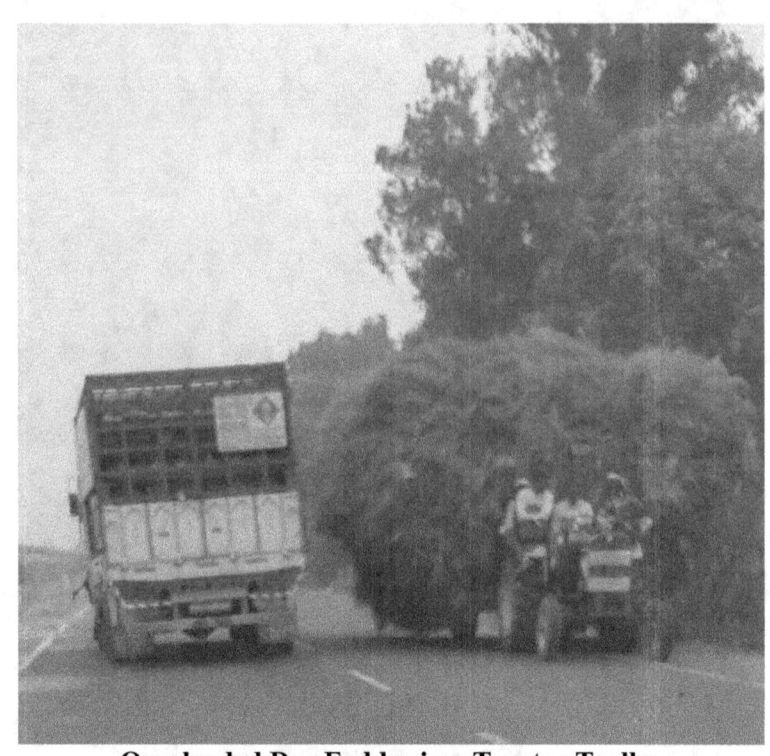

Overloaded Dry Fodder in a Tractor Trolley

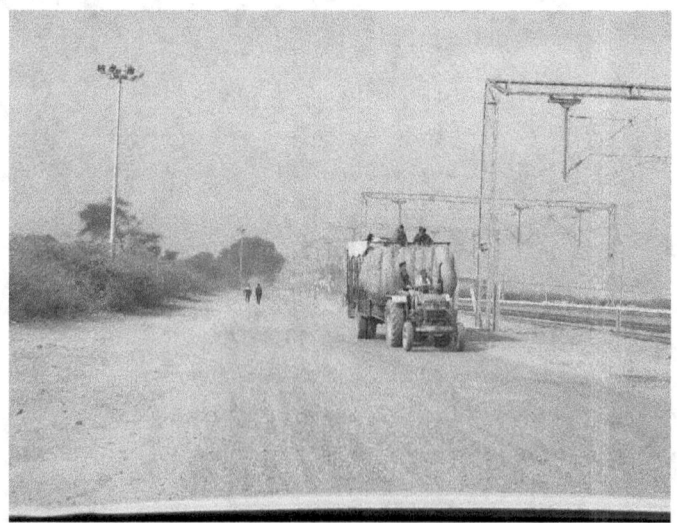

Overloaded Dry Fodder in a Tractor Trolley

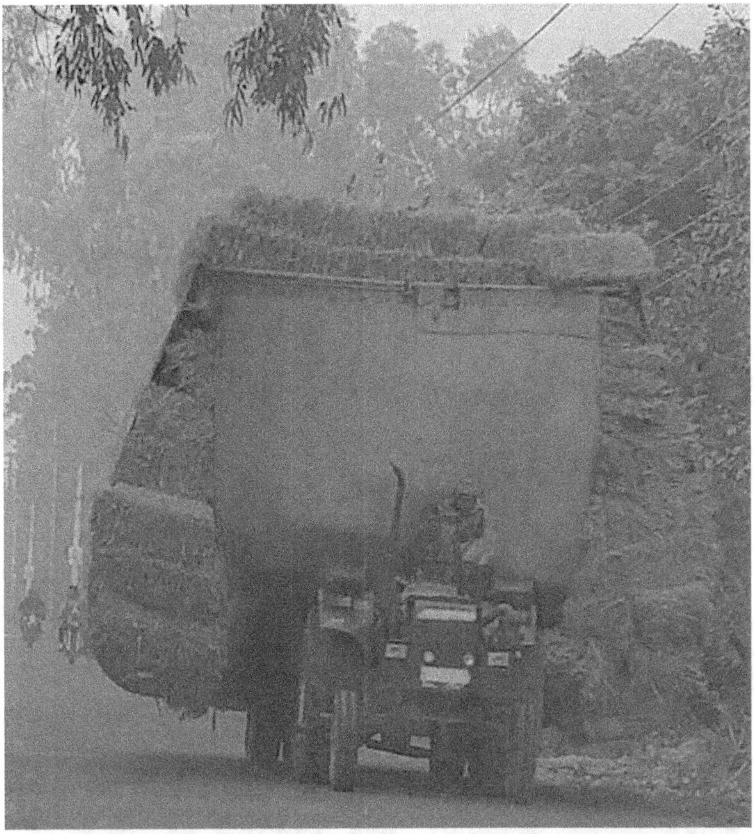

Overloaded Dry Fodder in a Tractor Trolley

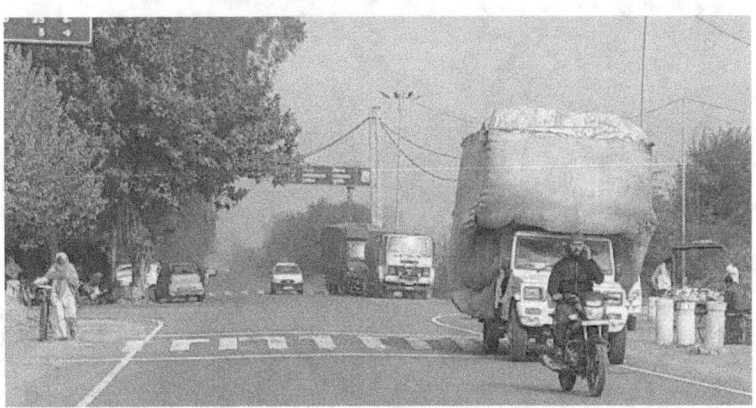

Overloaded Dry Fodder in a Mini Truck

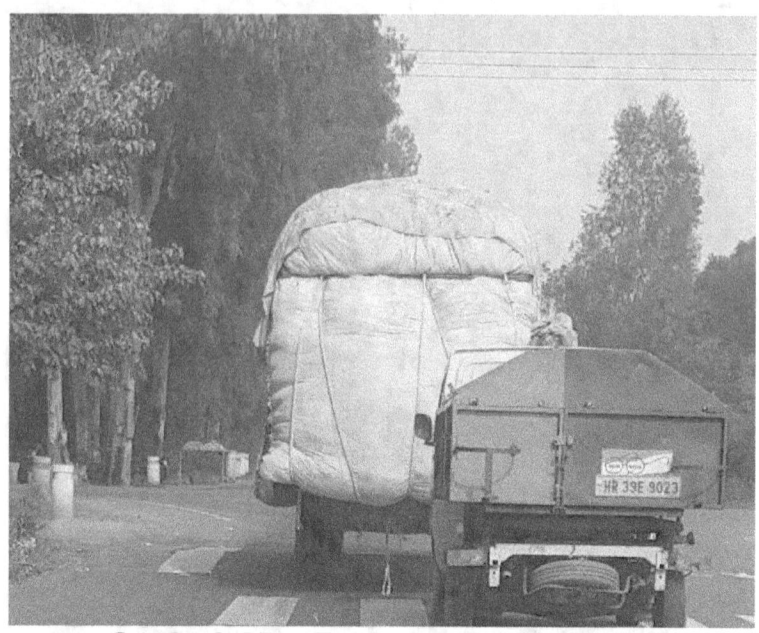

Overloaded Dry Fodder in a Tractor Trolley

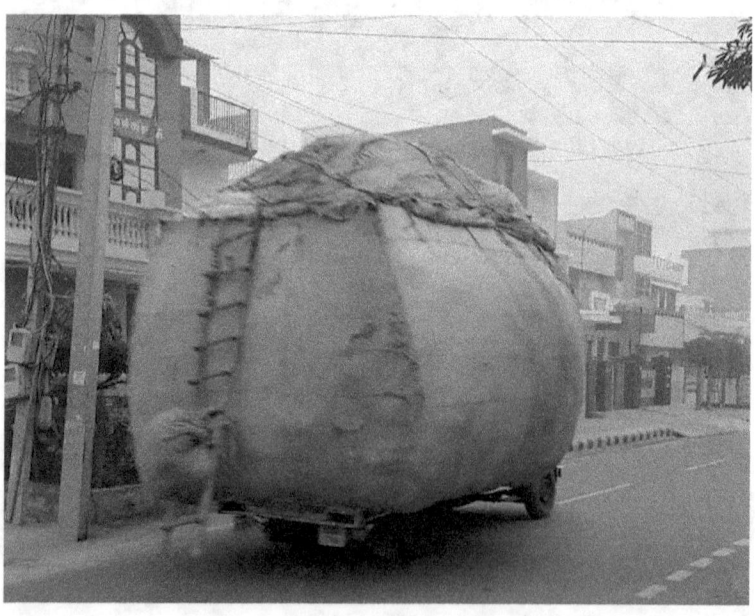

Overloaded Dry Fodder in a Tractor Trolley

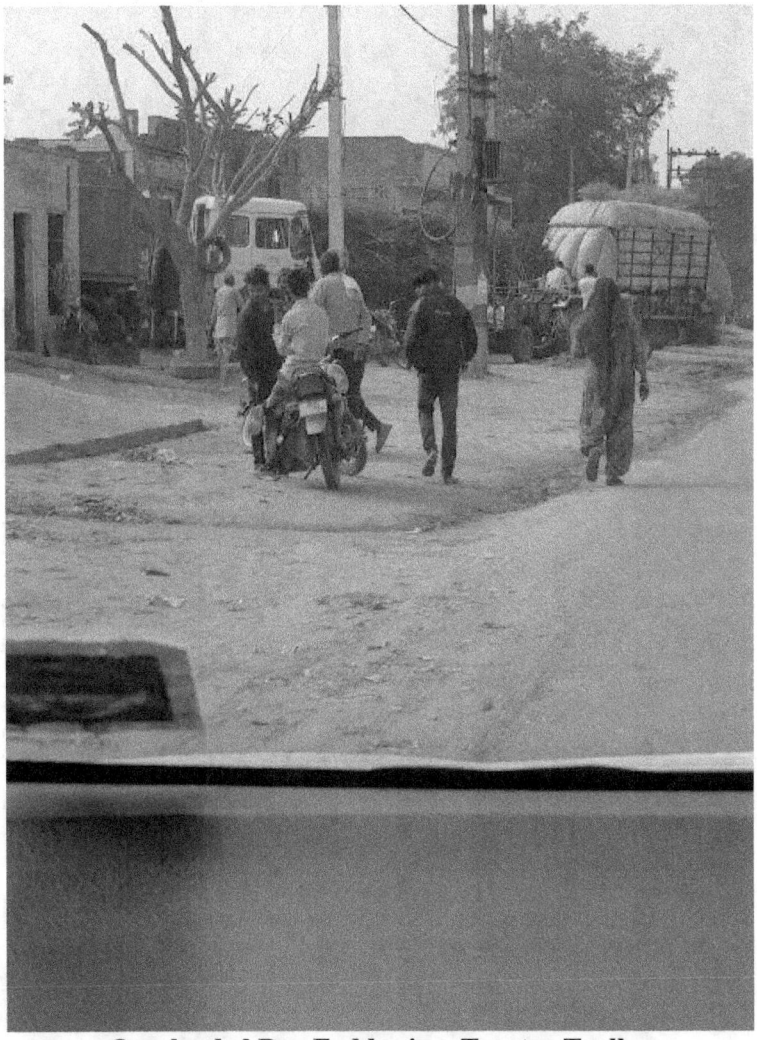

Overloaded Dry Fodder in a Tractor Trolley

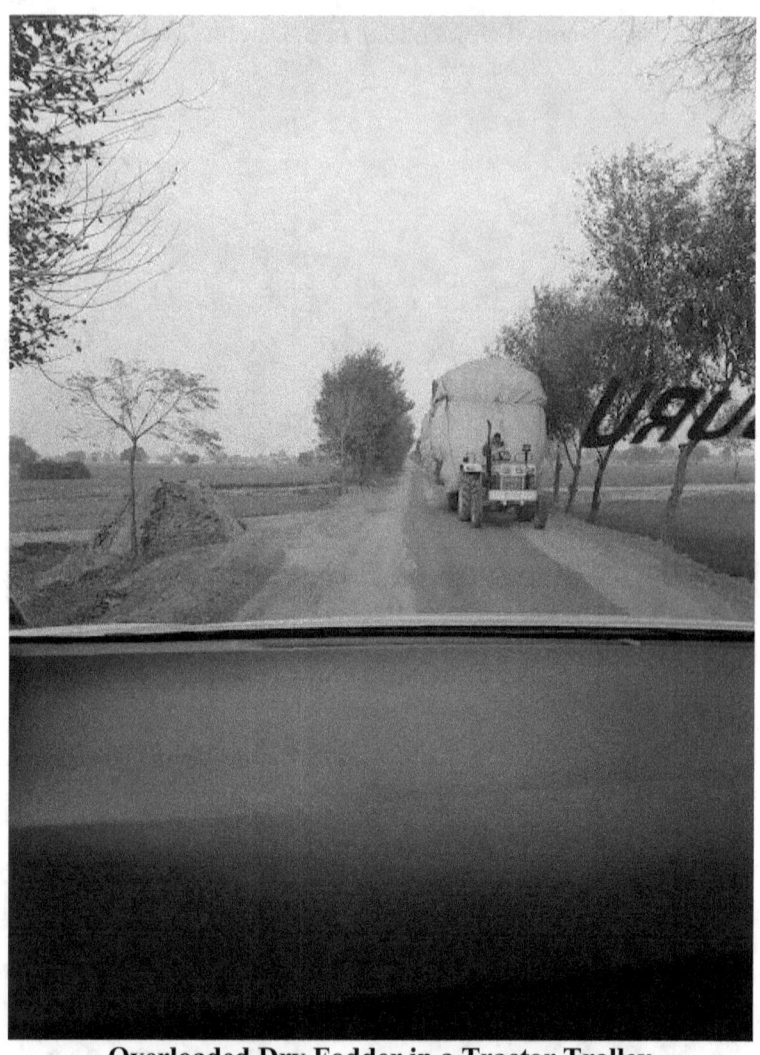

Overloaded Dry Fodder in a Tractor Trolley

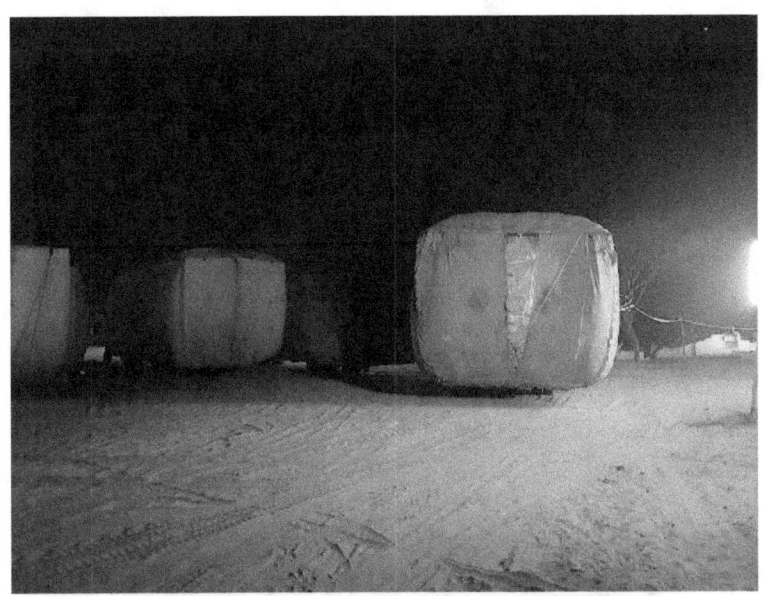

Overloaded Dry Fodder in a Tractor Trolley

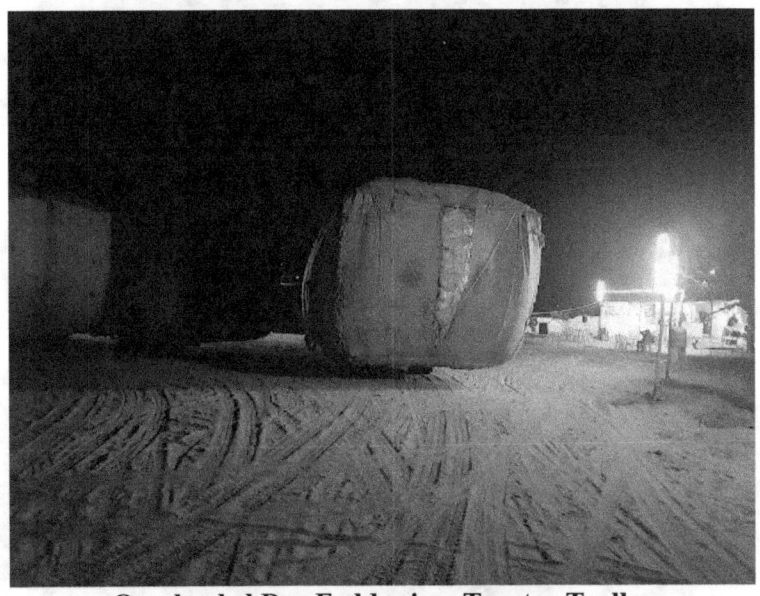

Overloaded Dry Fodder in a Tractor Trolley

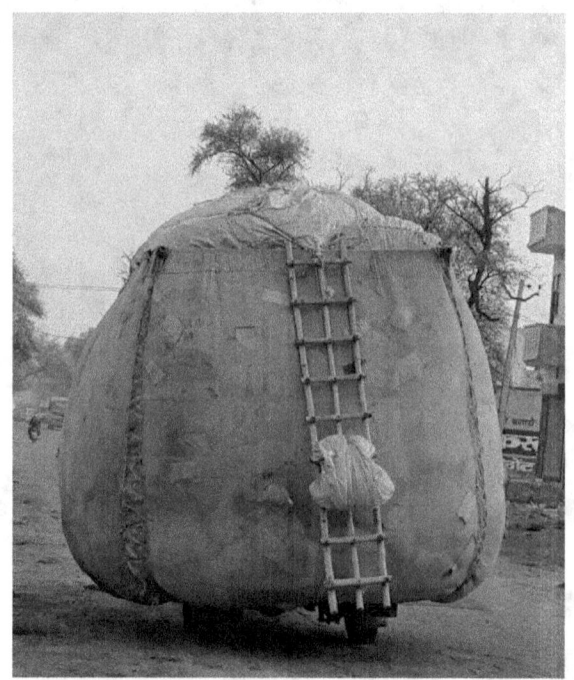

Overloaded Dry Fodder in a Tractor Trolley

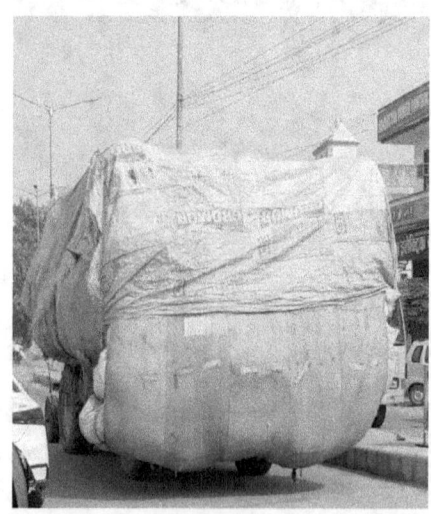

Overloaded Dry Fodder in a Tractor Trolley